The World Without a Self

The World Without a Self

Virginia Woolf and the Novel

by James Naremore

New Haven and London, Yale University Press

Designed by Sally Sullivan
and set in Linotype Granjon type.
Printed in the United States of America by
The Murray Printing Company, Forge Village, Mass.

Published in Great Britain, Europe, and Africa by
Yale University Press, Ltd., London.
Distributed in Latin America by Kaiman & Polon,
Inc., New York City; in Australasia and Southeast
Asia by John Wiley & Sons Australasia Pty. Ltd.,
Sydney; in India by UBS Publishers' Distributors Pvt.,
Ltd., Delhi; in Japan by John Weatherhill, Inc., Tokyo.

For Rita and Jay

What art was there, known to love or cunning, by which one pressed into those secret chambers? What device for becoming, like waters poured into one jar, one with the object one adored?
Lily Briscoe in *To the Lighthouse*

"How describe the world seen without a self?"
Bernard in *The Waves*

Contents

Acknowledgments

Portions of this book have appeared in *Novel: A Forum on Fiction,* and in *The Ball State University Forum.* I am grateful to the editors for permission to republish.

I wish to thank Indiana University for a grant that enabled me to complete the manuscript. Individuals have also helped: Paul Wiley, who interested me in writing about Virginia Woolf; L. S. Dembo and Bernard Benstock, who gave me encouragement; Mark Spilka, who read the manuscript and made valuable suggestions; and Jennifer Alkire, my editor at Yale, who did her work brilliantly.

I

Introduction

Virginia Woolf's fiction beautifully evokes her cultivated, slightly effete life among the *haute bourgeoise* of post-Edwardian England. And yet, for all the recognizable Bloomsbury influence, her novels contain other, stranger characteristics. There is first her extraordinary sensitivity: like Mary Carmichael, the writer she describes in *A Room of One's Own,* her imagination "responded to an almost imperceptible touch on it. It feasted, like a plant newly stood in the air on every sight and sound that came its way . . . her pages were full of that curious sexual quality that comes only when sex is unconscious of itself." [1] Whether unconscious or not, a highly sensitive, "curious sexual quality" is present everywhere in Mrs. Woolf's novels. It is reflected not only in the tales themselves, but in the ebb and flow of her prose rhythms, in her frequent references to acute pleasure or pain stimulated by the plainest domestic events, and in her loving attention to flowers, moths, and watery places. This vaguely erotic sensibility may be responsible for other distinctive traits—the remarkable moments of ecstasy that her characters

1. Virginia Woolf, *A Room of One's Own* (London: Hogarth Press, 1967), pp. 139–40. Unless otherwise noted, all references are to this edition.

feel, the frequent hints of fear, the preoccupation with brooding, dreamy experiences, rather like self-hypnosis. Whatever the cause, the naturally elegant milieu of her novels is often suffused with an atmosphere that is anything but comfortable and familiar.

Her attraction to a watery element gives her writing another of its unusual attributes. Reading her, one sometimes has the impression of being immersed in a constantly moving liquid, immersed so deeply that the people and things in her books become muffled and indistinct, like blurred and ghostly shadows. At these times, Virginia Woolf seems less "a plant newly stood in the air" than an exotic undersea flora. Indeed, hers is the preeminent example in English literature of what the French critic Gaston Bachelard calls "the material imagination of water." Such a characteristic of her mature fiction is precisely described in a later passage from *A Room of One's Own,* where, looking out her window, she detects "a signal pointing to a force in things which one had overlooked. It seemed to point to a river, which flowed past, invisibly, round the corner, down the street, and took people and eddied them along" (p. 144). At its extreme, this invisible river combines with the sleepy, hypnotic moods and the moments of exhilaration and fear to produce the strangest feeling of all: both the author and her characters appear on the verge of dissolving, or sinking forever into what Mrs. Ramsay famously calls a "wedge-shaped core of darkness."⁷

In the book that follows, I have tried to examine these idiosyncratic qualities of Virginia Woolf's fiction in some detail, and to suggest what it means to imagine life as she did. I have wanted to convey the unusual "world" of her novels, if we understand world to mean not just the physical trappings of her vision, but her way of seeing. It may be, as the late William Troy once suggested, that her whole approach to fiction comes down ultimately to a problem of style. Certainly her best known statements about writing—essays like "Modern Fiction" and "Mr. Bennett and Mrs. Brown"—indicate that the kind of things she wanted to express required a special attention to form, so that if we want to understand her, we must always return to the unusual manner of her writing and her celebrated technical experiments. But instead of relating these matters to familiar critical themes such as Mrs. Woolf's interest in time or psychology, I have wanted to connect them with other issues which are at least equally important, namely the erotic and visionary character of her novels, and her fascination with death.

My discussion is organized around six texts which represent both a cross section of Mrs. Woolf's work and her most significant achievement. The texts are arranged chronologically, except for *Orlando,* which I have moved out of place because its comedy, its prose style, and its overt preoccupation with English history seemed to make it a proper companion for *Between the Acts.* Normally, each chapter begins with observations about style and technique; again the treatment of *Orlando* is an exception, since I wanted to comment on Mrs. Woolf's interest in biography. I felt that this somewhat neglected, ostensibly quite different side of her personality was deeply related to the same issues I have treated elsewhere. A glance at the table of contents will show that I devote more space to *The Voyage Out* than to any of the later novels, but then Virginia Woolf herself seems to justify such a practice when she says in her essays that an author's first book is likely to be the least "guarded" and the most revealing. I move slowly and freely at first, trying to illustrate the apparently native aspects of her work, and setting down general arguments which can be seen to apply throughout. When I come to the later writings, I give somewhat less attention to small details of the prose, and spend more time with the techniques which are generally known as "stream of consciousness" or "interior monologue." I have taken pains to

show the limitations of such terminology, and to demonstrate
the special character of Mrs. Woolf's experiments.

Throughout, I have been aware that the peculiarity of Virginia Woolf's fiction is determined in large part by a number
of historical facts, not the least being that she spent much of her
life in a state of mind near madness and suicide.[2] Though granting the existence of these facts, I have been more interested in
the implications of Mrs. Woolf's writing than in its ultimate
causes. I have wanted to indicate the consistency of her mind,
as well as her struggle to shape the novel into a form that
would render an order of experience it had not dealt with before. Everywhere Virginia Woolf's fiction implies her need for
a union with what she sometimes called "reality." I hope to
show that she attained this union, but that her attitude toward
it was mixed, a commingling of love and sadness, fascination
and terror.

2. A great deal of new information is made available in Quentin Bell's
biography, *Virginia Woolf* (London: Hogarth Press, 1972). Bell's work
appeared just as this study was going to press.

2

A Passage from *The Voyage Out*

The yarns of seamen have a direct simplicity, the whole
meaning of which lies within the shell of a cracked nut.
But Marlow was not typical (if his propensity to spin yarns
be excepted), and to him the meaning of an episode was
not inside like a kernel but outside, enveloping the tale
which brought it out as a glow brings out a haze, in the
likeness of one of these misty halos that sometimes are
made visible by the spectral illumination of moonshine.

Conrad, *Heart of Darkness*

I

Five years after the publication of her first novel, Virginia
Woolf read it again, feeling a mixture of acute embarrassment
and pride. "If you ask me what I think," she wrote in her *Diary*,
"I must reply that I don't know—such a harlequinade as it is
—such an assortment of patches—here simple and severe—here
frivolous and shallow—here like God's truth—here strong and
free-flowing as I could wish. What to make of it, Heaven knows.
The failures are ghastly enough to make my cheeks burn—and

then a turn of the sentence, a direct look ahead of me, makes them burn in a different way. On the whole I think I like the young woman's mind considerably." [1]

This "harlequinade" displays many of the trappings that Mrs. Woolf was so concerned to do without in her later works. A great deal happens in the novel, including some comedy, some pathos, romantic love, and even a dramatic death scene toward the end. There is a large amount of dialogue, some of it brilliantly entertaining, and comparatively little of the extended treatment of the inner life that one associates with Virginia Woolf's mature period. The narrator is sometimes an expansive and self-assured commentator, there is a gallery of satirical character portraits, and there are some finely dramatized sequences of interplay between characters that are often reminiscent of Jane Austen. Yet in spite of all this, the novel tends to frustrate conventional expectations. Helen Ambrose, who demands our concentration at the beginning, remains in the background for the rest of the book. Richard and Clarissa Dalloway are introduced in the early chapters, treated in some detail, and then dropped altogether. Furthermore, an air of strangeness pervades the novel, a dark current that runs beneath the comedy-of-manners surface. The witty dialogue is often counterpointed with passages of somber reflection, and the novel ends on an elegiac note that is typical of Mrs. Woolf's subsequent fiction.

Certainly what plot *The Voyage Out* has is relatively simple. Rachel Vinrace, the central character, is at the beginning a profoundly inexperienced, naive girl of twenty-four, who has been educated "as the majority of well-to-do girls in the last part of the nineteenth century were educated." She has a superficial knowledge of several languages, but almost no comprehension of the world outside her cloistered school. Her mother is dead; her father and aunts have been overly protective; and though

1. Virginia Woolf, *A Writer's Diary* (New York: New American Library, 1968), p. 33.

her gift for music and her interest in novels like *Wuthering Heights* indicate her sensuality, she is quite ignorant of sex. (A good deal of her character is no doubt based on Virginia Woolf herself, just as Rachel's aunt and uncle are rather like Leslie Stephen and his wife, and the misanthropic St. John Hirst, whom we meet later, is a portrait of Lytton Strachey.) The major action of the novel involves a sea voyage Rachel takes from England to a small Latin American port where she spends some time with a small group of Englishmen. There, as a result of the guardianship of her newfound, liberal aunt, Helen Ambrose, and her love for a young would-be novelist, Terence Hewet, Rachel grows out of her isolation and experiences a moment of total communion with another person. But at virtually the same time as her sexual awakening is complete she contracts a virus, and soon after dies of a fever—a fever reminiscent of the typhoid that had killed Thoby Stephen before Virginia Woolf began work on the novel.

Death figures as a major theme in two ways: first, the dissolution of individuality through sexual love is linked, at least metaphorically, with death; and second, the death of the young girl is made to reverberate in the lives of the Englishmen at the hotel in Latin America, so that we sense their mortality and thus their relationship with something elemental in nature. Clearly, the title of the book suggests Rachel's voyage out of the social and sexual restrictions of her life in England, her voyage out of herself, and ultimately her voyage out of life. On the literal level, these themes are represented by Rachel's trip out from England on her father's ship, *Euphrosyne*. But as James Hafley and Harvena Richter have pointed out, the story places an almost equal emphasis on a voyage *in*—that of the two lovers, symbolically represented by their journey up a river deep into the heart of the Latin American countryside, together with Virginia Woolf's own voyage into the subjective lives of her characters. Hafley claims that "nearly every action, nearly every

event in *The Voyage Out* is made to be symbolical." [2] Certainly
the novel does exhibit at times an allegorical quality reminiscent
of a work like *Howard's End*. I do not know that one should go
too far in pressing an allegorical interpretation, but the full
import of the story cannot be understood unless we are aware
that the settings and events are rather carefully planned to illustrate a general thesis about life. Likewise, we must be aware that
the fact of death, far more than simply an expedient way to end,
is central to that thesis.

The Voyage Out has impressed many of its readers as a patch-
work of effects, and, until recently, has been regarded as the
novel of a gifted young writer who had not yet found her métier.
There is comparatively little criticism on the novel and few
serious analyses of its formal properties, the assumption apparently being that Virginia Woolf's career really began only with
the experimental sketches in *Monday or Tuesday,* or even later,
with her third novel, *Jacob's Room.* There are three critical
treatments which seem to me especially helpful: J. K. Johnstone,
in *The Bloomsbury Group,* discussing the novel as a voyage to
"reality," relates it to the philosophy of G. E. Moore and to
Virginia Woolf's particular values. James Hafley has written a
brief but intelligent commentary in an attempt to show that the
novel does just what it sets out to do, and, most interesting of
all, Harvena Richter has argued that "there is not a single mode
of subjectivity" in the later novels "which is not present" in
The Voyage Out.[3] In the treatment which follows, my approach
has been somewhat different from any of these. I offer first a
contemplation based on a single passage of Mrs. Woolf's prose.
I have tried to show that certain phenomena of the style can be

2. James Hafley, *The Glass Roof* (Berkeley: University of California
Press), p. 15.
3. Harvena Richter, *The Inward Voyage* (Princeton: Princeton University Press, 1970), p. 93.

linked to important themes in *The Voyage Out,* and to the special quality of Virginia Woolf's vision. In other words, I wish to indicate how the novel may be said to be characteristic in the most profound sense. No matter what metamorphosis his art may undergo, a serious writer of any real talent has some habit of mind that remains constant, though it may be manifested only in a recurrent rhythm or collection of images. In the case of Virginia Woolf, her first novel not only presents her major themes but is also in some ways highly characteristic of her style—this in spite of the many so-called conventional techniques she utilized. Too often it has been discussed in purely historical terms, as an odd mixture of the Edwardian and the modern. The historical approach is valid, of course, but it needs to be tempered with an understanding of how the reader senses Mrs. Woolf's special personality. Perhaps more important, we need to see that this personality has instincts which are darker than anything suggested in Bloomsbury's orderly rationalism.

II

Very often Virginia Woolf will set her characters off against some panoramic description of the world, a symbolic landscape. She is usually thought of as a novelist who explores the minutiae of individual sensibilities, a writer given to deep views of the insides of her characters; we tend to forget, or we do not sufficiently emphasize, that she habitually blends the flow of her character's thoughts with an omniscient, highly generalizing voice which seems to brood over a large scene, subordinating individuals to the broad eddies and currents of life. Sometimes she is like young Nancy Ramsay in *To the Lighthouse.* As Nancy is playing on the seashore, there comes a moment when she is virtually hypnotized by the contrast between "that vastness and this tininess"; on the one hand is the sea before her, and on the other is the little puddle where, "like God himself," she has been creating an imaginary world: "So listening to the waves, crouching over the pool, she brooded." [4]

In much the same way, Mrs. Woolf often seems hypnotized by a "vastness," usually in the form of a land or seascape. One can think of any number of examples: the skywriting scene in *Mrs. Dalloway,* for instance; or the "Time Passes" section of *To the Lighthouse*; or the descriptions of sun, sea, and land that are woven between the chapters of *The Waves*. The first definitive manifestation of this approach to her subjects comes fairly early in *The Voyage Out,* just after the *Euphrosyne* has set out to sea with its small party of passengers. I quote it here at length because it is worth considering in some detail; it suggests what might be called the landscape of Mrs. Woolf's imagination:

> The preliminary discomforts and harshnesses, which generally make the first days of a sea voyage so cheerless and trying to the temper, being somehow lived through, the succeeding days passed pleasantly enough. October was well advanced, but steadily burning with a warmth that made the early months of the summer appear very young and capricious. Great tracts of earth lay now beneath the autumn sun, and the whole of England, from the bald moors to the Cornish rocks, was lit up from dawn to sunset, and showed in stretches of yellow, green, and purple. Under that illumination even the roofs of the great towns glittered. In thousands of small gardens, millions of dark-red flowers were blooming, until the old ladies who had tended them so carefully came down the paths with their scissors, snipped through their juicy stalks, and laid them upon cold stone ledges in the village church. Innumerable parties of picnickers coming home

4. Virginia Woolf, *To the Lighthouse* (London: Hogarth Press, 1967, p. 119). Unless otherwise noted, all references are to this edition.

at sunset cried, "Was there ever such a day as this?" "It's you," the young men whispered; "Oh, it's you," the young women replied. All old people and many sick people were drawn, were it only for a foot or two, into the open air, and prognosticated pleasant things about the course of the world. As for the confidences and expressions of love that were heard not only in cornfields but in lamplit rooms, where the windows opened on the garden, and men with cigars kissed women with grey hairs, they were not to be counted. Some said that the sky was an emblem of the life they had had; others that it was the promise of the life to come. Longtailed birds clattered and screamed, and crossed from wood to wood, with golden eyes in their plumage.

But while all this went on by land, very few people thought about the sea. They took it for granted that the sea was calm; and there was no need, as there is in many houses when the creeper taps on the bedroom windows, for the couples to murmur before they kiss, "Think of the ships tonight," or "Thank Heaven, I'm not the man in the lighthouse"! For all they imagined, the ships when they vanished on the sky-line dissolved, like snow in water. The grown-up view, indeed, was not much clearer than the view of the little creatures in bathing drawers who were trotting into the foam all along the coasts of England, and scooping up buckets of water. They saw white sails or tufts of smoke pass across the horizon, and if you had said these were waterspouts, or the petals of white sea flowers, they would have agreed.

The people in ships, however, took an equally singular view of England. Not only did it appear to them to be an island, and a very small island, but it was a shrinking island in which people were imprisoned. One figured them first swarming about like aimless ants, and almost pressing each other over the edge; and then, as the ship withdrew, one figured them making a vain clamour, which, being unheard, either ceased, or rose into a brawl. Finally, when the ship was out of sight of land, it became plain that the people of England were completely mute. The disease attacked other parts of the earth; Europe shrank, Asia shrank, Africa and America shrank, until it seemed doubtful whether the ship would ever run against any of those wrinkled little rocks again. But on the other hand, an immense dignity had descended upon her; she was an inhabitant of the great world, which has so few inhabitants, travelling all day across an empty universe, with veils drawn before her and behind. She was more lonely than the caravan crossing the desert; she was infinitely more mysterious, moving by her own power and sustained by her own resources. The sea might give her death or some unexampled joy, and none would know of it. She was a bride going forth to her husband, a virgin unknown of men; in her vigor and purity, she might be likened to all beautiful things.[5]

Even a relatively casual reader ought to feel something in the whole manner of these paragraphs that is typical of Virginia Woolf—an air of elegant beauty, perhaps, or some hint of mystery; an emphasis on sensory impressions and a vibrating, self-consciously rhythmical prose. Even her favorite image, the sea, is here, and it is used in an overtly symbolic way. In fact, this particular excerpt is only the first of many instances of such techniques in *The Voyage Out,* which is full of mysterious land and seascapes.

Notice, however, that the first sentence of this passage conveys a very different impression from all the rest. It is an expository, almost conversational remark exchanged between author and reader: "The preliminary discomforts and harshnesses, which generally make the first days of a sea voyage so trying to

5. Virginia Woolf, *The Voyage Out* (London: Hogarth Press, 1965), pp. 27–29. Unless otherwise noted, all references are to this edition.

the temper, being somehow lived through, the succeeding days passed pleasantly enough." It establishes a personality; it could have been written only by a non-sailor, and it sounds very like a British lady of the upper middle class. Beginning with the second sentence, the narrator's mood changes: the voice loses some of that certainty and easy assurance about its subject and becomes more contemplative, subdued, less interested in exchanging information than in expressing a muted reverence for the vast scene—an extraordinarily panoramic view, at once general and microscopic. At the beginning, we are in the company of a more or less traditional narrator-confidant; but then the author seems to fall into a kind of reverie. It is still a very privileged and lofty view, but our vantage point is shifting and ambiguous, as if we were able to see the world from above and yet at the same time through the eyes of many anonymous people. A certain anonymity is in fact characteristic of the passage, or at least the major part of it. In the first sentence we are among the passengers on the *Euphrosyne,* but at the end we have reference only to "the ship," a sort of representative craft among the many that "people" are traveling in. We are still clearly in the presence of a controlling storyteller ("while all this went on by land"), but the speaker is caught up, subordinated to the view. The perspective is truly omniscient, but there is no more conversation with the audience. We simply look through the eyes first of one group and then of another; even the last lines, which have an especially lofty quality, grow out of the observations of "people in ships."

Erich Auerbach has said that the essential characteristic of Mrs. Woolf's style in *To the Lighthouse* "is that we are given not merely one person whose consciousness (that is the impressions it receives) is rendered, but many persons, with frequent shifts from one to the other." The passage at hand is a foreshadowing of such a technique, which later becomes much more complex. Even here the multipersonal point of view suggests, to quote Auerbach again, that we are "confronted with an endeavor to investigate an objective reality," but a reality which remains elusive, even when it is "encircled by the content of all the various consciousnesses" directed upon it, including the author's.[6]

With its attention to cadence and its liberal use of imagery, the greater part of the passage seems closer in spirit to the lyric poem than to the ordinary novel. Later I will want to consider some of the implications of this change of style, which here prefigures the way the novel as a whole oscillates between two kinds of experience; but first some general remarks about the qualities of Virginia Woolf's descriptive writing are in order. It is well known that, like nearly everyone in the modernist period, she was concerned to give her work more of that special intensity associated with lyric poetry. What needs to be stressed, however, is that her "poetry"—if prose can be called by that name for a moment—is qualitatively different from the writing of nearly all her great contemporaries. No matter how complex her style becomes, it retains a self-consciously lovely quality and a certain easy elegance that sets her apart from other important twentieth-century authors.

A good deal of this cultivated, graceful feeling probably stems from her social class and sex. There is such a thing as a Bloomsbury accent, and I think one can detect it in this passage. A particular station in life as well as a certain femininity is implied even by what the narrator chooses to describe. Out of the whole landscape of England, we are shown how the sun makes "stretches of yellow, green, and purple" on the earth and on the roofs of "great towns." No factories, no working-class details inhibit the pleasant view. The people and things singled out in this landscape belong almost exclusively to the world of well-bred domesticity: we are shown gardens, little old ladies, a

6. Erich Auerbach, *Mimesis* (Princeton: Princeton University Press, 1953), p. 536.

village church, and young men and women on picnics who speak genteel lines like "was there ever such a day as this." We are told that "all old people . . . prognosticated pleasant things about the course of the world," but Mrs. Woolf doesn't mean "all," and her diction here, as elsewhere, connotes a specific social class. She is the sort who gives less attention to "cornfields" than to "lamplit rooms" where "windows opened on the garden." The detail about men with cigars who kiss women with gray hairs cannot help, in this context, but evoke a secure English middle-class life, where people have the leisure to speculate on the sky as an "emblem."

The "Bloomsbury" quality is a result of the prose style, too. "I think writing must be formal," Virginia Woolf once noted in her *Diary*. "The art must be respected . . . for if one lets the mind run loose it becomes egotistic; personal, which I detest." [7] She never descends to the kind of colloquial idiom she would probably regard as chaotic or coarse; she always maintains a decorous tone, a shade of formality, which comes to the fore in characteristic phrases like "preliminary discomforts and harshnesses" or "confidences and expressions of love"; in words like "capricious" or "illumination" or "singular"; and in slightly formal turns of syntax such as "tracts of earth lay now." But at the same time, she never allows her prose to become severely formal—in the sense that T. S. Eliot is formal, for example—since the restrictions of this approach would preclude the quality of feminine elegance that she so admires. Her fondness for parallel syntax, for instance, is an obvious trait of her style. But her parallels seem to be there as much to beat out a hypnotic rhythm as to contrast ideas: "not only in cornfields but in lamplit rooms"; " 'It's you,' the young men whispered; 'Oh it's you,' the young women replied." And consider, too, how much her prose depends upon the formulae of polite

7. Woolf, *A Writer's Diary*, p. 73.

conversation: "somehow lived through," "lit up from dawn to sunset," "not to be counted," "not much clearer." As a result of these familiar phrases the language takes on a feeling of casual grace, an air of spontaneity. It is the very opposite of the highly formal language in, say, the opening stories of Joyce's *Dubliners.*

This tendency toward beauty and elegance can be found everywhere in Virginia Woolf's writing, and is reflected in her admiration for Jane Austen's finely-turned sentences. She believed, in fact, that there was a peculiarly feminine way of writing, and that women ought to cultivate it. In *A Room of One's Own,* Mrs. Woolf parodies a series of "man's sentences," which are full of abstract nouns like "grandeur" and "works." One of these sentences, " 'Success prompts to exertion; and habit facilitates success,' " is a perfect example of a trait learned from Johnson—an aphorism set down in a slow and exact parallel, three heavy measures on each side and a long pause between, the abstract, slightly latinate phrases balanced like two slabs of granite. There is nothing even politely conversational about this style; it is laden with quasi-political rhetoric, pompous calls to arms and manly words like "proceed," "exercise," "exertion," "success." It was the sort of language, Mrs. Woolf says, that no woman could be comfortable with. "Charlotte Brontë, with all her splendid gift for prose, stumbled and fell with that clumsy weapon in her hands. George Eliot committed atrocities with it that beggar description." Jane Austen, however, was an exception:

> Jane Austen looked at it and laughed at it and devised a perfectly natural, shapely sentence proper to her own use and never departed from it. Thus, with less genius for writing than Charlotte Bronte, she got infinitely more said. Indeed, since freedom and fullness of expression are of the essence of the art, such a lack of tradition . . . must have told enormously upon the writing of women. Moreover, . . . There is

no reason to think that the form of the epic or of the poetic play suits a woman any more than the sentence suits her. But all the older forms of literature were hardened and set by the time she became a writer. The novel alone was young enough to be soft in her hands . . . Yet who shall say that even now "the novel" . . . this most pliable of forms is rightly shaped for her use? No doubt we shall find her knocking that into shape for herself . . . providing some new vehicle, not necessarily in verse, for the poetry in her. For it is the poetry that is still denied an outlet. [pp. 115-16]

Here, with her interest in poetry, Mrs. Woolf drops her tongue-in-cheek pose; we have come to her central preoccupation with the novel—her desire, stated many times over, to make it more "poetic" and therefore more feminine. "The book," she says, "has somehow to be adapted to the body." Lyric poetry, it would seem, had more of the female body about it, and could be used to adapt the novel to the feminine way of seeing. In her more overtly poetic moods, therefore, Mrs. Woolf's prose is empurpled by a fairly mannered rhythm and a slightly ornamental imagery.

The passage at hand is noteworthy for its highly rhythmical quality, influenced by balance, repetition, and alliteration: "She was more lovely than the caravan crossing the desert; she was infinitely more mysterious, moving by her own power and sustained by her own resources." In all, it is a prose that loves the "poise and balance of the period itself," as young Stephen Dedalus once put it. Then, too, it is a prose that depends on the relationship of one sentence to another, with a sharp ear for the lulling effect of repetitions, pauses, and phrases like "travelling all day across an empty universe." "A book is not made of sentences laid end to end," Mrs. Woolf said, "but of sentences built, if an image helps, into arcades or domes." She claimed to be ignorant of metrics, yet her prose style is distinguished by its love of hypnotic rhythms and the way it seems to imitate the rhythm of whatever she is writing about. Bernard, the prose writer and chief voice in *The Waves,* says that the rhythm of his prose is the "most important" aspect of his writing. Indeed one has the sense that rhythm is what Virginia Woolf feels most of all when she writes; it is the thing that guides her pen.

There are not many modern authors (Joyce would be a qualified example) who adopt self-consciously lovely rhythms which seem to lull the reader into a dreamy state. Virginia Woolf's prose rhythms are reminiscent of the nineteenth century (particularly such writers as Austen, Peacock, De Quincey, and Thackeray) far more than of her own period. She can make her rhythms do various things; they can help produce the effects of cultivated irony or gaiety or hypnotic beauty. Sometimes she makes the rhythm imitate character—thus the staccato movement of Septimus Smith's mad visions, or the lurching, swaying rhythms associated with Mrs. McNab in *To the Lighthouse.* But she seldom tries to draw into her prose the cadences of uncultivated speech. Even when her language is at its most informal it takes its natural rhythm from the elegant conversation that is associated with a certain "good form" and literary good manners. We should remember that Yeats specifically rejected beautiful and dreamy rhythms in his late career; Eliot disapproved of them in Milton, in *Finnegans Wake,* and in most Victorian poetry, especially the poetry of Swinburne; and Dr. Leavis deplored anything of the kind in poetry or in the novel. Virginia Woolf was sensible of such criticism, and, as her diary shows, was quite conscious that her prose was open to charges of "fine writing." [8] Yet throughout her career she continued to write the highly rhythmic, lyrical prose which became one of the distinguishing marks of her style.

8. See, for example, William Troy's essays, "The Poetic Method," *Symposium* 3 (1932): 53–63; and "The Poetic Style," *Symposium* 3 (1932): 153–66. Also W. H. Mellers, "Mrs. Woolf and Life," *The Importance of Scrutiny,* ed. Eric Bentley (New York: New York University Press, 1948), pp. 378–82.

Her imagery, too, is quite unlike that of her great contemporaries. The language in the passage above, like that in many passages one could draw from her work, appeals more to the auditory sense than the visual. There is hardly a sentence that does not present some new image, but most of these are of a relatively predictable kind: "men with cigars," "women with grey hairs," "sky was an emblem," "houses where the creeper taps on the bedroom window," "white sails or tufts of smoke," "swarming about like aimless ants," "vain clamour," "empty universe;" the list could be made much longer. There is little of what Victor Shklovsky called "defamiliarization" in this sort of language.[9] Virginia Woolf's words seem to be controlled more by the impulses of a literary convention than by a need to capture a special and peculiar experience, and the language flows along with the ease of something highly comfortable and familiar. In fact, Mrs. Woolf does not have any specific memory in her mind's eye as she writes; her picture is based wholly on fancy, and not on any lived or felt experience. Instead of a language put to the scrupulous service of presenting life, she offers a language which trusts to cultivated literary associations, language depending on language. Of course there are many exceptions to this manner in her work, but, generally speaking, when she falls into the mood I am considering here—as in the "Time Passes" section of *To the Lighthouse* or the interchapters of *The Waves*—her imagery conveys just this sort of mannered, ornate, "literary" feeling.[10]

9. See Shklovsky's essay, "Art as Technique," in L. T. Lemon and M. J. Reis, *Russian Formalist Criticism* (Lincoln: University of Nebraska Press, 1965), pp. 3–25.

10. William Troy, who makes these same observations, feels that *The Voyage Out* is a "distinguished" work, but he condemns the "poetic" aspects of Mrs. Woolf's style, specifically as it appears in her later novels. He concludes her language is "detached from experience," that it attains "no more substantial beauty than that of a charming virtuosity of style," and that "its charm seems false, its authority invalid, and its beauty sterile" ("The Poetic Style," pp. 164–65). It is true that Virginia Woolf's imagery

Whatever the virtues of Mrs. Woolf's fiction—and I believe they are considerable—one cannot argue that her descriptions have the power, exactness, and almost revelatory quality of those in Joyce or Pound or Eliot. Furthermore, the defects to which she is most prone are the defects of "charm." And yet Mrs. Woolf chose to differ from her contemporaries not simply as a matter of taste or because she could not write the way they did. In some ways, her attitudes toward life were quite unlike theirs. The art of Joyce and Pound is based on a profound faith in the reliability of carefully employed language. Later in this study, I hope to show that Virginia Woolf had no such faith. In place of a "luminous silent stasis of aesthetic pleasure," to use Stephen Dedalus again, Mrs. Woolf sought a semi-transparent envelope, or, in another famous metaphor, "a luminous halo." Instead of hard, Parnassian clarity, she chose evocation, generalization, a prose in which things are slightly blurred, as in a fine mist. Her experience commanded of her a language which is always in fluid motion, never asking us to pause and contemplate a brilliant image, forever carrying us forward by the beat of the rhythm, by connections, repetitions, transitions. She was critical of T. S. Eliot precisely because his poetry did not connect things: "As I sun myself upon the intense and ravishing beauty of one of his lines, and reflect that I must make a dizzy and dangerous leap to the next, and so on from line to line . . . I cry out, I confess, for the old decorums." [11] The "old decorums," in the sense of a fading and never very vital nineteenth-century tradition of "manners," are in fact never

-----

is less compelling than that of Shakespeare, Yeats, Baudelaire, and Emily Brontë—the writers Troy compares her with. But the quality of the imagery does not account for the power of her best writing. I doubt that Hemingway, an author Troy places above Mrs. Woolf, could survive the same test.

11. Virginia Woolf, quoted by T. Holliday in the introduction to the Modern Library edition of *To the Lighthouse* (New York, 1937), p. ix.

missing from her style. But she did not simply want to make literature easy. In her later work, she goes to extremes to make everything she describes blend together. Her descriptions of this effect, and the effect itself, have been related to the philosophy of Bergson; and there is a connection, though there is no evidence that Mrs. Woolf ever actually read Bergson.[12] If one wishes to conjecture about sources, Marlow's notions about storytelling, quoted as the epigraph to this chapter, are in some ways very appropriate to Mrs. Woolf's fiction—even to the watery metaphor and a reference to "misty halos." In any case, the most important single characteristic of Virginia Woolf's later style is her tendency to blur outlines and fill up the spaces between things, to blend her voice so subtly with that of her subject that one often cannot be sure if a given line is something a character said or thought or felt, or something Mrs. Woolf herself is saying as she muses over her imaginary world. She dislikes stasis and hard, clear definition; and she has a terror of separateness that is perhaps intimated in her remark about the "dizzy and dangerous leap" she has to make between Eliot's lines.

Nevertheless, while most of the imagery in the passage I have quoted from *The Voyage Out* is so ordinary that it is unobtrusive, there are exceptions. Consider the last sentence of the first paragraph: "Longtailed birds clattered and screamed, and crossed from wood to wood, with golden eyes in their plumage." Perhaps this does not rank very highly qua image, but the line, coming as it does at the end of a paragraph, is calculated to affect us strongly. The fantastic and even violent sound of the birds' cries is meant to disrupt the quiet picture of people contemplating the warm autumn sky. The fact that the birds, clearly peacocks, are not named as such only adds to the strangeness of the moment. The beauty of the afternoon, therefore, is

12. See Hafley, *Glass Roof*, p. 174, n. 21.

tempered by a kind of elemental force that operates at the periphery of the scene. Indeed the passage is filled with hints of fear, suggestions of a more or less primitive and destructive power hovering at the edges of ordinary life. Notice the picture of the old lady gardeners: "millions of dark-red flowers were blooming, until the old ladies who had tended them so carefully came down the paths with their scissors, snipped through their juicy stalks, and laid them upon cold stone ledges in the village church." There is both sexuality and death in this description, something in the way the scissors cut through the "juicy stalks" of the "dark-red flowers" that disturbs the tranquillity of the scene.

Similarly, the sea is meant to remind us of an elemental force that can dwarf human beings. We are told that "very few people thought about the sea." But we are reminded of those houses where "the creeper taps on the bedroom windows," where the couples experience a mutual shudder as they kiss. Sexuality here is again associated with the fear of death and destruction, even if sex and death do not seem to be causally related. And toward the end of the passage, where the ship becomes more and more like the virgin Rachel Vinrace, the effect recurs: "The sea might give her death or some unexampled joy, and none would know of it." One of the essential qualities of Mrs. Woolf's fiction is the intrusion of these fantastic, eerie, potentially violent forces upon a tranquil and beautiful mood. Usually, too, the elemental forces which underlie the orderly, everyday patterns of British domesticity are emphatically sexual, as in the image of old ladies cutting flowers.

It is no accident that sex and death are linked so many times in this passage. Late in the novel, Rachel discovers sex in the jungles of Latin America; but she also acquires a fever, probably in the same steamy bower where she embraces her lover, so that she is quite literally given both an "unexampled joy" and death. For Rachel, the voyage out of the social and sexual restrictions of her life among maiden aunts in England, out of her lonely room toward the embrace of something "outside," is ultimately a voyage out of life. Usually, however, the theme of sex is approached in a highly indirect manner—often too indirectly, so that images of water and trees or flowers and insects carry the whole burden of Mrs. Woolf's meaning. Perhaps the best example of such a technique elsewhere in her writings would be her sketch "Kew Gardens," which sets off ordinary visitors to a park against the minutely observed, highly sexual life of the plants and insects. In any case, it is typical for her to use images of nature to indicate a beautiful, primitive, and often dangerous unity beneath ordinary life.

Throughout the passage at hand, there is a feeling, achieved in part by repetitions and rhythms in the prose, that everything is moving in a mysterious union. Much of this effect probably stems from the author's consistent use of the plural: "Great tracts of earth lay now beneath the autumn sun," "even the roofs of the great towns glittered," "In thousands of small gardens, millions of dark-red flowers were blooming." We are told of "Innumerable parties of picnickers," "men with cigars," "women with grey hairs," "little creatures in bathing drawers who were trotting into the foam all along the coasts of England, and scooping up buckets of water." The picture is rich with details, but details presented nearly always in the plural, to emphasize how each particular is multiplied many times over until it finds a place in a great pattern. Even the snatches of speech are spoken by many people at once. These speeches, quite banal out of their context, gain a mysterious quality because they seem to be repeated by choruses.

Indeed, evidence of Virginia Woolf's habit of describing details in the plural crops up everywhere in *The Voyage Out.* Even in passages of more or less conventional commentary vestiges of the technique appear. On the first page of the novel, for example, we are cautioned not to walk down narrow London streets arm-in-arm: "If you persist, lawyer's clerks will have to make flying leaps into the mud; young lady typists will have to fidget behind you." There is nothing unusual about such grammar in itself; now and then every writer will express habitual, typical, or repeated actions by means of a plural. But with Virginia Woolf the device becomes a mannerism. One thing it implies is a certain off-handedness, a willingness to step back and type people, as in this sentence from the scene focusing on the Prime Minister's car in *Mrs. Dalloway*: "Tall men, men of robust physique, well dressed men with their tailcoats and their white slips and their hair raked back, who, for reasons difficult to discriminate, were standing at the bow window of White's with their hands behind the tails of their coats, looking out, perceived instantly that greatness was passing." But in many cases, the language has a more serious tone, and we sense its deeper importance. Thus, in *The Voyage Out,* Virginia Woolf often refers to her characters as "they," as if "they" were a single organism. In the second half of the novel, as the characters voyage upriver into the heart of a jungle darkness, her descriptions are full of sentences like, "They seemed to be driving into the heart of the night . . . after walking round the deck three or four times, they clustered together, yawning deeply and looking at the same spot of gloom on the banks." Or there are related sentences such as this remarkable example: "The gentlemen, having smoked a certain number of cigarettes, dropped the glowing ends into the river and looked for a time at the ripples wrinkling the black water beneath them, undressed too, and lay down at the other end of the boat." Nearly every one of Mrs. Woolf's novels includes similar moments, where the style suggests mass hypnosis, with people not only acting but thinking in unison. People, she implies, are not so separate or individual as they might seem. Certain elemental emotions—call them the "id," or the "racial memory," or "Nature," or, as Rachel Vinrace does, "Reality" —cluster at the root of their lives. And whenever these emotions are touched, whether by a sunset or a dark river or a skywriting airplane, the group becomes like a single person.

In the passage I am considering from *The Voyage Out,* the reader is told that the people on land and the people at sea felt very different things. But the technique almost belies the notion that human beings are individual entities. Perhaps it is significant that the people on land are divided into various groups, whereas in the last paragraph the author adopts the impersonal pronoun "one" to describe the reactions of people at sea, people who are far enough removed from ordinary life to have common reactions. Indeed, the farther we move out into the vast sea, the more the differences between people dissolve; and ultimately the passage conveys a sense of some great unity in life.

Such visions of a vast natural pattern are central to the novel, and they remain a central preoccupation in all of Mrs. Woolf's fiction. They are related to the theme of love, with the understanding that the meaning of the word is as much spiritual as physical. *The Voyage Out* contains many references to the gulf that separates people from anything outside themselves. Occasionally, however, the narrator will step back from her characters, subordinating their individuality to a great community. By this means she attempts to suggest that a kind of unity exists outside the ego; to capture that heightened feeling of reality which Bernard in *The Waves* calls a "splendid unanimity."

Likewise, some people in *The Voyage Out*—especially Rachel Vinrace and Terence Hewet—seek to realize a sense of unity with the world outside themselves, to share their deepest feelings with at least one other person. But here is a difficult problem for Virginia Woolf; indeed, it is the crucial problem in all her fiction: the gulf between people or between the ego and the world outside is not to be traversed without some cost. Once the voyage is made, a certain loss of individuality, a dissolution of the self, is the inevitable result. One cannot, at least not in the terms of Virginia Woolf's fiction, come to a heightened awareness of one's unity with what is "out there" and at the same time conceive of significant individuals. Mrs. Woolf suggests that beneath the surface of civilization there runs a current of emotion, a general truth that unites all men who submit to it. To make oneself fully aware of this current is to subordinate reason to feeling, and to lose awareness of the self.

In *The Voyage Out,* the loss of self through contact with an outside reality takes place not only in the one-to-one relationship between people, as in a love affair, but also in the very fabric of Virginia Woolf's prose, in the relationship of the author to her subject matter. In the passage at hand, for example, Virginia Woolf is obviously attempting to portray a scene which she believes is of some emotional importance. If she has not been vouchsafed a mystic vision, she at least has drawn near to a deeply-felt sense of unity in life which gives rise to an imaginative awe; and in attempting to portray this unity, her style, her whole role as narrator undergoes a transformation. As I indicated at the beginning of this discussion, her transition from a more or less conventional exposition to an emotional, lyric presentation of landscape is accompanied by a kind of self-effacement. The first sentence of the passage implies an author whose personality can be felt quite openly. Its style leans toward the epigrammatic; the speaker remarks upon "The preliminary discomforts and harshnesses, which generally make the first days of a sea voyage so cheerless and trying to the temper." From the moment the description of landscape begins in the second sentence, however, the narrator becomes more subdued, almost like a ghostly voice. Particularly toward the end of the passage, where the ship is being described, there is a curious ambiguity about the whole status of the narration: "An immense dignity had descended upon her . . . she was more lonely than the caravan crossing the desert . . . The sea might give her death or some unexampled joy . . . She was a bride going forth to her husband, a virgin unknown of men." These remarks do not seem to come from a lofty authorial presence, but from a person who feels deeply what some character on board the ship might feel. The words, ostensibly about the ship, make as much or more sense if they are regarded as the thoughts of Rachel Vinrace about herself—or as the narrator's thoughts about Rachel. It is Rachel who is in fact a virgin ("unknown of men" is the sort of redundancy that appears now and then in these descriptive passages), and her virginity is one of the central issues of the novel. At any rate, by this point the narrator is interfused with the scene and living in it, so much so that distinctions between things become a bit hazy. The passage as a whole, after the opening sentence, seems an attempt to assimilate various experiences into an elemental pulse felt in the prose rhythms. The author, Rachel Vinrace, and the *Euphrosyne* are no longer separate entities.

This submission of the narrator's ego to the world she writes about, this blurring of boundaries, has been observed many times by Mrs. Woolf's critics, though it is not always described in the terms I have used here. However they account for the phenomenon, many readers have discovered that it can be difficult to tell where the voice of Mrs. Woolf's persona leaves off and where the voices of her characters begin.[13] In *The Voyage Out,* for example, she describes a small European community asleep in the hotel at Santa Marina as follows:

One could almost hear a hundred people breathing deeply, and however wakeful and restless it would have been hard to escape sleep in the middle of so much sleep. Looking out

[13]. Auerbach has placed the strongest emphasis on this trait of style. See also M. C. Bradbrook, "Notes on the Style of Mrs. Woolf," *Scrutiny,* May 1932, pp. 33–38.

of the windows, there was only darkness to be seen. All over
the shadowed half of the world people lay prone, and a few
flickering lights in empty streets marked the places where
their cities were built. [p. 127]

We seem to view this scene through the eyes of a character, or
perhaps the eyes of a hypothetical interloper, who begins to
feel drowsy, looks out the windows, and contemplates "the
shadowed half of the world." But the indefinite "One could"
at the beginning of the passage leaves us in doubt as to whether
some people in the hotel are "wakeful," or whether Virginia
Woolf herself has been drawn into the fictional cosmos by the
sheer force of sympathy.

In the later novels especially, such ambiguities imply a *communion* between the author and the world she has envisioned,
a relationship that is different, at least in degree, from anything
in traditional English fiction. It is true that in Virginia Woolf's
novels, as in a great deal of modern fiction, the narrator's personality is effaced, her role as a commentator greatly reduced.
But her reasons for employing this technique are quite different from the ones that motivated James or Ford or Joyce to
withdraw from the scenes they created. In fact Virginia Woolf
does not withdraw; she is pulled into the fiction by the intensity of her emotions. Far from being a silent and aloof
author, she seems to wander through the story like a ghostly but
unprivileged observer, often sharing in the thoughts and sensations of the characters. Her narration is "impersonal" only
in the sense that she makes relatively few overt judgments.
Otherwise she gives the impression of being intimately involved, sympathetic to such a degree that her voice becomes
selfless, disembodied.

And this effect is in some ways analogous to what happens
to people in the novels. In *The Voyage Out,* for example,
whenever the characters feel a sense of love or communion,

they lose themselves in trances or sleep. Rachel is constantly pre-occupied with a desire to escape the confines of individuality and share her deepest feelings with someone else: "It appeared that nobody ever said a thing they meant," she thinks, "or even talked of a feeling they felt, but that was what music was for." Rachel's movement toward sexual love, toward a condition where her feelings are in absolute harmony with something or someone outside herself, is reflected in a series of contrasts between the "surface," the everyday world of conventional relationships, and the "depths," the primitive, communal flow of life that Mrs. Woolf emphasizes throughout. The beautiful depths, however, are dangerous. They are like the storm at sea which troubles the passengers of the *Euphrosyne*: "after their view of the strange under-world, inhabited by phantoms, people began to live among tea-pots and loaves of bread with greater zest than ever." Perhaps not surprisingly, Rachel's desire for love leads eventually to a total loss of self in death.

3

The Artist as Lover:
The Voyage Out Continued

*Love is the mysterious vital attraction which draws things
together, closer, closer together. For this reason sex is the
actual crisis of love. For in sex the two blood systems, in
the male and female, concentrate and come into contact,
the merest film intervening. Yet if the film breaks down,
it is death. . . .*

  *In spiritual love, the contact is purely nervous . . . . the
pitch can rise higher and higher. But carry this too far, and
the nerves begin to break, to bleed, as it were, and a form
of death sets in.*
D. H. Lawrence, *Studies in Classic American Literature*

I

The difference between the "surface" and the "depths" of life
in *The Voyage Out* is much the same as the difference between
England and the South American country Rachel voyages to.
In a summary of the history of that place (pp. 100–03), Virginia Woolf suggests how the settings echo the theme. The

major part of the novel takes place in a lush, sexual landscape which is also sinister and destructive. The land has been impervious to the activity of European colonialism. "Men like Richard Dalloway," "Indians with subtle poisons," "vengeful Spaniards and rapacious Portuguese" have poured over the country like so many insects. All that remains as a vestage of their invasion is the village of Santa Marina, which, we are told, is "not much larger than it was three hundred years ago." Only the tiny village with its resort hotel shelters the Europeans from the dark beauty around them.

The Latin American landscape is set off against the English landscape through a series of basic contrasts—night and day, for example, or water and land. By means of these contrasts, Virginia Woolf develops a kind of metaphor for her view of experience. At the risk of seeming overly obvious or simpleminded about this metaphor, I want to state as clearly as I can its primary significance: the human personality is divided, having both a civilized exterior of manners and routine, of tea cakes and prime ministers, and a profound, obscured inner life of passion and feeling. So in the novel there is a light half of the world and a dark half—on the one hand a world of manners, politics, and reason, where the masculine will dominates and where a few individuals like the Tory politician Richard Dalloway wield power; and on the other hand a world of primitive feeling, where the more feminine impulse toward being is strongest and where individuals, usually isolated, desire to be united and subordinated under a natural law. In departing from the brightly-lit, busy streets of London and voyaging to a village with the exotic, watery name of Santa Marina, the characters of the novel enter a strange, passionate, half-obscured world which is analogous to the private self. Thus the literal voyage out represents a psychological or spiritual voyage inward.

Significantly, the South American landscape is depicted as

both frightening and beautiful. The violence and fear that we sensed in the picture of the English landscape are here made much more evident. In the description of night at the hotel in Santa Marina (pp. 127–28), we are told that in the "dark half of the world" there was for the space of six hours a "profound beauty," but that it was "more mysterious than the earth colored and divided by roads and fields." Wild and dangerous animals are abroad; an owl flies past and we catch an eerie glimpse of the moon. All the elements of human life seem attenuated by sleep, and the description of the hundred people breathing, which I have already quoted, exerts a hypnotic fascination: "however wakeful and restless it would have been hard to escape sleep in the middle of so much sleep." In this nether-world we are closer in spirit to what Virginia Woolf saw as an intense and true form of experience, an ultimate reality. But at the same time we are very close to extinction as individuals: there is a frightening and destructive quality in all this beauty, which is not very far from death itself.

As we have seen, even the prose style of the novel ranges back and forth as the writer attempts to capture two views of experience. On the one hand is a personable narrator with an elegant, somewhat ironic style and a more or less detached view of life (visible in the opening paragraphs of the novel), and on the other is a dreamy, poetic voice which expresses a muted awe toward nature and a desire to be united with it. The author remains in the book as a presence, but instead of providing a traditionally discursive, epigrammatic commentary, she sometimes speaks like a poet. She muses over the scene and imparts its meaning through nuances of rhythm and image; she paints symbolic landscapes and speaks to us in metaphor. The commentary is still there, but it is slightly veiled, more intense than ordinary prose, and often impressive as only poetry is impressive.

Thus far, however, I have been considering only passages of

description, where the author stands at some remove. A great deal of *The Voyage Out* is made up of the internal, purely subjective experience of the characters, especially the experience of Rachel. Through Mrs. Woolf's depiction of Rachel's sensibility, we can see perhaps even more clearly the themes I have been discussing. At the same time, we can study the first instance of Mrs. Woolf's treatment of consciousness, a subject I want to treat at length in terms of the later novels.

Early in the book, Rachel is seen drifting toward sleep in a state of "dreamy confusion":

> [H]er mind seemed to enter into communion, to be delightfully expanded and combined, with the spirit of the whitish boards on deck, with the spirit of the sea, with the spirit of Beethoven Op. 112, even with the spirit of poor William Cowper there at Olney. Like a ball of thistledown it kissed the sea, rose, kissed it again, and thus rising and kissing passed finally out of sight. The rising and falling of the ball of thistledown was represented by the sudden droop forward of her own head, and when it passed out of sight she was asleep. [p. 35]

In this case, as in many scenes where Mrs. Woolf presents an inner view of her characters (compare Clarissa Dalloway working over her sewing or Mrs. Ramsay seated at the window), we are caught on a borderline between sleeping and waking. The narrator leans very close to Rachel and tries to evoke the emotional quality of the moment. We know that Beethoven's Op. 112, Cowper at Olney, the sea, the white boards of the ship have all become intermingled in Rachel's mind; more important, however, is the stress on the way the mind, as it enters this twilight area on the border of sleep, feels in "communion" with the objects around it, seems "expanded and combined" with the very boards on the deck. There is a good deal of emphasis on rhythm; the repetitions of "rising" and "kissing," the suggestion of floating thistledown and undulating wave, are meant to reinforce the slightly sexual mood that draws Rachel toward sleep.

This passage is clearly not a direct quote from Rachel's mind; it is spoken by the same narrative voice which renders the descriptions of landscape. But beyond this fact, it is sometimes difficult to say exactly how much of the passage represents notions or images that are actually in Rachel's thoughts. We know that the last sentence, describing the rise and fall of Rachel's head and announcing the moment when she falls asleep, is not something Rachel could be aware of. But we have to read the passage carefully to determine whether Rachel actually thinks her mind is like a ball of thistledown or whether the simile is applied from outside by the narrator. Indirect quotation, whether it occurs in Dostoyevsky, Flaubert, or Joyce, always results in this sort of ambiguity. But in Virginia Woolf's later novels, as we shall see, the ambiguity takes on greater dimensions and importance.

Anyone who has read Mrs. Woolf's novels can cite several passages roughly comparable to the one I have quoted. Something in this sort of moment seems to have exerted a powerful hold over her imagination. Such occasions, when the vestiges of individuality begin to fall away and the character is pulled toward a somewhat erotic communion with the world itself, can be found everywhere in her fiction. That these passages are something more than a simple evocation of sleepiness, that they are related to a concept of reality, is often explicitly affirmed by internal evidence. Just a line or so above the passage I have quoted, for example, Rachel has these thoughts: "Reality dwelling in what one saw and felt, but did not talk about, one could accept a system in which things went round and round quite satisfactorily to other people, without often bothering to think about it, except as something superficially strange." While there is clearly a distance between Rachel and Virginia Woolf

—the author has already indicated that the girl is sheltered, badly educated, and prone to girlish fantasies—nevertheless Rachel in such moments expresses something which is not very far from Virginia Woolf's own view of experience. "Reality," in this view, dwells in "what one saw and felt, but did not talk about." Virginia Woolf, of course, does talk about it, or at least she tries to indicate its presence, but she conceives of reality as something quite apart from the social order of experience, removed from the dialectic of active personal relationships. This does not mean, however, that her reality is solipsistic; on the contrary, it can be seen and felt by everyone who will open themselves to it, as *The Voyage Out* attempts to show.

In the page and a half leading up to the moment when Rachel falls asleep, Mrs. Woolf has been following her train of thought in a fairly literal way. "Lying in the hot sun her mind was fixed upon the characters of her aunts, their views, and the way they lived. . . . Why did they do the things they did, and what did they feel, and what was it all about? Again she heard Aunt Lucy talking to Aunt Eleanor . . ." So the passage goes, through Rachel's meditations on the nature of reality and until she falls asleep. There is nothing unusual about this form. It is an indirect quotation of Rachel's thoughts, something like what the Germans call *erlebte Rede*. Auerbach cites examples as early as Boccaccio. But the occasion here is different, and it demands a different use of the technique, in a striking departure from the traditional English novel. Rachel is doing nothing but lazing in the sun; she is not even under the pressure of any immediate problem, and we are shown how thoughts can range freely beyond the particular situation. She begins by reading *Tristan,* becomes bored, picks up *Cowper's Letters,* and reads "something about the smell of broom in his garden." This image evokes an almost completely unrelated picture in her mind: "the little hall at Richmond laden with flowers on the day of her mother's funeral, smelling so strong that now any flower-scent brought back the sickly horrible sensation." This in turn associates with another image, Aunt Lucy arranging flowers in the drawing-room:

> "Aunt Lucy," she volunteered, "I don't like the smell of broom; it reminds me of funerals."

And so we come to Rachel's thoughts about her aunts. We have here, in other words, *erlebte Rede* used to evoke an idle mind adrift on a sea of impressions. Auerbach describes the moment perfectly: "an insignificant exterior occurrence releases ideas and chains of ideas which cut loose from the present of the exterior occurrence and range freely through the depths of time." [1]

The master of this style is, of course, Proust, and it is with Proust, not Joyce or Richardson, that Mrs. Woolf must be compared. Even so, she is interested in something more than the past remembered; the first part of this scene is quite different from the dreamy mood evoked as Rachel falls asleep—in spite of the fact that the method of viewing the character remains essentially the same. Virginia Woolf begins with the Proustian moment only to take it a step further, to report a state of almost pure feeling, something beneath words and ideation. Indeed, the mature stages of her career are marked by an increasing tendency to render purely emotional states, where she is less interested in what her characters think than in how they feel. The Proustian novel shows the personality being liberated from time and space, but Mrs. Woolf goes even further until the personality itself becomes dissolved in total communion with what is "out there." Ultimately, the sense of being in contact with "reality" is replaced by a vast and peaceful darkness.

The temptation to link her with Joyce is always very strong, if only because the two are exact contemporaries and are so often

---

1. Auerbach, *Mimesis,* p. 540.

put in the same camp. But whereas Joyce put primary value on the ability to name a thing exactly and therefore know it, Virginia Woolf's emphasis seems quite the opposite. In Joyce, the meaning of experience is often related to encounters with words (see the opening chapters of *A Portrait of the Artist* or any page of *Finnegans Wake*), while in Virginia Woolf words seem at times superfluous, sometimes even false to the experience of something that is non-verbal. That is why Virginia Woolf's treatments of consciousness, here and in her later works, depends so greatly on indirection and on metaphors used to describe a character's state of emotion, as in the following passage, occurring late in the novel. Rachel, who has contracted a fever but does not yet know it, is again found sitting drowsily in the sun:

> Many books had been tried and then let fall, and now Terence was reading Milton aloud, because he said the words of Milton had substance and shape, so that it was not necessary to understand what he was saying; one could merely listen to his words; one could almost handle them.
>
> There is a gentle nymph not far from hence,
>
> he read,
>
> > That with moist curb sways the smooth Severn stream.
> > Sabrina is her name, a virgin pure;
> > Whilom she was the daughter of Locrine,
> > That had the sceptre from his father Brute.
>
> The words, in spite of what Terence had said, seemed to be laden with meaning, and perhaps it was for this reason that it was painful to listen to them; they sounded strange; they meant different things from what they usually meant. Rachel at any rate could not keep her attention fixed upon them, but went off upon curious trains of thought suggested by words such as "curb" and "Locrine" and "Brute," which

brought unpleasant sights before her eyes, independently of
their meaning. [pp. 398–99]

Here again Virginia Woolf reports thought in a manner rather
like the "free indirect" style, which allows the author to adopt
the mode of the character's thinking almost literally, while still
retaining the form of a third-person narrative. Again we have
a near-Proustian moment, or the frustration of that moment,
prompted by literature. The last sentence, however, describes a
free-associative state of mind, and the narrator departs from
indirect quotation in order to comment on the quality of
Rachel's mood. In this mood, words, floating along like
trinkets to stimulate the sensibility, have become detached
from any immediate experience.

Of course Mrs. Woolf did not choose the lines from Milton's
Comus arbitrarily. Rachel, like the lady in the poem, is a virgin
in need of help; it is appropriate that she, too, should call on
the water-nymph Sabrina, another "Virgin pure," whose home
is "Under the glassy, cool, translucent wave." But Harvena
Richter points out that in Milton's poem the young virgin is
not ill of a fever—she is enchained by the lusts of the flesh, in
the person of the evil magician Comus. "It is not coincidence
that the 'saving' of Rachel consists of being released through
her own death from . . . the fulfilling of the fleshly self from
which she shrank earlier in the novel when Richard Dalloway
kissed her. . . . At the novel's end, Rachel and Sabrina join
as the sheets of her bed turn to water . . . Sabrina, the water
spirit, a lovely death-wish, has come for her." [2] This strikes me
as a brilliant observation which reveals the central issue of the
novel. I would stress, however, that I do not believe Virginia
Woolf herself saw Rachel's death with the same critical detachment. There is an extraordinary ambivalence in her approach
to death and sexuality in *The Voyage Out,* and it is not

2. Richter, *Inward Voyage,* p. 124.

exclusively a product of Rachel's shrinking from the flesh; it derives also from the author's own implicit attitudes. Indeed, in a sense Rachel's tendency to shrink from sex is balanced by her eventual initiation into its mysteries. Her embrace of Hewet in the jungle is treated as a fulfillment, and there is no real evidence that she wants to avoid marriage, though she and Hewet waver back and forth between feeling "divisions" and feeling "indivisible." On the other hand, the correlation between sex and death is stressed at every turn—in Rachel's imagination, in the events of the plot, even in the imagery of the descriptive passage I discussed in the previous chapter. Furthermore, the experience of sex is made to resemble in many ways the experience of those hypnotic, almost self-destructive moods that repeatedly overcome Rachel and some of the other characters.

At several points in the book Virginia Woolf details these trancelike moods, each time trying to imitate the character's feeling by means of the various devices that give her prose its pronounced rhythmical effects. In chapter 10, for example, we again find Rachel sitting in the heat of the day, in a state of mind near sleep or hypnosis: "The sounds of the garden outside joined with the clock, and the small noises of midday, which one can ascribe to no definite cause, in a regular rhythm. It was all very real, very big, very impersonal, and after a moment or two she began to raise her first finger and to let it fall on the arm of her chair so as to bring back to herself some consciousness of her own existence." She undergoes a kind of "dissolution" which is so complete that

> she could not raise her finger anymore, and sat perfectly still, listening and looking always at the same spot. It became stranger and stranger. She was overcome with awe that things could exist at all. . . . She forgot that she had any fingers to raise. . . . The things that existed were so immense and

so desolate. . . . She continued to be conscious of these vast
masses of substance for a long stretch of time, the clock still
ticking in the midst of the universal silence. [p. 145]

Such passages help to prefigure Rachel's death, but they also
demonstrate how the individual—in Virginia Woolf it is usually
a female individual—can be mesmerized by the strokes of a
clock or a lighthouse beam and thus experience a different,
timeless world. Sometimes these moments of awareness are
induced by strong emotions such as anger or love; but no
matter what emotion prompts them, they are always associated
with a hypnotic rhythm that is potentially destructive. Thus in
chapter 13 Rachel falls into a euphoric state, this time described
as hypnosis, brought on by her sexual awakening and her
growing love for Hewet. She watches a butterfly opening and
closing its wings, and this establishes a rhythm for the moment.
Again Virginia Woolf employs metaphor to describe an emotional condition: "each word as it came into being seemed to
shove itself out into an unknown sea." Again, though we are
taken very far inside the girl, the quality of the experience is
not such that it can be captured by a quotation from her mind.
Instead we are told only that Rachel has discovered love, and
that she has found "a terrible possibility in life." The emphasis
here should fall on "terrible," a word which is repeated later on
during the climactic love scene between Rachel and Hewet. In
every case, such emotional states entail a danger to the self,
manifested either through sexual love or through a "dissolution" into something outside the self.

The Voyage Out often counterpoints scenes which show
Rachel among people and scenes which show her in sedentary
moods of discovery, playing off a social comedy against the
more poetic and even mystic ramifications of the theme. Thus
in chapter 12 there is a very fine episode depicting the relationship between Rachel, Hewet, and St. John Hirst at a dance

given at the hotel. Hirst would like to be in love with Rachel, but his ugliness and shyness prevent him, so that he masks his awkwardness behind his intellectual superiority. The scene, which begins with Hirst trying to talk with Rachel and ends with him making her hurt and angry, is a good indication of how well Mrs. Woolf could handle a conventionally realistic technique rendered largely through dialogue and event. It is also another variation on the theme of love and communication, since Rachel, after being offended, complains to Hewet, " 'It's no good; we should live separate; we cannot understand each other.' " Hewet, amused by the incident, has to explain to Rachel that Hirst was in fact " 'trying to make friends.' " The result is an effective picture of the interplay between two young people who are frightened of one another—Hirst growing defensive and aloof because Rachel is a pretty girl at a dance, Rachel becoming withdrawn and angry because of Hirst's air of superiority.

This dance is effectively juxtaposed with an episode that takes place the following morning, when Rachel goes walking along a riverbed with volumes of Gibbon and Balzac: "The constraint of being among strangers in a long silk dress made it unusually exciting to stride thus alone." Again we have Rachel in solitude, and again the narrator remains unobtrusive, describing Rachel's thoughts and sensations. Our attention, however, is directed mostly to the landscape, which is primitive and harshly beautiful: "In this land where the population was centered in the towns it was possible to lose sight of civilization in a very short time, passing only an occasional farmhouse, where the women were handling red roots in the courtyard; or a little boy lying on his elbows on the hillside surrounded by a flock of black strong-smelling goats." I have mentioned before that there are hints of sexuality in Mrs. Woolf's landscapes, but here the sexual motif is especially strong: "On the bank grew those trees which Helen had said it was worth the voyage out merely to see. April had burst their buds, and they bore large blossoms among their glossy green leaves with petals of a thick wax-like substance coloured by an exquisite cream or pink or deep crimson" (p. 204). It is in this landscape that Rachel falls into another of her dreamy moods, encounters the butterfly I have mentioned, and discovers a "terrible possibility" in life.

That such a scene does not represent any very close rendition of Rachel's consciousness should be fairly clear. Mrs. Woolf's point is made entirely by innuendo and indirection. Nevertheless in this particular case the indirection is not altogether justified. One could wish that the "terrible possibility"—in this case love brought on by sexual passion—might have been treated with less palpitation and more openness.[3] Indeed, where sex is concerned, the method and manner are sometimes more evasive than perceptive. Though sexuality is often the very basis of her novels, few of her characters are ever shown thinking directly about it. Where this novel is concerned, the voyage out clearly represents in part a sexual awakening for Rachel, who is guided by Helen Ambrose. But although the theme of sex is inseparable from the contrasts between the surfaces and the depths of character, from the emphasis on the process of life and death, sex itself never receives anything but an indirect treatment from Mrs. Woolf. To a large extent, Rachel's growth into sexual maturity is suggested by her reactions to the lush landscape. From the time Helen Ambrose discovers that Rachel has been profoundly disturbed by a kiss from Richard Dalloway until the time she learns that Rachel is in love with Hewet, we are not shown that Helen plays any really active role in Rachel's education. Presumably Mrs. Woolf wants to suggest

3. I do not mean that Mrs. Woolf should attempt to model herself after D. H. Lawrence (though she has more in common with him than is generally recognized). Her decision to treat sex indirectly is not fundamentally wrong; my quarrel is with the *degree* of indirection, especially in a novel that purportedly criticizes Victorian morality.

that Helen did play such a role, but she offers only hints, as in "those trees which Helen had said it was worth the voyage out merely to see."

Of course it could be that Rachel does not in fact receive any active education from Helen, that her growth is perfectly natural and Helen's tutelage quite indirect. If so, then Virginia Woolf has emphasized too strongly the inadequacy of nineteenth-century educations for young girls. For it is clear that one reason for Rachel's ignorance of sex is that people have assiduously avoided *telling* her anything about it. She is physically mature, but, Virginia Woolf makes plain, she cannot be expected to learn simply by a process of osmosis. Her initial experience with sex—Richard Dalloway's kiss—leaves her mystified and in considerable anxiety, not because of any sense of sexual inadequacy, but simply because she is so very ignorant. Her subsequent experience with sex—falling in love with Hewet at Santa Marina—is, however, not attended by the same kind of anxiety. Something has intervened, and presumably that something is Helen Ambrose, since it is not plausible that a dance, an excursion, and a love of landscape could tell the girl all she needs to know about her emotions. Nevertheless Virginia Woolf remains vague about this point, half-guilty herself of the faults she finds in nineteenth-century British life, shrinking from the flesh. Her rhythmic prose and sexually symbolic landscapes are made to bear too much of the task of illustrating the sexual theme, and the technique of indirection is at times a serious flaw.

Mrs. Woolf seems to have been conscious of some of her difficulties over sexuality. In a paper she delievered to The Women's Service League, she once spoke of her two greatest problems as a novelist: "These were two of the adventures of my professional life. The first—killing the Angel in the House—I think I solved. She died. But the second, telling the truth about my own experiences as a body, I do not think I solved. I doubt that any woman has solved it yet." [4] Nevertheless the passionate life, the life of the body, is central to her vision as a novelist. In attempting to deal with it, she developed many of the crucial elements in the "luminous halo" of her technique—as can be seen in her treatment of the love affair between Rachel and Hewet.

In the final third of the book, in the episodes describing the flowering of Rachel's love for Hewet and her subsequent death, the theme of sexuality is blended with a more general treatment of the power of nature itself, and we can see most clearly Virginia Woolf's preoccupation with states of emotion that dissolve the ordinary world of social relationships. At the same time, we are given confirmation of Helen Ambrose's thoughts on the quality of life: "Aimless, trivial, meaningless, oh no— what she had seen at tea made it impossible for her to believe that . . . the inanities of the afternoon shrivelled up before her eyes. Underneath the likings and the spites, the comings together and the partings, great things were happening—terrible things . . . a moment's respite was allowed, a moment's make-believe, and then again the profound and reasonless law asserted itself" (p. 322).

As the party of people from Santa Marina is about to make

---

4. Virginia Woolf, "Professions for Women," *Collected Essays*, 4 vols. (London: Hogarth Press, 1966), 2:288. Another passage from this essay is worth quoting, since it touches on hypnosis, watery depths, and sexuality: "I want you to imagine me writing a novel in a state of trance. . . . figure to yourselves a girl sitting with a pen in her hand . . . The image that comes to my mind when I think of this girl is the image of a fisherman lying sunk in dreams on the verge of a deep lake with a rod held out over the water . . . letting her imagination sweep unchecked round every rock and cranny that lies submerged in the depths of our unconscious being. Now came the experience which I believe to be commoner with women writers than with men. The line raced through the girl's fingers. Her imagination rushed away. It had sought the pools, the depths, the dark places where the largest fish slumber. And then there was a smash. . . . The girl was roused from her dream . . . she had thought of something, something about the body, about the passions which it was unfitting for her as a woman to say" (pp. 287–88).

the voyage inland upriver, we encounter the peculiar use of
"they" which I have remarked upon before. "When they all
stood upon its deck they found that it was a very small boat
which throbbed gently beneath them for a few minutes, and
then shoved smoothly through the water. They seemed to be
driving into the heart of the night." The emphasis on rhythm
and darkness and sleep is very pronounced in the passage. The
boat "throbbed gently beneath them," Mrs. Flushing speaks in
a "rhythmical tone" and begins to wonder "where they were to
sleep, for they could not sleep downstairs, they could not sleep
in a doghole smelling of oil, they could not sleep on deck, they
could not sleep—She yawned profoundly" (p. 325). There
are a number of sounds which work to lull the passengers toward sleep: the "rustling" of leaves, the "murmuring" of Mrs.
Flushing, the "thin and small" sounds of words. The boat seems
to voyage into the "heart of the night," where there is a "great
darkness." (I have mentioned *Heart of Darkness* once before
in regard to Mrs. Woolf's style; here there is not only Conrad's
insistence on mood, but even images that seem to owe vaguely
to his story.) We are told that the dark night takes away "all
desire for communication by making their words thin and
small." But in fact a deeper kind of communication seems to
have been achieved, for all the passengers share the one feeling.
Their individualities have been muted and the technique makes
them appear to move together for a few moments like a school
of fish, or like the separate parts of a single organism. The
style here becomes not only a foreshadowing of the sense of
total communion that the young lovers will feel at the heart of
the darkness, but also a means of representing the theme. The
Europeans, who have journeyed outward to a dark, passionate,
and sometimes frightening side of the earth, now commence a
journey inward which for a time will unify them with all nature. The dark and beautiful setting of the chapters which follow has a general import; it is a state of feeling objectified.

The travelers, and especially Rachel and Hewet, seem to fall
into a trance. Hewet, as he lies on deck watching the dark
shapes of the sky drift ceaselessly across his eyes, is "drawn on
and on away from all he knew, slipping over barriers and past
landmarks into unknown waters." This total relaxation of the
ordinary self, the sinking into a "deeper consciousness," is
analogous to several scenes noted earlier, where Rachel sinks
into sleep or reverie. Again, as in those scenes, the language
emphasizes sexual imagery and rhythm or undulation: "watching the tree-tops change their position slightly against the sky,
and arch themselves, and sink and tower huge." The repetitions, the rhythmic prose, the vaguely apprehended images, all
evoke a drowsy state of consciousness that is not conducive to
active thinking or the formation of words in the mind. We are
more interested in what the character "saw and felt" than in
what his mind might be saying.

The settings of the novel, as I have been attempting to indicate, are always used in a symbolic fashion. This is not to deny
that they have some realistic qualities, but only to insist that
details like the crowded London streets, the wide sea, the box-
like rooms of the hotel at Santa Marina, and the winding river
that carries the party of Europeans into a tropical forest are
meant to objectify a kind of internal landscape. Terence and
Rachel's love scene, for example, is set in a richly sensual bower:

> The path narrowed and turned; it was hedged in by dense
> creepers which knotted tree to tree, and burst here and there
> into star-shaped crimson blossoms. The sighing and creaking
> up above were broken every now and then by the jarring cry
> of some startled animal. The atmosphere was close and the
> air came at them with languid puffs of scent. The vast green
> light was broken here and there by a round of pure yellow
> sunlight which fell through some gap in the immense um-
> brella of green above, and in these yellow spaces crimson and

black butterflies were circling and setting. Terence and Rachel hardly spoke. [p. 331]

The scene has a number of characteristics I have noticed before. For example, in this moment of intense emotional communion words are either unnecessary or inadequate. The natural scene displays not only beauty but a kind of barely-contained power, and, in the "jarring cry of some startled animal," as in the scream of peacocks in the passage quoted earlier, an element of terror and violence. The circling and setting butterflies are reminiscent of the butterfly that appeared when Rachel experienced a dawning sexual knowledge. Here, as in that scene, the sexual passion of the two young people has been transferred to the landscape; there is no doubt of the sexuality in the surroundings, but the characters' behavior has been etherealized. The young lovers confront each other with professions of love, they embrace in a somewhat melodramatic fashion, tears roll down Hewet's cheeks, Rachel feels the pulse of life around her, and both make what they no doubt think are profound statements.

As I have already indicated, I believe that the treatment of sexuality in the novel is inadequate, or at least mismanaged; this scene is symptomatic of that inadequacy. The indirection of the method, although obvious in its intent, suggests a hesitancy to fully explore the sexual relationship between the two young people. The technique in itself is not at fault; indeed, it is deeply grounded in a view of experience that Virginia Woolf develops with great force and consistency in all her novels. But this scene is shamelessly overwritten, like a parody of a slick romantic story in a lady's magazine. It is given over entirely to what Dr. Leavis, in referring to Conrad, once called an "adjectival insistence," which implies in this case a reluctance to tell the truth about the body.

The snatches of dialogue have the unusual character I have

already cited as typical of Mrs. Woolf's most lyrical moments. Considered alone, the dialogue is reminiscent of the tentative conversation of lovers as they experience the sexual act, and we are probably supposed to keep this quality in mind as we read: " 'Does this frighten you?' . . . 'No . . . I like it.' . . . 'I like it.' . . . 'Do you like being with me?' . . . 'Yes, with you' " (pp. 331–32). These bits of talk seem to bubble up out of a vast silence, which, we are told, has "fallen upon the world." (An unfortunate phrase, but typical of the style of the passage.) The remainder of the talk is not really talk at all, but states of feeling that have been given a voice: " 'We are happy together,' " " 'Very happy,' " " 'We love each other,' Terence said." " 'We love each other,' she repeated." In Virginia Woolf's later novels, this mysterious kind of dialogue reappears in other contexts. It is related to the unusual technique employed in *The Waves,* as I hope to show, and it represents simply a declaration rising out of deep feeling, usually in a context where conventional conversation is unnecessary.

The speeches also help to impose a rhythm on the passage, in the way they echo one another: " 'I like it'—'I like it,' " "with me?'—'with you,' " " 'happy together'—'very happy,' " " 'we love each other'—'we love each other.' " Here, as in every other comparable passage in Virginia Woolf, there is a hypersensitivity to rhythm, prose verging upon poetry, and in this case the rhythms and indeed the whole pacing of the scene are designed to roughly approximate the curve of passion in sexual intercourse. Terence and Rachel walk for a time in the forest, their voices confessing affection. Then, "their steps unconsciously quickened . . . Faster and faster they walked; simultaneously they stopped, clasped each other in their arms, then, releasing themselves, dropped to the earth" (p. 332). There is a pause, during which the two draw close, quietly repeating one another's names; of Rachel we are told, "She was thinking as much of the persistent churning of the water as of her own feeling. On and on it went in the distance, the senseless and cruel churning of the water." After this "a very long time seemed to have passed." The two lovers rise from the ground, drowsy, and walk "as people walking in their sleep" (pp. 332–33).

Many details in the scene are meant to suggest a primitive and frightening power that is awe-inspiring and potentially destructive. Rachel's murmured "Terrible—terrible," reflects her awareness of that power, an awareness that colors her recognition of the beauty and force of sexual love. We have encountered this quality, however, in passages where Virginia Woolf is dealing not just with Rachel but with all the characters together: when the boat sets off up the river, for example, and even in the long passage contrasting the *Euphrosyne* with the landscape of Britain. It is, as I have already pointed out, central to the observation Helen makes about the "frightening things" that underlie the apparently trivial surface of life. Through a deep sense of sexual love, Terence and Rachel glimpse an elemental terror which Virginia Woolf suggests is the primitive biological force of life itself, terrible because it asserts itself over any human will, any individuality. An analogous point can of course be made concerning the great emphasis on sleep in this or any of Mrs. Woolf's novels. Here, the young couple feel drowsy after their passion has reached a kind of climax, and in this drowsiness, as at the height of their passion, they seem almost to have lost a sense of themselves. Hewet leads Rachel along, dimly anxious to get back to the rest of the party, but with no clear idea of where he is going: " 'I don't want to be late,' he said, 'because—' He put a flower into her hand and her fingers closed upon it quietly. 'We're so late—so late—so horribly late,' he repeated as if he were talking in his sleep" (p. 333).

In Virginia Woolf's fiction the more intense and meaningful states of feeling are always associated with dimness and depth, with some sort of drowsiness or hypnotic effect, with a blurring or effacing of the ordinary visible world, and with something very near to a death of the self. In their first euphoric recognition that they are in love, Rachel and Hewet are said to feel that they have "dropped to the bottom of the world together." They are mildly conscious of two layers of existence: the profound depths and the air above, where one finds "the Flushings talking, talking . . ." (p. 335). When the day of their adventure alone in the forest is fading, Rachel and Hewet still luxuriate in the depths: "as the dark descended, the words of others seemed to curl up and vanish as the ashes of burnt paper, and left them sitting perfectly silent at the bottom of the world. Occasional starts of exquisite joy ran through them, and they were peaceful again" (p. 338). They seem to have become one person, and in such sentences as this last one, they are described almost as if they were stirring in the peace of the womb, only dimly aware of the world outside. Even on the next day, Rachel is still withdrawn, and her condition is described as a kind of dream state: "The eyes of Rachel saw nothing. Yellow and green shapes did, it is true, pass before them, but she only knew that one was large and another small; she did not know that they were trees. These directions to look here and there irritated her, as interruptions irritate a person absorbed in thought, although she was not thinking of anything" (p. 339).

We are used to seeing young girls in love portrayed as somnambulists, but here there is something more serious involved. For one thing, the note of irritation is a precursor of the illness which Rachel has no doubt already acquired; for another, Rachel's feelings closely resemble those trancelike moods to which she has been prone from the start of the novel, moods that Virginia Woolf links to her apprehension of reality. In almost every way, however, the reality Rachel perceives is associated with death. Significantly, we are told in this passage that "she was not thinking of anything." Indeed whenever

Virginia Woolf's characters approach this hypnotic state they cannot be said to think in the ordinary sense. They yield up their wills entirely, so that nearly all active contact of the mind with the world is forsaken. They become passive agents, sensibilities, interested only in being. They enter a realm of experience which is common to everyone, where all emotion is reduced to a single essence comparable to the elemental forces in nature; and like the sheltering depths of the South American forest, their condition is at once joyful, peaceful, and destructive. Helen Ambrose seems to comment on this fact when she describes the jungle landscape as "very beautiful, but also sultry and alarming" (p. 340).

This strangely disturbing quality is perhaps emphasized most strongly at the climax of the voyage upriver, when the party of white men visits an Indian village. Life here is primitive, elemental, and, at first glance, beautiful. Women are squatting on the ground, plaiting straw, regarding the Europeans with inexpressive stares. Mr. Flushing has a conversation with a "lean majestic man, whose bones and hollows at once made the shapes of the Englishman's body seem ugly and unnatural." A native woman uncovers her breast to a baby, and "harsh, unintelligible cries" rise up amid the voices of the place. The pulse of life can be felt in the prose, which is heavy with parallels and repetitions:

> If they moved, it was to fetch something from the hut, or to catch a straying child, or to cross a space with a jar balanced on their heads; if they spoke, it was to cry some harsh, unintelligible cry. Voices rose when a child was beaten, and fell again; voices rose in song, which slid up a little way and down a little way, and settled upon the same low and melancholy note. . . . Peaceful, and even beautiful at first, the sight of women, who had given up looking at them, made them now feel very cold and melancholy. [p. 349]

The reactions of the members of the party to this scene are revealing: "Well," Terence sighs to Rachel, "it makes us seem insignificant, doesn't it?" Hirst, on the other hand, is almost unaware of the village; he can be seen wandering off, "absorbed in his own thoughts, which were bitter and unhappy, for he felt himself alone." And Helen, standing among the native women, feels "presentiments of disaster." "The cries of the senseless beasts rang in her ears high and low in the air . . . she became acutely conscious of the little limbs, the thin veins, the delicate flesh of men and women, which breaks so easily and lets the life escape compared with these great trees and deep waters" (pp. 349–50). Male and female sexuality are of course implicit in "great trees and deep waters." Hewet, as we have seen, is brought to a dreamy state by contemplating the masculine image of trees, and Rachel is associated with the sea and the "rushing waters" of the forest. These vital forces of nature are, however, greater than individuals, and anyone who commands more than a temporary knowledge of their power must pay with extinction. Perhaps that is why, after their union in the forest, Rachel and Hewet do not remain in their trance, but rather fluctuate between a sense of union and a sense of separateness.

For Rachel, however, there does come an ultimate union with Hewet, which results indirectly in her death. Her bout with fever begins like a troubled sleep; in fact she has a dream very like the one she experienced as a result of sexual anxiety after Richard Dalloway's kiss. The voyage toward the knowledge of sex and the voyage toward death have similar premonitions: "Rachel again shut her eyes and found herself walking through a tunnel under the Thames, where there were little deformed women sitting in archways playing cards, while the bricks of which the wall was made oozed with damp" (p. 404). Through much of the fever, Rachel feels an intense isolation from the rest of the world: "She was completely cut off, and unable to communicate with the rest of the world, isolated alone with her body" (pp. 402–03). But at the same time the quality of the imagery, the atmosphere of her emotions, suggests that she is being drawn into a world that has something in common with that deeper, more meaningful state which elsewhere in the book is contrasted to the relatively trivial surface of things.[5] As when she and Hewet felt their intense emotional communion, Rachel senses herself sinking to the bottom of the world. Her condition is painful and unpleasant, but ultimately it leads to an extinction of the personality and a kind of peace: "The sights were all concerned in some plot, some adventure . . . Now they were among the trees and savages, now they were on the sea; now they were on the tops of high towers . . . At last the faces went further away; she fell into a deep pool of sticky water, which eventually closed over her head . . . There she lay, sometimes seeing darkness, sometimes light, while every now and then someone turned her over at the bottom of the sea" (p. 416). Death, like sleep and intense union in love, has the attraction of the return to the womb. And ultimately, death has the power to bring about an intense communion; at the moment when Rachel dies, Terence feels that "their complete union and happiness filled the room with rings eddying more and more widely" (p. 431).

Here, as in *Jacob's Room, Mrs. Dalloway, To the Lighthouse,* and *The Waves,* death is seen in relation to the effect it has upon the living. Terence, finally recognizing the fact of Rachel's death, rushes out of the sickroom crying " 'Rachel, Rachel!' "—a cry very like the one that runs through *Jacob's Room* and *To the Lighthouse.* In the wake of the young girl's death, the community at the hotel huddles together; old Mrs.

5. See, for example, p. 343.

Thornbury feels drawn closer to her husband; and Evelyn
Murgatroyd, normally given to chatter and mild flirtation, feels
a sudden misgiving about the nature of her life: "Were these
proposals and intimacies and adventures real, or was the con-
tentment she had seen on the faces of Susan and Rachel more
real than anything she had ever felt?" The last pages of the
book, however, are devoted to the defensively cold and misanthropic St. John Hirst, who, having failed at his attempt to
"make friends" with Rachel, has since withdrawn even more
from others. After Rachel's death and a climactic thunder-
storm which seems to confirm Helen's speculations on nature's
"profound and reasonless law," Hirst sits, weary, in the common room of the hotel, and experiences his own moment of
being:

> All these voices sounded gratefully in St. John's ears as he
> lay half-asleep, and yet vividly conscious of everything around
> him. Across his eyes passed a procession of objects, black and
> indistinct, the figures of people picking up their books, their
> cards, their balls of wool, their work baskets, and passing
> him one after another on their way to bed. [p. 458]

And, the implication is, on their way to death. For the first
time, Hirst experiences one of those passive, drowsy moods
that have been typical of Rachel and Hewet. But Hirst's vision,
perhaps to show that for the first time he has yielded to the
impulse of love, perhaps to show that he is potentially more
wise, has people in it; and thus may be seen as analogous to
Virginia Woolf's vision. Indeed, Hirst is allowed to see things
in much the same way as the narrator of the passage I quoted
in the previous chapter: he has a vision of a procession of
people, somewhat indistinct, viewed from afar and obscured by
a dreamy mood, moving along in accordance with an elemental
pattern of life and death.

II

I hope now that it is possible to see how certain habits of Virginia Woolf's technique have a special relevance to the actions and events she describes. The sleepy, hypnotic moods that she renders so lovingly in all of her writings exerted a powerful hold on her imagination; so much so that often her novels can be understood in terms of the uneasy compromises the characters make between the will to live in the world and the temptation to dissolve all individuality and sink into a deathlike trance. Her first novel seems an unconscious reflection of these compromises, wavering between two kinds of experience: the rational, orderly, mannered world of regular proportions and social relationships, and the deeper world of intense feeling where individuals lose their sense of separateness and blend with nature. Very clearly, however, it is the latter emotional, feminine world that attracts Virginia Woolf most powerfully. She finds that this world represents something more real and intense than ordinary life can afford; or, to put it another way, it represents what ordinary life is all about. Her novel is not, therefore, simply about Rachel Vinrace. It concerns the elemental forces of sexuality, of life and death, that stir far down beneath the civilized and orderly exterior of British life. Rachel is a personification of that theme—a young virgin who journeys out to meet a bridegroom who is death. And Rachel's experience is seen ultimately in relation to the community at large, so that through her death that community, including its most rational member, Hirst, is able to sense the elemental affinities which are the pattern and meaning of life.

Sleep, death, and elemental passion are the means which enable the characters to apprehend reality. In life such apprehension endures only briefly; thus, once the first flush of her experience in the forest begins to wear off, the world takes on different proportions for Rachel. The sense of communion is valuable and important, but difficult to sustain, as Rachel notes. Perhaps the sort of communion we see in Helen and Ridley Ambrose is the best compromise life can offer in the long run. The most intense feelings of union with others or with the world are not achieved without a cost; either they are short-lived or they lead to extinction.

It was this kind of experience, however, which determined the whole character of Virginia Woolf's special approach to the novel, and which helps account for the peculiar nature of her style. Nearly all of her writings are governed by her belief in some essential rhythm in life; one feels the hypnotic pulse throughout her prose, but it becomes strongest during moments of emotional intensity. She has an antipathy toward aesthetic stasis, which inhibits the flow of a constant rhythm, and even in her essays she seems naturally drawn from the analytical to the emotional, from the ethical, judicial plane to the substance of life itself. Likewise, her most sympathetic characters are creatures of sensibility, embodiments of the feminine principle of being, who want most of all to give themselves up to feeling, to find unity between themselves and the world. But it is also true—and here is a crucial point—that these characters exemplify a death wish. Thus we have Mrs. Ramsay's famous meditation:

> To be silent; to be alone . . . one shrunk, with a sense of solemnity, to being oneself, a wedge-shaped core of darkness. . . . Losing personality, one lost the fret, the hurry, the stir; and there rose to her lips always some exclamation of triumph over life when things came together in this peace, this rest, this eternity. [*To the Lighthouse,* pp. 99–100]

To illustrate how the attraction of death influenced the character of Mrs. Woolf's prose and the development of her peculiar narrative method, I offer one last passage from *The Voyage*

Out. It appears in chapter 25, as Rachel briefly regains consciousness after a particularly severe attack of her fever:

> a wave seemed to bear her up and down with it; she had ceased to have any will of her own. . . . It was true that she saw Helen and saw her room, but everything had become very pale and semi-transparent. Sometimes she could see through the wall in front of her. . . . The room had an odd power of expanding. . . . It sometimes took an hour for Helen to raise her arm, pausing long between each jerky movement, and pour out the medicine. [p. 423]

I would suggest that the effects of Rachel's fever are akin to the "semi-transparent" view of life in Virginia Woolf's later novels, where one seems borne along upon a wave of finely-modulated prose, where time and the proportions of things appear greatly distorted, and where the narrator, if she has not exactly suspended her will, at least seems to have merged with her characters and her subjects. Indeed, Rachel's peculiar, feverish sensibility almost epitomizes the kind of atmosphere Mrs. Woolf said she wanted to convey in the modern novel.

One is tempted at this point to indulge in psychoanalysis. The events of Mrs. Woolf's life—her frailty, her mental breakdowns, some of the records she has preserved in her diary, and of course her suicide—all provide evidence for conjecture on the close relationship between her life and her fiction. She has described in her diary, for example, a "nervous breakdown in miniature," in which she appears to have felt a loss of "character and idiosyncrasy as Virginia Woolf," a blankness of mind and wish to be alone. In this state she had "no pleasure in life whatsoever; but felt perhaps more attuned to existence." [6] Without, however, placing too much emphasis on the private aspects of Mrs. Woolf's life, it is clear enough that as a writer she was

6. Woolf, *A Writer's Diary,* p. 97.

given to a kind of presentation that almost dissolves the boundaries of character—even, as we shall see, the boundaries that separate the fictional characters from the narrator. She was attracted to death, like the narrator of her sketch, "A Mark on the Wall":

> Yes, one could imagine a very pleasant world. A quiet, spacious world, with the flowers so red and blue in the open fields. A world without professors or specialists or housekeepers with the profiles of policemen, a world which one could slice with one's thought as a fish slices water with his fin, grazing the stems of the water-lilies, hanging suspended over the nests of white sea eggs. . . . How peaceful it is down here, rooted in the centre of the world and gazing up through the grey waters, with their sudden gleams of light, and their reflections—if it were not for Whitaker's Almanack—if it were not for the Table of Precedency! [7]

One can sympathize with a dislike for Whitaker's Almanack, and even respond to the touch of humor in such a passage; but there is something a bit frightening about this seaworld, a retreat from active contact with life which implies a kind of death. Virginia Woolf recognizes the dangers implicit in abandoning oneself to such a world, but at the same time it represents for her an intense vision of reality, and much of her fiction reflects her desire to be united with it.

By referring to "A Mark on the Wall," however, I am anticipating the subject matter of the next section, where I hope to indicate how Mrs. Woolf developed an increasingly impersonal and poetic technique that accords with her vision of reality. "A Mark on the Wall" is an experiment in what we can safely call the *monologue interieur,* a sketch in which the protagonist in-

7. Virginia Woolf, "A Mark on the Wall," *A Haunted House and Other Stories* (London: Hogarth Press, 1967), p. 46.

dulges in what appears to be a Freudian daydream. But Virginia Woolf was not satisfied with this particular method; her problem was to show that such individual fancies were more than daydreams—that the strange visions of such a character represented reality and not solipsism or aberration. In an attempt to solve this problem, she engaged in the technical experimentation which produced *Mrs. Dalloway, To the Lighthouse,* and *The Waves.*

4

Virginia Woolf and the Stream
of Consciousness

Few things in Virginia Woolf's fiction have received so much attention from critics as her method of treating the inner lives of her characters. There have been a number of sensitive discussions of specific passages in her work, and a whole series of papers and books have been devoted to the *monologue interieur* and its variants in modern literature. Mrs. Woolf is still popularly known as a "stream-of-consciousness" writer, but even so there is comparatively little critical agreement over what such labels mean, and even less accord about how accurate they are as descriptions of her method.

The primary cause for the problem is a simple inability to agree on definitions of terms. Everyone acknowledges by now that stream of consciousness and interior monologue are troublesome phrases, often applied inaccurately, but there is still some disagreement about how they ought to be cleared up. Robert Humphrey, Melvin Friedman, Frederick Hoffmann, Wayne Booth, and several other writers either say or imply that stream of consciousness should designate a literary genre which subsumes interior monologue and several other possible techniques.[1] This, indeed, is coming to be the generally accepted notion. But Lawrence Bowling and Erwin Steinberg both contend that stream of consciousness is a rare technique, different from interior monologue, and that each term can be defined precisely.[2] Still another critic, Leon Edel, says that the terms have to do with a method that had better remain loosely defined, since few twentieth-century psychological novels are susceptible to any rigid classification.[3] And when one turns from theory to practical criticism, the confusion is magnified. Thus Virginia Woolf is called either a stream-of-consciousness writer or a writer of interior monologue by all of the people named above (though they disagree about specific novels), and by several commentators who have written at length about her work, including J. K. Johnstone and Ralph Freedman. But one of her best critics, James Hafley, who has his own rather narrow definition of the terms, states categorically that Virginia Woolf never at any time wrote stream-of-consciousness fiction;[4] and Walter

1. Robert Humphrey, *Stream of Consciousness in the Modern Novel* (Berkeley: University of California Press, 1954); Melvin Friedman, *Stream of Consciousness: A Study in Literary Method* (New Haven: Yale University Press, 1955); Frederick Hoffmann, *Freudianism and the Literary Mind* (Baton Rouge: Louisiana State University Press, 1945), pp. 126–29; Wayne Booth, *The Rhetoric of Fiction* (Chicago: University of Chicago Press, 1961), p. 54.

2. L. E. Bowling, "What is the Stream of Consciousness Technique?" *PMLA* 65 (1950), pp. 333–45; Erwin Steinberg, "the steady monologue of the interiors; the pardonable confusion . . . ," *James Joyce Quarterly* 6 (Spring 1969): 185–200. For additional attempts to define the terms, see Derek Bickerton, "Modes of Interior Monologue: A Formal Definition," *MLQ* 28 (1967): 229–39, and "James Joyce and the Development of Interior Monologue," *Essays in Criticism* 18 (1968): 32–37; H. A. Kelly, "Consciousness in the Monologues of *Ulysses*," *MLQ* 24 (1963): 3–12; Keith Leopold, "Some Problems of Terminology in the Analysis of the Stream of Consciousness Novel," *AUMLA* 13 (May 1960): 23–32; John Spencer, "A Note on the 'Steady monologue of the interiors,'" *A Review of English Literature* 6 (1965): 32–41.

3. Leon Edel, *The Psychological Novel, 1900–1950* (Philadelphia: Lippincott, 1955), p. 86.

4. Hafley, *Glass Roof*, pp. 73–75.

Allen seems to agree.[5] In the face of all these conflicting judgments, one wishes for some majestic edict which would fix the
necessary and sufficient characteristics of the terms once and for
all. But no such dictate is forthcoming.

The present study is not an attempt to rescue terminology
from its quagmire. At this stage, a new definition would do no
good at all, since it would have no more inherent value than
any of the others, and would only confuse the issue more. It is
far better to stay with the definitions we already have, since all
of them offer interesting insights, and they are not altogether
contradictory. It is, in fact, possible to find areas of implied
agreement in what the critics say about stream of consciousness
and interior monologue; and because of what this agreement
suggests, it is possible to isolate parts of Virginia Woolf's fiction
that might be included under the terminology. Nevertheless,
surprisingly little of her work actually conforms to the descriptions sometimes applied to it. This is especially true of *The
Waves,* which, it seems to me, is the quintessential example of
Mrs. Woolf's style during this period of her career. In *Mrs.
Dalloway* and *To the Lighthouse* Virginia Woolf develops and
refines a technique that is peculiar to her fiction, and *The
Waves* represents in many ways the ultimate refinement, the
purest example of what is idiosyncratic about her work.

It is wrong to simply label Virginia Woolf a "stream-of-
consciousness writer," but not because literary pigeonholes are
misleading. On the contrary, at a certain stage in the criticism
of art it is useful and even liberating to be able to classify styles
by means of broadly descriptive terms; and stream of consciousness is probably at least as good a description for a collective

5. Walter Allen, *The English Novel: A Short Critical History* (New
York: Dutton, 1954), p. 336. Allen makes an interesting point here when
he notes how Mrs. Woolf's characters seem "abnormally self-aware, watching their thoughts and feelings the whole time."

style as "baroque" or "decadent." (The term, it seems to me, does refer to a style rather than simply a kind of subject matter; even those who define it as a subject imply that it generates a specific variety of techniques.) It is misleading to apply it to Virginia Woolf, however, because there is evidence to show that she was temperamentally opposed to any detailed or extended literary excursion into consciousness, even while she was herself experimenting with such a method. Her reservations about Joyce, for example, cannot be written off as simply a case of rivalry or prudishness, though both of these motives were no doubt operative in an indeterminate sense. Mrs. Woolf was excited by the way Joyce, in the early chapters of *Ulysses,* was able to capture what she called the "tremor of susceptibility" in the self, but at the same time she felt his experiments tended to imprison the reader inside an individual ego. In her later fiction, as we shall see, the ego sometimes becomes a kind of antagonist, or at least something she has mixed feelings about. As a result of her dislike for what she called the "egotistic" quality in modern fiction, she tried to evolve a related style, but one more in keeping with what she called "life itself." In the preface to the first New York edition of *Mrs. Dalloway* she says her experiments preceded any philosophic commitment.[6] By the time of *To the Lighthouse,* however, she had come more and more to describe a reality which transcends the self; and this notion of a transcendant reality—implicit in her work all along —causes her to depart more and more from the early methods of Joyce.

Before I consider the novels, however, let me review the definitions of stream of consciousness. William James is credited with having coined the term, in *Principles of Psychology,* after rejecting such expressions as "train of thought," which he felt

6. Virginia Woolf, *Mrs. Dalloway* (New York: Harcourt, Brace, 1925), p. 15.

connoted a logically connected sequence.[7] James wanted to emphasize the fluid ramblings of the mind's conversations with itself, the jumble of instantaneous thoughts and impressions, and therefore his term suggests both a subject and a particular style. Though his metaphor is not always an accurate representation of what novelists have taken to be the texture of consciousness, it has stayed with us, in conjunction with the French *monologue interieur*—the two terms are sometimes used interchangeably.

Edouard Dujardin is named by Joyce as an originator of the interior monologue; Joyce, who was a bit perverse about hinting at his sources, claimed that Dujardin's *Les Lauriers sont coupés* (1887) inspired some of the techniques used in *Ulysses*. Dujardin, in the wake of Joyce's statement, issued a monograph with the lengthy academic title, *Le monologue interieur, son apparition, ses origines, sa place dans l'oeuvre de James Joyce* (1931). Dujardin claims in this work to have invented interior monologue, but his definition of the term is unclear, and seems based more on Joyce's practice than on his own. He defines the technique as "the speech of a character in a scene, having for its object to introduce us directly into the interior life of that character, without authorial intervention through explanations or commentaries; . . . it differs from traditional monologue in that: in its manner, it is an expression of the most intimate thought that lies nearest the unconscious; in its form, it is pro-

---

7. "Consciousness does not appear to itself chopped up in bits . . . It is nothing jointed; it flows . . . *let us call it the stream of thought, of consciousness, or of subjective life*" (William James, *Principles of Psychology* [New York: Henry Holt & Company, 1890], 1: 239; James' italics). Note also that James stresses the separateness of thought: "Absolute insulation . . . is the law. . . . Neither contemporaneity, nor proximity in space, nor similarity of quality and content are able to fuse thoughts together which are sundered by this barrier of belonging to different minds" (p. 226).

duced in direct phrases reduced to the minimum of syntax." [8]
What has puzzled critics most about his definition, and undoubtedly led to the interchangeable use of stream of consciousness and interior monologue, is that while at one point Dujardin
emphasizes that the technique represents the "speech" (*parole*)
of a character (even his name for the method implies a high
level of verbal awareness), he goes on to say that it expresses
"the most intimate level of thought that lies nearest the unconscious." Most critics agree that thoughts "nearest the unconscious" are not expressed by speech; to them consciousness implies a broad area of mental life with various degrees of conscious control, and they see the speech-making faculty as distinct
from that faculty which simply receives images or sensations.
Thus Dujardin's definition seems contradictory.

There have been several attempts to repair the vagueness of
Dujardin's commentary; purely for the sake of economy, we
might consider two of the more ambitious efforts, those by
Lawrence Bowling and Robert Humphrey. I choose these two
because in some ways they represent opposite solutions: Bowling
offers a very narrow definition of stream of consciousness, and
Humphrey believes that the term embraces several different
methods. All the other definitions are simply variations of these,
and where Bowling and Humphrey agree, so do the other
theorists.

Bowling observes that critics have had difficulty in using
stream of consciousness as a descriptive counter, because "they
have failed to recognize different variations within the . . .
technique." [9] To solve the problem, he argues that interior
monologue and pure stream of consciousness should represent

8. Edouard Dujardin, *Le monologue interieur* (Paris: A Messein, 1931),
pp. 58–59, trans. and quoted by Humphrey in *Stream of Consciousness in
the Modern Novel.*

9. Bowling, "What is the Stream of Consciousness Technique?", p. 333.

two slightly different things. Interior monologue, he contends, should apply to the level of mental life which is nearest ordinary speech; it describes, he says, "only that part of a character's interior life *farthest from* the unconscious." [10] It is devoted entirely to the verbal area of the mind, and does not take into account sensations and images. Furthermore, Bowling implies, interior monologue is characterized by a high degree of verisimilitude. "To be convincing," he says, "interior monologue must be no more logical and formal than ordinary speech." [11] And a bit later, he offers this rule:

> As we walk down the street and pass a house, we are aware that we are walking and we are aware that we see the house, but we do not bother to say silently to ourselves, "I am walking down the street; there is a house; I am passing the house." This type of awareness we do not normally express to ourselves in language form, and any attempt on the part of a writer to lift such phenomena to the same level of consciousness as ordinary interior monologue seems cumbersome and formal.[12]

According to this notion of what the term should represent, Bowling calls Molly Bloom's soliloquy in *Ulysses* an interior monologue. He also calls *The Waves* "a novel rendered exclusively in the form of interior monologue," [13] though he does not go on to say whether he thinks it a cumbersome and unconvincing work—*The Waves* is quite formal and full of statements like "I am walking down the street; there is the house."

At another level of consciousness is what Bowling calls sensory impression. When a writer wants to show this area of the

10. Ibid., p. 334.
11. Ibid., p. 336.
12. Ibid., pp. 337–38.
13. Ibid., pp. 339–40.

mind at work he focuses, according to Bowling, entirely on images and sensory data; and, presumably, his character does not think "I am walking down the street; there is the house," but something more like "street . . . house" in order to suggest that awareness on this level is not purely verbal. As an example, Bowling quotes a passage from Dorothy Richardson's *Honeycomb,* where the character Miriam steps out onto the street:

> grey buildings rising on either side, feeling away into the approaching distance—angles sharp against the sky . . . softened angles of buildings against other buildings . . . high moulded angels soft as crumb, with deep undershadows . . . creepers fraying from the balconies . . . strips of window blossoms across the buildings. [(1917), p. 137]

Stream of consciousness is, for Bowling, something of a mixture of interior monologue and sensory impression. It is to be recognized by the fact that it "includes *all* conscious mental processes," including "such non-language phenomena as images and sensations." [14] In other words, stream of consciousness incorporates interior monologue, and augments it by suggesting other mental activity. And this other activity is presented in such a way as to indicate that it takes place on a different level of the mind than the making of speech.

Bowling adds that it is important not to confuse stream of consciousness or interior monologue with what he calls "internal analysis," where "the author stands as an interpreter between us and the character's mind and gives us his *interpretation* of what the character thinks." [15] This, he points out, is the method Dorothy Richardson most often uses (it is Virginia Woolf's typical method, too, though he does not say so), and it is a method "fundamentally different" from stream of conscious-

14. Ibid., p. 334.
15. Ibid., p. 343.

ness; "the one *summarizes*, the other *dramatizes*; the one is
abstract, the other is *concrete*." [16] Stream of consciousness and
interior monologue, as he defines them, give *"a direct quotation
of the mind,"* but interior analysis, like the German *erlebte
Rede*, is indirect. "If . . . the author intervenes in any way
between the reader and the character's consciousness in order
to analyze, comment, or interpret, then he is employing not the
stream of consciousness technique, but . . . *internal analysis*." [17]

Bowling's definitions of stream of consciousness and interior
monologue rule out much of the literature to which the terms
have been applied. The only example he cites to illustrate
stream of consciousness where several levels of conscious awareness are suggested at once comes from Dujardin, whose method
is normally what Bowling calls internal analysis. An opposite
solution to the problem, however, is found in the slightly more
recent work of Robert Humphrey, who implies that since
writers like Joyce, Woolf, Richardson, and Faulkner have all
been called stream-of-consciousness novelists, we should aban-
don Dujardin's confused discussion and construct a new definition based on what the aforementioned novelists have in common. It is perhaps debatable that Joyce, Woolf, et al. are really
that much alike, except in general ways that would preclude a
detailed discussion of their very different styles; but once we
grant Humphrey this assumption, his argument has much in its
favor. Because these several novelists use different techniques,
Humphrey concludes that stream of consciousness is less a
method than a subject matter. For him, stream of consciousness
is a variety of psychological fiction, differing from other psychological literature—James, for example, or Proust—"precisely in
that it is concerned with those levels of consciousness that are
more inchoate than rational verbalization—those levels on the

16. Ibid., p. 344.
17. Ibid., p. 345.

margin of attention." [18] The apparent technical differences from writer to writer and novel to novel can be reconciled, he argues, by simply regarding them as slightly different means to get at the same end. Thus he indicates four major techniques which are instruments of the stream of consciousness novel: direct and indirect interior monologue, omniscient or conventional treatments, and soliloquy.

Direct interior monologue he describes as the most dramatic of the techniques: it gives the impression of unedited material, with no overt clue indicating that the author is present. Indirect interior monologue is essentially the same, but it allows for a third-person view of the character as well as occasional minor interpolations from the author (presumably similar to *erlebte Rede*). Humphrey cites Joyce's treatment of the last chapter of *Ulysses* as an example of direct monologue, and *Mrs. Dalloway* and *To the Lighthouse* as examples of the indirect method. The omniscient technique is just what the name implies; the author stands between the character and the reader and describes consciousness in the third person. The difference between this method and the ordinary omniscient view, Humphrey says, is that it is devoted to an essentially disorganized subject. He cites Dorothy Richardson as an example of the technique, and points out how she always remains "within the mind of the character" and uses a primarily "descriptive" method. The difference between *Pilgrimage* and *Robinson Crusoe,* he says, is that Miriam's consciousness is represented in all its "unformulated, unspoken, incoherent state." [19] The fourth major technique, soliloquy, he defines as "presenting the psychic content and processes of a character directly from character to reader without the presence of an author, but with an audience tacitly assumed. . . . The point of view is always the character's, and the level of con-

18. Humphrey, *Stream of Consciousness in the Modern Novel*, pp. 2–3.
19. Ibid., p. 34.

sciousness is usually close to the surface." [20] He refers to *The Waves* and William Faulkner's *As I Lay Dying* as examples of the method.

In his discussion of these four techniques, Humphrey emphasizes that the focus is primarily on the mental wanderings of the characters, and that the author records the thoughts more or less in the sequence they occur. Though Humphrey would allow for considerable artificiality in the transcription of thought, he contends that all stream-of-consciousness techniques have something in common: they suggest "the actual texture of consciousness." [21] Stream-of-consciousness writers, he says, all make use to some degree of free association, discontinuity, or imagery that has private connotations for the characters, in order to show the "inchoate" nature of their subject.

Thus, while Bowling would limit considerably the use of terms like stream of consciousness or interior monologue, Humphrey tends to broaden their use. Nevertheless, in spite of the broad areas of disagreement between these two critics, they do concur on two fundamental points: first, that stream of consciousness, whether it is a technique or a subject matter (and one cannot easily separate the two), is especially concerned with a private and essentially disorganized part of the mind; second, that stream-of-consciousness fiction always focuses on the contents of a character's mind at a given point in space and time, in order to suggest a record of thought as it occurs, as it rises out of a circumstantial context. If stream of consciousness is not always represented by a direct quotation, it involves at least some kind of quote from the mind.

These points, I should think, are implied by any definition of the stream of consciousness. Even by this general standard, however, Virginia Woolf's novels do not always meet the neces-

20. Ibid., p. 36.
21. Ibid., p. 63.

sary qualifications. And though it seems to me that she can be called a stream-of-consciousness writer, especially if we employ Humphrey's useful terminology, it is important to emphasize that her most highly experimental fiction, from *Mrs. Dalloway* to *The Waves,* reflects a steady movement away from the more-or-less direct rendition of thought streams toward methods which allow her considerable latitude to express what lies outside the character's ego.

Critics often try to describe Mrs. Woolf's novels by referring to her criticism. Certainly there is nothing wrong in this procedure, so long as her comments are read with care. Humphrey, for example, quotes this famous passage from "Modern Fiction," calling it "the best possible description of her method":[22]

> Let us record the atoms as they fall upon the mind in the order in which they fall, let us trace the pattern, however disconnected and incoherent in appearance, which each sight or incident scores upon the consciousness.[23]

Out of context, this sounds rather like a call to arms. Melvin Friedman also quotes the passage in his book on the stream of consciousness, and comments that it has "become for the stream of consciousness tradition what Andre Breton's *Le Manifeste du surrealisme* was for surrealism or what Rimbaud's two 'lettres du Voyant' . . . were for symbolism." [24] But to claim there is something called a "stream of consciousness tradition," and to urge that it is a "school" like surrealism is highly misleading. It is even more inaccurate to say that Virginia Woolf

22. Ibid., p. 31.

23. Virginia Woolf, "Modern Fiction," *The Common Reader* (New York: Harcourt, Brace, 1953), p. 155. Note the all-important qualifier, ignored by most critics: "Anyone who has read *Ulysses,* now [April, 1919] appearing in the *Little Review,* will have hazarded some theory of this nature as to Mr. Joyce's intention."

24. Friedman, *Stream of Consciousness: A Study in Literary Method,* p. 189.

wrote its manifesto. The passage under consideration has become one of Mrs. Woolf's most famous statements, and has
been quoted out of context over and over again to describe her
technique.[25] In its proper context, however, it is clear that the
passage is an abstract of what Virginia Woolf thinks *Joyce's*
method tells us. She herself was seldom predisposed to "record
the atoms as they fall." She rather dislikes such a method, and
she explains why a few lines later:

> Is it the method that inhibits the creative power? Is it due
> to the method that we feel neither jovial nor magnanimous,
> but centered in a self which, in spite of its tremor of sus-
> ceptibility, never embraces or creates what is outside itself
> and beyond? . . . This method has the merit of bringing us
> closer to what we are prepared to call life itself; did not the
> reading of *Ulysses* suggest how much of life is excluded or
> ignored, and did it not come with a shock to open *Tristram
> Shandy* or even *Pendennis* and be by them convinced that
> there are not only other aspects of life, but more important
> ones into the bargain.[26]

Here is where the emphasis should lie if we are to properly
understand the course Mrs. Woolf's experimentation took; and
yet this part of her famous essay has received comparatively
little attention.

Notice that her objection to the stream of consciousness is
that it is "centered in a self." It is therefore, in her mind, a
claustraphobic and essentially egocentric method. (I have already remarked on her ambivalent attitude toward the ego.)
One of the distinctive traits of Mrs. Woolf's novels is that even

25. See Steinberg, "the steady monologue . . . ," p. 189; F. R. Leavis,
"After *To the Lighthouse*," *Scrutiny* 10 (January, 1942):295–97; Morris
Beja, *Psychological Fiction* (Glenview, Ill.: Scott Foresman, 1971), pp.
150–51.
26. Woolf, "Modern Fiction," p. 156.

when she is depicting a kind of inner emotional life, she seems to stress that this life is not confined to individuals. Her books are full of scenes where whole groups of people share thoughts and become like a single organism—one remembers examples like the skywriting airplane sequence in *Mrs. Dalloway*. The method has its antecedent, however, in *The Voyage Out,* as in the passage quoted at the beginning of chapter 2; or in the repeated use of plurals and "they" to describe the feelings of the characters; or in scenes like the voyage upriver, where for a time all the passengers seem to have a single body.

Here Virginia Woolf comments on the mind in *A Room of One's Own*—she has just been looking out a window:

> The mind is certainly a very mysterious organ, I reflected, drawing my head in from the window, about which nothing whatever is known, though we depend upon it so completely. Why do I feel that there are severances and oppositions in the mind, as there are strains from obvious causes on the body? What does one mean by "the unity of the mind," I pondered, for clearly the mind has so great a power of concentrating at any point at any moment that it seems to have no single state of being. It can separate itself from the people in the street, for example, and think of itself as apart from them, at an upper window looking down on them. Or it can think with other people spontaneously, as, for instance, in a crowd waiting to hear some piece of news read out. It can think back through its fathers or through its mothers, as I have said that a woman writing thinks back through her mothers. [pp. 145–46] 168 - 69

This passage shows clearly that Virginia Woolf's interest in the mind should not be confused with the typical post-Freudian concern for depth psychology, repression, or motivation. She is intrigued by the imaginative and emotional powers of the mind, the way it can attach or detach itself from those people in the

street, can think back to times before it even existed. She emphasizes that the mind can break down the divisions of time
and space to establish a total unity} thus, in her essay on modern
fiction, she argues for a literature which will show how the
"self" of the interior monologue "embraces or creates what is
outside itself or beyond."

But the two words "embraces" and "creates" are something
of a problem, since they postulate two different attitudes toward
what is outside. Is the world around us an ultimate order
which we can "embrace" by somehow getting outside the ego,
or is it a chaos out of which we "create" order through the
effort of imagination? Mrs. Woolf is never very clear about her
answer, and her fiction provides plenty of evidence to support
both notions. Mrs. Ramsay, for example, is clearly "embracing"
the world outside when she sits alone by the window and feels
herself becoming the trees, streams, and flowers. We are told
that a "mist" curled up from her mind like a "bride to meet a
lover." Likewise Rachel Vinrace feels herself merge with the
objects around her when she falls into her dreamy moods. But
on the other hand, Bernard remarks at a particularly intense
moment in *The Waves* that "We are creators," and certainly
Mrs. Ramsay's Boeuf en Daube, like Lily Briscoe's painting,
functions to create order out of apparent disorder.

These two views of experience may indicate a very deep uncertainty, or they may not be so contradictory as they seem. It
is likely that Virginia Woolf regarded the aesthetic act, whether
in the form of a party or a painting, as a means of apprehend-
ing an underlying order in life which is concealed from us by
everyday existence. Such a view is not incompatible with the
novels. There is, for example, very little difference between the
hypnotic mood that overtakes Lily Briscoe as she paints and the
trance Mrs. Ramsay seems to enter as she sits at her window.
In any case, Virginia Woolf's desire to achieve an "embrace" of

the world has a central importance in her experiments with the novel.

In the *Writer's Diary* Mrs. Woolf is quite blunt about "the damned egotistical self" which she says "ruins Joyce and Richardson to my mind." [27] There is, then, something paradoxical about Virginia Woolf's relation to her contemporaries. She is like them in her desire to make her fiction closer to "life itself," but she reacts against, or at least is unsympathetic toward, their methods because she seems to have a different conception of what "life" is. Out of her disagreement with her fellow novelists, she tries to evolve a technique which will allow her to present the "luminous halo" of experience, even the "tremor of susceptibility" in the self, without neglecting what is "outside . . . and beyond."

To describe this technique, Harvena Richter has suggested that we set aside the conventional terminology and "approach the question of *voice*," which, in Virginia Woolf, "is at once conscious and unconscious, personal and impersonal, individual and collective." [28] In what follows, I have tried to indicate how the narrator of Mrs. Woolf's novels modulates between these extremes until it seems to become the voice of everyone and no one. It is probably impossible to find a term that would accurately characterize this voice. Virginia Woolf herself was unable to name it, though she wrote the best description of its effect:

Certainly it is difficult to find a name for that which is in a room, yet the room is empty; for that which perceives . . . knife and fork, also men and women; and describes them; and not only perceives but partakes of [the]m, and has access to the mind in its darkness. And further goes from mind to mind and surface to surface, and from body to body, creating

27. Woolf, *A Writer's Diary*, p. 129.
28. Richter, *Inward Voyage*, p. 129.

what is not mind or body, not surface or depths, but a common element in which the perishable is preserved, and the separate become one.[29]

The emphasis here is on the "creative" rather than the "embracing" function of the novelist's method, but, as I have said, it often seems to make little difference which word Virginia Woolf uses. The point is that she tends to write a fiction which is not made from the language in a single consciousness or even a set of consciousnesses. Most of her later novels are narrated by what she has called a "nameless spirit," [30] which, by its very existence, asserts a "common element" in life—something not isolated, not separate, not perishable. Obviously the motives for such a technique are less psychological than metaphysical, though they do suggest something about Mrs. Woolf's personality. Her experiments, as we shall see, lead her from the stream of consciousness to a different sort of watery world where the "common element" sometimes dissolves all sense of individuality.

29. Woolf, early ms. of *Between the Acts,* quoted by Richter, *Inward Voyage,* p. 138.
30. Ibid.

5

Mrs. Dalloway

The opening of *Mrs. Dalloway* is a good example of what Robert Humphrey calls indirect interior monologue. The method has a reasonably high degree of verisimilitude, at least in that Mrs. Dalloway's thoughts seem to follow one another by free-association. She is preparing for a rather large party; since her servant, Lucy, has many things to do, and since it is an unusually fine summer's day, Clarissa has decided to buy the necessary flowers herself. She thinks about the work planned for the day and the beauty of the morning. The freshness of the air and the squeak of a hinge on the door lead to a Proustian evocation of her youth at Bourton, and this makes her remember Peter Walsh, whom she characterizes by his eyes and his smile, his pocketknife and his epigrams. (Incidentally, details such as Walsh's nervous habit of playing with his pocketknife suggest that Mrs. Woolf was well aware of the psychopathology of everyday life.) The method also gives the impression that the controlling author has tried to efface her personality. When the author's voice separates itself from the mental life of Clarissa Dalloway, it offers only rather prosaic rhetorical asides, as in the following lines, where I have italicized the relevant phrases: "And then, *thought Clarissa Dalloway,* what a morning"; *"For so it had always seemed to her,* when, with a little squeak of the hinges, *which she could hear now";* "How fresh, how calm . . . the air was . . . (for a girl of eighteen *as she then was)."* [1] It seems that the author wants to avoid confusion as much as possible by providing the necessary signposts for the scene. She wants to make clear that Clarissa Dalloway's thoughts are the subject; to offer a suggestion of the exterior surroundings—a lady with a servant girl, the lady stepping out of her door on a fresh morning; and to distinguish reverie from the here and now, past from present. The technique is economical and unobtrusive. Indeed, once the reader has established for himself the perspective of the first pages, he reads on almost without noticing the author's brief guides. Even so, the method creates a certain ambiguity. "Thought Clarissa Dalloway" clearly is spoken by the author alone; but what about the other phrases I have underlined? Are they simply statements by the author or are they too a part of Clarissa's thoughts, a reflection of her self-consciousness?

As I say, the technique here easily fits Humphrey's definition of indirect interior monologue (it is, in fact, the model he cites), but there is some question as to how long it is sustained in the novel. Even here, the impression we get from Virginia Woolf's handling of consciousness is quite different from the impression we sometimes get in Joyce, where every atom is accounted for as it falls. This is chiefly because it is characteristic of Virginia Woolf to interpret the mental life of a character rather than transcribe it. Hence in the first pages of *Mrs. Dalloway* the technique is fairly realistic, but while the author refrains from analysis of the action, there is nevertheless a

1. Virginia Woolf, *Mrs. Dalloway* (London: Hogarth Press, 1968), p. 5. Unless otherwise noted, all references are to this edition.

feeling that all the materials have been given form by a controlling authorial personality that is sometimes self-consciously
artistic.[2] It is true that a sense of random thought pervades
the opening pages of the book, but this quality is barely suggested. Clarissa Dalloway's transitions from one subject to another are in fact quite orderly and smooth. The metaphor of
the stream might be quite inappropriate when applied to the
actual movement of thought, but it is singularly apt when we
come to describe Virginia Woolf's method. Even when Clarissa
Dalloway is busy and relatively gay, as in these opening pages,
the style has a high degree of order. It is a polished, elegant,
rhythmic prose; not even the literary, Hamletesque young
Dedalus in *Ulysses* thinks in such beautifully modulated pe-
riodic sentences. The reason for this quality in the style is obvious enough from the brief authorial asides: Mrs. Dalloway
and the other characters are seen as third persons, and all the
thoughts are rendered by an ever-present narrator, who endows
the novel with its poetic rhythms and unity of style.

Though the prose remains clear, there are hints of the random
flux of thought, as on the first page:

How fresh, how calm, stiller than this of course, the air was
in the early morning; like the flap of a wave; the kiss of a
wave; chill and sharp and yet (for a girl of eighteen as she
then was) solemn, feeling as she did, standing there at the
open window, that something awful was about to happen;
looking at the flowers, at the trees with the smoke winding
off them and the rooks rising, falling; standing and looking
until Peter Walsh . . .

Here the language conveys a special sort of mood, a kind of
hypnosis which, while perhaps more intense and excited than

2. See Stuart Rosenberg, "The Match in the Crocus: Obtrusive Art in
Virginia Woolf's *Mrs. Dalloway*," *Modern Fiction Studies* 13 (Summer,
1967): 211–20.

the hypnotic moods in *The Voyage Out,* is nonetheless like them in kind. The sentence is drawn out by the addition of participial phrases, which create a flow of impressions and help measure out a rhythm: "feeling as she did," "standing there," "looking at the flowers," "standing and looking." Other repetitions, together with several of the important words and images, help induce a dreamy effect ("the flap of a wave; the kiss of a wave; chill and sharp and yet . . . ," "the trees with the smoke winding off them and the rooks rising, falling"). This effect is all the more interesting for the way it differs from the light, bustling mood established at the start. It has taken only a moment for Mrs. Dalloway, eager to be off and buy the flowers herself, to fall into a daydream. And once she has attained this state of mild trance, the figure of Peter Walsh appears to her like some premonition or intuition.

Almost all of the characters' thoughts in *Mrs. Dalloway* are daydreams of one kind or another. Relatively little of the inner monologues are related to or determined by the actual circumstantial context, the West End of London on a summer's day. It takes only a squeak of the hinge to set Mrs. Dalloway off, to transport her to another time and place. She seems to have surrendered herself to "the kiss of a wave"; "What a plunge," she thinks, and for the next three pages, until she encounters Hugh Whitbread, she is aware only of the fresh June day, of standing on a curb while Durtnall's van passes, and of the striking of Big Ben. Her extended reverie is only dimly related to what goes on around her. Her thoughts do reflect the quality of life on the London streets, but only indirectly:

> The King and Queen were at the Palace. And everywhere, though it was still so early, there was a beating, a stirring of galloping ponies, tapping of cricket bats; Lords, Ascot, Ranelagh and all the rest of it; wrapped in the soft mesh of the grey-blue morning air, which as the day wore on,

would unwind them, and set down on their lawns and pitches the bouncing ponies, whose forefeet just struck the ground and up they sprung, the whirling young men, and laughing girls in their transparent muslins who, even now, after dancing all night, were taking their absurd wooly dogs for a run; and even now, at this hour, discreet old dowagers were shooting out in their motor cars on errands of mystery; and the shopkeepers were fidgeting in their windows with their paste and diamonds, their lovely old sea-green brooches. [p. 7]

This vision of London is contained wholly in Clarissa Dalloway's fancy, stimulated only by some vague quality in the air and in the street sounds. It is a sentimentalized picture that owes everything to Mrs. Dalloway's fashionable female sensibility, and it is set off by her complacent observation that "the War was over." It is in beautiful contrast to the mad visions of the veteran Septimus Smith, Mrs. Dalloway's alter ego. The loose syntax of the long second sentence is no doubt intended to suggest the random quality of actual thought, but otherwise the passage is stylistically analogous to the authorial comment in *The Voyage Out*—a series of images conjured up in the plural, forming a sketch of the landscape. Thus we have "bouncing ponies," "whirling young men," "laughing girls in their transparent muslins," "wooly dogs," "discreet old dowagers," "shopkeepers . . . fidgeting in their windows with their paste and diamonds, their lovely old sea-green brooches." Clarissa Dalloway, like Virginia Woolf, senses an emblematic pattern in the landscape, and the pattern has very little to do with what she *actually* sees. Mrs. Dalloway is always being carried off into these flights of sensibility, and must be forcibly returned to the real world by the explosive backfire of an automobile or the sudden ring of a doorbell.

It is true that the novel does evoke life on the streets of Lon-

don, but it seems to me that J. K. Johnstone considerably over-
states the case when he says that one of the prime virtues of
the book is its recreation of the West End of twentieth-century
London.[3] One has only to recall Leopold Bloom's meanderings
through Dublin to see how much of the physical surroundings
Mrs. Woolf leaves out, how little she is concerned with the
sustained reaction of a character to the shower of physical
stimuli around him. Joyce's characters daydream too, but even
when Stephen Dedalus is walking alone on a beach he is more
in contact with the sights and sounds around him than Mrs.
Dalloway is on a busy London street. I am speaking relatively,
of course. Certainly Mrs. Woolf does depict London, but in no
sense is she "numbering the atoms as they fall," a method she
found unsuitable for the particular vision of life she wanted to
project.

Because so much of the novel is given over to the relatively
uninterrupted flow of daydreams and meditations controlled
by an authorial voice, the book has an almost seamless quality.
Many things besides the inner monologues contribute to this
effect. There is hardly any good stopping place in the novel;
there are no chapters, and except for an occasional space inserted
between paragraphs to alter a mood or change the scene we
have a completely uninterrupted stream of prose that begins in
the middle of an action ("Mrs. Dalloway said she would buy
the flowers herself") and does not come to rest until the last
sentence, where everything pauses like the brief one-beat hesita-
tion at the end of a ballroom dance ("For there she was.").

So far as I can determine, the spaces that occasionally mark
a change of scene were not added until Mrs. Woolf saw the
first page proofs of the book.[4] In any case, the steady, almost

3. J. K. Johnstone, *The Bloomsbury Group* (London: Secker and Warburg, 1954), p. 338.
4. Proof pages of *Mrs. Dalloway*, first edition, Lilly Library, Blooming-
ton, Indiana.

uninterrupted flow of the novel obviously depends upon the author's ability to make orderly transitions. One thinks immediately of the motorcar travelling down Piccadilly, carrying the thoughts of the crowd with it; also of the skywriting airplane which, like the car, "grazed something very profound" in the emotions of the crowd. For a moment everyone is united by an elemental emotion of wonder and curiosity, and we move easily from Clarissa to Sara Bletchely to Mrs. Coates to Mr. Bowley to Rezia and finally to Septimus Smith again. This atmosphere is reminiscent of several scenes in *The Voyage Out*; the skywriting plane creates or at least discloses a kind of ideal realm where the message has less to do with what is actually being spelled in the sky (Glaxo? Kreemo? Toffee?) than with the emotions which unite the separate individuals.

> Every one looked up.
> Dropping dead down the aeroplane soared straight up, curved in a loop, raced, sank, rose, and whatever it did, wherever it went, out fluttered behind it a thick ruffled bar of smoke which curled and wreathed upon the sky in letters. But what letters? A C was it? an E, then an L? Only for a moment did they lie still; then they moved and melted and were rubbed out up in the sky, and the aeroplane shot further away and again, in a fresh space of sky, began writing a K, an E, a Y perhaps? [p. 23]

What is important here is not so much the actual writing as the diving, swooping dance of the airplane, which attracts everyone and as the passage develops seems to hold them in a trance, much as the dark river in *The Voyage Out* held the excursion party in a kind of union. The author herself seems to be caught up in the collective consciousness, watching the event with a dreamy wonder. In the next few pages, the sense of union is emphasized as the reader moves easily from one mind to another.

The prose style in the passage I have just quoted merits a brief comment. Again it is clear that Virginia Woolf's prose depends heavily upon a rhythm that lends an emotional significance to whatever is being described. The sentences here are beautifully designed to capture the lighthearted grace of the plane, the curiosity of the onlookers, and the almost hypnotic wonder that the smoky letters induce. I would point out especially the author's ability to imitate the dips and dives of the plane's flight and the feeling she has for certain elegant repetitions and phrasings that almost put one to sleep: "smoke which curled and wreathed upon the sky in letters," "they moved and melted and were rubbed out up in the sky." As good as the passage is, however, it seems a shade too artful, and it demonstrates the problem Virginia Woolf always faces in trying to write a prose that will incorporate the virtues of poetry. The alliteration in "Dropping dead down," for example, creates the proper effect, but the reader is conscious of it *as* an effect. To me it seems too literary, composed with too much stress on the elegance of the phrase. Beautifully-mannered and poetic prose styles are legitimate when they seem to be generated by some special intensity of vision, as in Conrad, Faulkner, Joyce, and in places in Virginia Woolf. To a lesser extent, they are also legitimate when the author has a deliberately self-indulgent or ironic purpose, or when he is in active rebellion against nature, as Wilde, Huysmans, and sometimes even Joyce seem to be. But Virginia Woolf is not playing the role of a self-conscious aesthete in this passage; she seems to be striving for a certain natural beauty and intensity, and her mannered prose does not further this purpose. Rather, it tends to confirm William Troy's judgment that she depends too much on "associations to the cultivated mind" and too little on "the fullness and immediacy of concrete experience." Remarkable as her prose is, she is something of a "phrasemaker," like her character Bernard in *The Waves*; and her style often involves what Troy calls "a resuscitation rather than a re-creation of language." [5]

The whole conception of the skywriting scene is perhaps a bit arty. Nevertheless it is in some ways a very typical moment in Mrs. Woolf's fiction, an important manifestation of the emotional undercurrent that seems to dissolve the boundaries between people. Most of the transitions in the novel contribute to just such an effect. Not all are so spectacular, but nearly every one of them enables the author to move discreetly from one character to another, to shift our viewpoint from one scene to another. Some part of the first scene is usually carried over into the next. Thus we are shown two characters looking at the same object—the airplane, for example, or the sun striking a bank of clouds, which fascinates both Elizabeth Dalloway and Septimus Smith later in the novel—and we move from one character to another over the bridge that the object affords. In most cases a transition is effected by brief snatches of dialogue; we move from speaker to listener and back again by means of the sound of a word:

> Sounds made harmonies with premeditation; the spaces between them were as significant as sounds. A child cried. Rightly far away a horn sounded. All taken together meant the birth of a new religion—
>
> "Septimus!" said Rezia. He started violently. People must notice.
>
> "I am going to walk to the fountain and back," she said.
>
> For she could stand it no longer. Dr. Holmes might say there was nothing the matter. Far rather would she that he were dead! She could not sit beside him when he stared so . . . [p. 26]

The "For" which opens Rezia's meditations is one of Mrs. Woolf's favorite words, and she uses it often to make one thing

5. Troy, "The Poetic Style," p. 156.

carry over into another with hardly a sense of pause. Similar
techniques accomplish the transitions from one character to
another in most scenes that involve dialogue, but even when
the characters in question are not within speaking distance
Mrs. Woolf strives to bridge the gaps smoothly. The skywriting plane takes us from Mrs. Dalloway to the Smiths and
then back again to Mrs. Dalloway, who has returned home.
Peter Walsh visits her there, and when he leaves Clarissa calls
out to him over the sound of clock bells. These sounds carry us
into his mind, where we hear the "downright" masculine echo
of Big Ben, followed by the feminine, Clarissa Dalloway-like
sound of St. Margaret's. We follow him to Regent's Park, where
he dozes and dreams.

> Still, the sun was hot. Still, one got over things. Still, life
> had a way of adding day to day. Still, he thought, yawning
> and beginning to take notice—Regent's Park had changed
> very little since he was a boy, except for the squirrels—still,
> presumably there were compensations—when little Elsie
> Mitchell, who had been picking up pebbles to add to the
> pebble collection which she and her brother were mak-
> ing . . . , plumped her handful down on the nurse's knee
> and scudded off again full tilt into a lady's legs. Peter Walsh
> laughed out.
>
> But Lucrezia Warren Smith was saying to herself, It's
> wicked; why should I suffer? She was asking as she walked
> down the broad path. No; I can't stand it any longer, she
> was saying, having left Septimus, who wasn't Septimus any
> longer, to say hard, cruel, wicked things, to talk to himself,
> to talk to a dead man, on the seat over there; when the child
> ran full tilt into her. [p. 72]

Little Elsie Mitchell serves no other purpose than to form a
bridge between Septimus and Rezia; and because the author's
voice is always present, describing the character's thoughts in-

directly, the transition makes us feel as though Mrs. Woolf's world were made of a single thread. Elsie is altogether too patent a contrivance, of course, and for that reason the transition seems forced. But it is important to realize that such transitions occur not because Mrs. Woolf is arty or has what David Daiches calls a "tidy mind," though in some ways both of these statements are true. More significantly, such transitions help Virginia Woolf to convey the impression that life is what Mrs. Ramsay will later describe as "all one stream." Even the rhythmic pulse we feel in Peter's thought, expressed by the repetition of "still," is emphasized by the repetitions in the paragraph describing Rezia's thought; so that the inner lives of these two characters, who are very different (she is a foreigner) and who do not know one another, seem attuned to the same elemental beat, which fluctuates according to their emotions.

An even more remarkable example of transition occurs later in the novel, when Elizabeth Dalloway is about to board a bus:

> Of course, she would not push her way. She inclined to be passive. It was expression she needed, but her eyes were fine, Chinese, oriental, and, as her mother said, with such nice shoulders and holding herself so straight, she was always charming to look at; and lately, in the evening especially, when she was interested, for she never seemed excited, she looked almost beautiful, very stately, very serene. What could she be thinking? Every man fell in love with her, and she was really awfully bored. For it was beginning. That she did not care more about it—for instance for her clothes —sometimes worried Clarissa, but perhaps it was as well with all those puppies and guinea pigs about having distemper, and it gave her a charm. And now there was this odd friendship with Miss Kilman. Well, thought Clarissa about three o'clock in the morning, reading Baron Marbot for she could not sleep, it proves she has a heart. [p. 149]

Just prior to this passage, we have been following Elizabeth's
thought. But then—it is impossible to say precisely where—
we find ourselves reading Clarissa's meditation on her daughter.
The last sentence places us at a new point in time and space,
but a rereading of the passage suggests that the transition took
place long before. It is not at all clear who asks, "What could
she be thinking?" One's first assumption is probably that the
question comes from Elizabeth or the narrator; but when the
passage is read a second time, keeping the transition in mind,
the question seems to issue from Clarissa. In any case, it should
not be surprising that the opening of the next paragraph returns us gracefully to Elizabeth: "Suddenly Elizabeth stepped
forward and most competently boarded the omnibus."

These transitions entail no major change in prose style between the meditations of one character and those of another,
and the characters sometimes seem to feel the same rhythmic
pulse; but this does not mean that the prose has a monotonous
regularity or that the rhythms remain the same. It is true that
during this period Mrs. Woolf's novels often suffer from a lack
of variety in the quality of experience she depicts, even though
her characters are ostensibly quite different. This, however, is
an aesthetic problem related to her wish to show life as a single
thread, and should be understood in that context. On the other
hand her prose does undergo some changes, and her rhythms
are subject to variation. For example, in the passage concerning
Elsie Mitchell, the rhythms of Peter Walsh's thought are not
exactly the same as those in Rezia's mind, although in this case
the difference is minimal.

Significant changes of style emerge, however, when there is
an important change in the emotional lives of the characters;
as on the first page, where the brisk, short sentences that accom-
pany Mrs. Dalloway's departure from her house give way to
the long and complex section that describes her memory of
Bruton. There is a fluctuation, too, in the moods of the char-

acters at different times of the day. After a good lunch at Lady
Bruton's, for example, Richard Dalloway listens to his hostess
discourse on emigration, and the effect of her words, long and
heavy and rife with parallels, is distinctly soporific:

> She exaggerated. She had perhaps lost her sense of propor-
> tion. Emigration was not to others the obvious remedy, the
> sublime conception. It was not to them (not to Hugh, or
> Richard, or even to devoted Miss Brush) the liberator of the
> pent egotism, which a strong martial woman, well nourished,
> well descended, of direct impulses, downright feelings, and
> little introspective power (broad and simple—why could not
> everyone be broad and simple? she asked) feels rise within
> her, once youth is past, and must eject upon some object—it
> may be Emigration, it may be Emancipation; but whatever
> it be, this object round which the essence of her soul is daily
> secreted, becomes inevitably prismatic, lustrous, half looking
> glass, half precious stone; now carefully hidden in case people
> should sneer at it; now proudly displayed. Emigration had
> become, in short, largely Lady Bruton. [p. 120]

Here Virginia Woolf begins by mimicking Lady Bruton's conversation. We are looking at Lady Bruton through Richard's
eyes and listening to her speech. But early in the fourth sentence
comments on her character appear (a strong martial woman,
etc.), and by the end of the passage she has become a Goddess
of Divine Proportion and the object of Mrs. Woolf's sarcasm.
But the source of most of the passage is highly ambiguous;
one can't be sure if the reflections are those of Virginia Woolf
or Richard Dalloway. In any case, during the fourth sentence,
longwinded and full of pompous phrases like "liberator of the
pent egotism" and "well nourished, well descended," the
reader's mind tends to wander. A striking contrast is presented
by the brisk chatter at Clarissa's evening party:

> She and Peter had settled down together. They were talk-
> ing: it seemed so familiar—that they should be talking. They
> would discuss the past. With the two of them (more even
> than with Richard) she shared her past; the garden; the
> trees, old Joseph Breitkopf singing Brahms without any
> voice; the drawing-room wallpaper; the smell of the mats.
> A part of this Sally must always be; Peter must always be.
> But she must leave them. There were the Bradshaws, whom
> she disliked.
>
> She must go up to Lady Bradshaw (in grey and silver,
> balancing like a sea-lion at the edge of its tank, barking for
> invitations, Duchesses, the typical successful man's wife), she
> must go up to Lady Bradshaw and say . . . [p. 200]

A very different pace, but not what one would call a basically
different prose style. Again there is a curious ambiguity about
the source of commentary. Who speaks or thinks the material
in parenthesis—Clarissa, Virginia Woolf, or all the characters
sitting there and the author besides?

It is characteristic of Virginia Woolf's so-called psychological
novels that most of the time it is impossible to distinguish one
character from another by the manner of their thoughts. Thus
we recognize the difference between Clarissa and Septimus, between Mr. Ramsay and Mrs. Ramsay, between Bernard and
Susan, not so much by changes of style as by changes of preoccupation. When Virginia Woolf's style changes, it usually
does so only slightly, and only in order to imply an intensified
emotion, as when Septimus sees the vision of Evans in Regent
Park:

> But the branches parted. A man in grey was actually
> walking towards them. It was Evans! But no mud was on
> him; no wounds; he was not changed. I must tell the whole
> world, Septimus cried, raising his hand. [p. 105]

The short sentences here serve not so much to characterize Septimus as to generate some of the excitement and terror that the moment holds for him. In other words, the reader is never invited to leave the presence of the author, who, by muting the exterior setting, speaks virtually throughout the novel in a single voice.

This single voice dominates all the scenes that in almost any other novel would be taken up with dialogue. Virginia Woolf seldom gives us a direct transcription of anything that is said. Except for occasional snatches of speech, all we get are summaries of conversations. Usually the interplay between characters is twice removed from direct presentation: every scene is refracted through the minds of the characters, and their thoughts in turn are refracted through Mrs. Woolf's elegant voice. The result is a curious qualitative unity; much of the time the reader seems to hear only muffled words, as if he were under water. For example, we are given few details of the conversation between Peter and Clarissa when they are reunited (pp. 45–54). The circumstantial context, the conversation itself, has little bearing on the way Virginia Woolf presents their thoughts. Such a technique might be explained by the fact that what Peter and Clarissa actually say is insignificant—the important reactions all take place in their minds. But the technique remains substantially the same even in scenes where all the irony is on the surface. Consider Sally and Peter's conversation with Clarissa, quoted above, or the interview (pp. 106–09) between the Smiths and Dr. Bradshaw. It is, I think, unnecessary to quote lengthy examples of such scenes. The book is full of them, the author rendering the interplay between characters indirectly, so that objective events are distilled for the reader. I have already noted in another context that Mrs. Woolf recorded in her *Diary* a desire to make *Mrs. Dalloway* a finished work of art which yet retained the quality of a sketch.[6] In scenes of potentially dramatic interplay between characters her intent is especially clear; but her reports of consciousness are also somewhat generalized, refined, indirect.

And the authorial voice, which often supplies what might be called indirect interior monologues, is not by any means an impersonal voice. Wayne Booth has remarked that in a very large number of modern novels—he includes the novels of Virginia Woolf—the author and the reader often meet, but, like Voltaire and God, they do not speak.[7] Yet this is not quite true where Mrs. Woolf is concerned; only in *The Waves* is she totally noncommittal. In her other works, Virginia Woolf and the reader are always face to face, and while usually far from assertive, she sometimes engages in traditional analysis or makes lofty ironic judgments about her characters. Generally speaking, of course, the author of *Mrs. Dalloway* stands very close to the central figures, rendering their thoughts in the indirect style we have been considering—partly, no doubt, because to give the voice a great deal of freedom would be to "materialize" the novel, to turn it from its essential subject matter and theme: the subtly related inner lives of the characters. Sometimes, when an objective outlook is required or an ironic point needs to be made, the novelist simply shifts the viewpoint. Thus on the second page the first description of Clarissa is provided when we pass briefly into the mind of Scrope Purvis, who thinks she has "a touch of the bird about her . . . light, vivacious, though she was over fifty, and grown very white since her illness." And later in the novel an ironic comment is made by transferring our view from the Smiths to Peter Walsh when they encounter one another in the park. At times, however, a more conventional omniscience is implied;

6. Woolf, *A Writer's Diary*, p. 71.
7. Booth, *Rhetoric of Fiction*, pp. 271–72.

the author straightforwardly describes a character, provides necessary information, or makes a series of arch comments. Consider, for example, our introduction to Septimus: "Septimus Warren Smith, aged about thirty, pale-faced, beak-nosed, wearing brown shoes and a shabby overcoat, with hazel eyes which had that look of apprehension in them which makes complete strangers apprehensive too" (p. 19). Or this direct offer of information: "The violent explosion which made Mrs. Dalloway jump and Miss Pym go to the window and apologize came from a motor car which had drawn to the pavement precisely opposite Mulberry's shop window" (p. 16). And here is part of a lengthy and bitter character sketch of the physician Bradshaw:

> Proportion, divine proportion, Sir William's goddess, was acquired by Sir William walking hospitals, catching salmon, begetting one son in Harley Street by Lady Bradshaw, who caught salmon herself and took photographs scarcely to be distinguished from the work of professionals. Worshipping proportion, Sir William not only prospered himself but made England prosper, secluded her lunatics, forbade childbirth, penalised despair, made it impossible for the unfit to propagate their views until they, too, shared his sense of proportion—his, if they were men, Lady Bradshaw's if they were women (she embroidered, knitted, spent four nights out of seven at home with her son), so that not only did his colleagues respect him, his subordinates fear him, but the friends and relations of his patients felt for him the keenest gratitude for insisting that these prophetic Christs and Christesses, who prophesied the end of the world, or the advent of God, should drink milk in bed, as Sir William ordered; Sir William with his thirty years' experience of these kinds of cases, and his infallible instinct, this is madness, this sense; in fact, his sense of proportion. [p. 110]

Bradshaw is, of course, a peripheral figure and can be treated differently than the central characters; to judge them so categorically would be difficult if not impossible. Nevertheless a passage like this one reminds us, if we need to be reminded, that the materials of the novel are being controlled by an omniscient narrator, who is free to make her animus strongly felt. Indeed, a number of critical passages, like the whole sketch of Septimus' past leading up to his visit with Bradshaw (pp. 93–104), are not centered in any single consciousness, but are composed of running commentary by the narrator. And even in the reunion between Clarissa and Peter, which entails so much description of thought, the author's presence is often clearly evident.

> Then, just as happens on a terrace in the moonlight, when one person begins to feel ashamed that he is already bored, and yet another sits silent, very quietly, sadly looking at the moon, does not like to speak, moves his foot, clears his throat, notices some iron scroll on a table leg, stirs a leaf, but says nothing—so did Peter Walsh now (p. 48).

> So before a battle begins, the horses paw the ground; toss their heads; the light shines on their flanks; their necks curve. So Peter Walsh and Clarissa, sitting side by side on the blue sofa, challenged each other (p. 50).

> But the indomitable egotism which forever rides down the hosts opposed to it, the river which says on, on, on; even though, it admits, there may be no goal for us whatever, still on, on; this indomitable egotism charged her cheeks with colour. [pp. 50–51]

The first two excerpts above reveal that personable, elegant, ladylike narrator we have observed in *The Voyage Out*. She is self-consciously literary; although the epic simile in the second passage concerns battle, it is the aesthetic elements of battle, like the graceful curve of the horses' bodies, that are stressed and not the bloody conflict. The third excerpt, however, is somewhat different in tone—more serious, more sad. It is in fact a comment that rises out of one of Virginia Woolf's deepest concerns: the contest for life between the ego and the undifferentiated forces which threaten to dissolve or destroy it. While most of her characters seem to long for a mystic unity, they are also capable of fighting to protect their identity. This battle goes on even though there is a temptation to surrender: "There may be no goal for us whatever." Notice that the picture of the ego as an equestrian warrior who "rides down the hosts opposed to it" is reminiscent of the more spectacular image that ends *The Waves,* where Bernard fancies himself riding indomitably into the face of death.

Yet in spite of the indirection, the sketchy details, and the occasional open declarations of an authorial personality, *Mrs. Dalloway* fits Robert Humphrey's definition of stream-of-consciousness writing. Clearly the book is designed to present the flux of several character's thoughts; but, granted that the conventional terminology may be applied here, it may also tend to obscure or oversimplify Virginia Woolf's technique. True, she tries to approximate the aimless pattern of consciousness, but her voice is often so far removed from the actual contents of a mind that it verges on a traditional omniscience. The result is an unusually flexible method, well-suited to the novelist's special purposes.

Norman Friedman, in his useful and widely-reprinted essay, "Point of View in Fiction," says that most stream-of-consciousness fiction involves what he calls a selective omniscience. This selective method differs from ordinary omniscience, he says, in that the author shows us what is going on rather than telling us about it. "The one renders thoughts, perceptions, and feelings as they occur consecutively and in detail passing through the mind (scene), while the other summarizes and explains after they have occurred (narrative)." [8] Friedman points out that stream-of-consciousness writers, even when they assume an omniscient view, dramatize mental states rather than summarizing them (the passage he chooses for an example is from *To the Lighthouse*). This is a useful and it seems to me a crucial distinction; even Humphrey, I believe, would agree with it. Yet in *Mrs. Dalloway* the technique functions artfully to cloud this distinction. Compare, for example, these two passages:

> "That is all," she repeated, pausing for a moment at the window of a glove shop where, before the War, you could buy almost perfect gloves. And her old Uncle William used to say a lady is known by her shoes and her gloves. He had turned on his bed one morning in the middle of the War. He had said, "I have had enough." Gloves and shoes; she had a passion for gloves; but her own daughter, Elizabeth, cared not a straw for either of them (pp. 13–14).

> Quiet descended on her, calm, content, as her needle, drawing the silk smoothly to its gentle pause, collected the green folds together and attached them, very lightly, to the belt. So on a summer's day waves collect, over-balance, and fall; collect and fall; collect and fall; and the whole world seems to be saying "that is all" more and more ponderously, until even the heart in the body which lies in the sun on the beach says too, That is all. Fear no more says the heart. Fear no more says the heart, committing its burden to some sea, which sighs collectively for all sorrows, and renews, begins, collects, lets fall. And the body alone listens to the passing bee; the wave breaking; the dog barking, far away barking and barking. [pp. 44–45]

8. Norman Friedman, "Point of View in Fiction: The Development of a Critical Concept," *PMLA* 70 (1955): 1176.

We can use "stream of consciousness" to describe both these passages, arguing that the difference between them is only a technical one. But it seems to me that this difference needs emphasis. After a certain point, technique begins to imply something about the special nature of the subject matter. The first passage attempts to present the mental life of the character in a relatively realistic fashion, and nothing more. But in the second passage, with its carefully modulated syntax, its hint of detachment from the actual verbal content of Clarissa Dalloway's mind, the author is doing something more complicated. It opens by focusing on Clarissa ("quiet descended on her"), but then goes on to develop an elaborate image that falls just short of general commentary: "So on a summer's day waves collect . . . until even the heart in the body which lies in the sun on the beach says too, That is all." Who says this? Is this a report, a dramatization of Clarissa's thought, or is it a summary, a general comment by the author? The image is related to several ideas which have been running through Clarissa's head all day—the summer; the refrains "That is all," and "Fear no more the heat of the sun"—so we can assume that what is said here is related to what is actually happening in Clarissa's mind. Yet at the same time the status of the passage is not clearly defined; it seems to hover somewhere between an evocation of Clarissa's drowsiness and a broader statement about the novel as a whole. The carefully-wrought images of sun and wave and beach imply that the passage is more than a description of Clarissa's mind, that it relates her consciousness to a reality outside the individual ego and thus goes beyond Clarissa to the ultimate meaning of her experience. The moment described here is exactly like those in *The Voyage Out* where Rachel Vinrace seems to be falling asleep and giving herself to the things around her. "That is all" signals the passive surrender of the self to the general sea, until one is aware of only a vast empty landscape and casual faraway sounds. Indeed,

some of these images are used later in the novel to describe
Septimus Smith's thoughts as he is hypnotized by the play of
sunlight on his wall: "while far away on shore he heard dogs
barking and barking far away. Fear no more, says the heart in
the body; fear no more" (p. 154).

Passages like the first, which suggest disorder and free-
association, which dramatize the actual movement of a character's mind, are relatively few by actual count. The larger
part of the novel has more in common with the second passage,
where we are not sure at what point a stylized report of consciousness ends and a summary begins. Often, in fact, Mrs.
Woolf employs the same method to present her character's
thoughts as in *The Voyage Out,* using image, metaphor, and
rhythm to evoke a special emotional state resembling hypnosis
or sleep. Mrs. Dalloway working at her knitting is an example
of this method, as is the description of Lady Bruton's mind
after lunch, "hazy with the sounds of bells," like "a single
spider's thread . . . blotted with raindrops," which "sags
down." Only a moment later the same image is applied to
Richard Dalloway's thoughts: "And as a single spider's thread
after wavering here and there attaches itself to the point of
a leaf, so Richard's mind, recovering from its lethargy, set now
on his wife." Thus the minds of the characters can be shown
to have a unity not only through subtle transitions and a consistent prose style, but also by means of the very images which
are used to evoke their states of mind.

A number of passages, like the accounts of the crowds watching the Prime Minister's car and the skywriting airplane, are a
mixture of indirect interior monologue and omniscient comment. But consider the curious imagery Mrs. Woolf develops
when Peter Walsh drops off to sleep on a park bench seated
next to an elderly nurse (pp. 63–65).

The grey nurse resumed her knitting as Peter Walsh, on
the hot seat beside her, began snoring. In her grey dress,

moving her hands indefatigably yet quietly, she seemed like
the champion of the rights of sleepers, like one of those
spectral presences which rise in the twilight in woods made
of sky and branches. The solitary traveler, haunter of lanes,
disturber of ferns, and devastator of great hemlock plants,
looking up, suddenly sees the giant figure at the end of the
ride. [p. 63]

The author—and the style here strongly suggests a ghostly
presence that is not Peter though it may be speaking for him
in some way—goes on to discuss the vague yearnings and
frustrations of the solitary traveler, who may well be Peter's
vision of himself. The passage is no doubt related to Peter's
dreams, but in exactly what way? Is it an evocation of the
unconscious, a more or less exact rendition of the images that
are going through Peter's mind? When Peter awakes we are
told he has been dreaming of "some scene, some room, some
past," but this does not suggest anything like what we have
just read. Or is the association with "some past" hidden in the
symbols of the dream? To what extent does the solitary traveler
represent Peter Walsh, and to what extent is he simply an
archetypal male sleeper?

Or again, what are we to make of the treatment of memory?
Clarissa and Peter, for example, both remember at length
scenes from their youth at Bourton, and these scenes are always
coherent, self-contained, much like the sort of reminiscence
one finds in Proust. Should we then call Peter's memory of
Bourton (pp. 65–72) or Clarissa's recollection of Sally Seton
(pp. 37–40) streams of consciousness? There is very little in
these passages which could be said to provide a circumstantial
context for thought or to imitate the disordered texture of a
remembering consciousness; in some ways the opening pages
of *The Mill on the Floss* give a better sense of the strangeness
of the past, though in that case it is the narrator who remembers and not a character.

To me it seems that Virginia Woolf's use of traditional omniscience and the very large number of ambiguous passages in *Mrs. Dalloway* require that we qualify the terms we use to describe the novel—too often the author does not make a clear distinction between a refined, stylized report and an aloof summary or commentary. Mrs. Woolf has lent her voice to what she writes about; thus the reader is almost never certain whether the narrator or a character is speaking—a problem he would seldom encounter with the ordinary novel. Furthermore, Mrs. Woolf's style focuses one's attention on the rhythm of a scene, adding just enough detail to suggest a picture of what is happening. Her desire to keep her touch light, her love of the sketch, is one of the basic characteristics of her personality. It is a quality that can be felt at the most elementary level of her prose. Anyone who has read her essays or her fiction will have encountered passages like these:

> In my little street, however, domesticity prevailed. The house painter was descending his ladder; the nursemaid was wheeling the perambulator carefully in and out back to nursery tea; the coal-heaver was folding his empty sacks on top of each other; the woman who keeps the green-grocer's shop was adding up the day's takings in red mittens.[9]

> She could see people laughing and talking; the great men she had known; Dryden, Swift, and Pope; and statesmen in colloquy; and lovers dallying in the windowseats; and people eating and drinking at the long tables; and the wood smoke curling round their heads and making them sneeze and cough. . . . An organ boomed. A coffin was borne into the chapel. A marriage procession came out of it. Armed men with helmets left for the wars.[10]

9. *A Room of One's Own*, p. 60.
10. *Orlando: A Biography* (London: Hogarth Press, 1964), p. 287. Unless otherwise noted, all references are to this edition.

And Richard Dalloway and Hugh Whitbread hesitated at the corner of Conduit Street . . . Some newspaper placard went up in the air, gallantly, like a kite at first, then paused, swooped, fluttered; and a lady's veil hung. Yellow awnings trembled. The speed of the morning traffic slackened, and single carts rattled carelessly down half-empty streets.[11]

All of these passages—lifted almost at random from very different sources—have in common the impression of a sketch, a swift but accurate summary, a series of impressions strung out in apposition. And this style is indicative of a habit of mind that can be felt in almost every aspect of Virginia Woolf's art. It is analogous to her whole approach in her more experimental fiction, where there is rarely any sense of a direct, literal rendition of either thought or action. Of course the method of such novels as *Jacob's Room, Mrs. Dalloway,* and *To the Lighthouse* evolved from Mrs. Woolf's experiments with sketches in *Monday or Tuesday*—although, as I have tried to indicate, the feeling of a sketch was implicit in her style even as early as *The Voyage Out.*

One point to be made about Mrs. Woolf's fondness for the sketch, her tendency to list impressions, is that in some ways it makes her temperamentally indisposed to the style we normally associate with the stream of consciousness. The stream of consciousness, though it can be rendered by indirect means, requires of the author an essentially dramatic technique, as opposed to a summary method. What is more, it tends to number the atoms as they fall, rather than to show how the mind in certain instances can select and combine certain atoms or even merge with them in a kind of harmony. Thus Mrs. Woolf's need to develop a style that sometimes suggests consciousness but never directly reports it, that can give the feeling of both the particular and the general, moving easily be-

11. *Mrs. Dalloway,* pp. 124–25.

tween the thoughts of several characters and the ruminations of the author without changing its quality; in sum, a style that makes us feel both the individuality of the character and his relation to the whole of life.

But it remains to be seen what particular vision of life determined this style. The primary motive behind *Mrs. Dalloway,* I hope to show, is the same one already detected in *The Voyage Out.* Clarissa Dalloway, like so many of Virginia Woolf's characters, is beset by the problem of aloneness and separateness in life: "the supreme mystery which Kilman might say she had solved, or Peter might say he had solved, but Clarissa didn't believe either of them had the ghost of an idea of solving, was simply this: here was one room, there was another. Did religion solve that, or love?" This, in fact, is the central problem that Mrs. Woolf tries to deal with in all her fiction. It is intimately related, of course, to the problem of death, the ultimate separation and from one point of view the ultimate confirmation of the separateness of things.

Virginia Woolf's fiction repeatedly offers two related responses to this problem. The first is indicated in this passage, which shows Peter musing upon Clarissa:

> Clarissa had a theory in those days—they had heaps of theories, always theories, as young people have. It was to explain the feeling they had of dissatisfaction; not knowing people; not being known. For how could they know each other? You met every day; then not for six months, or years. It was unsatisfactory, they agreed, how little one knew people. But she said, sitting on the bus going up Shaftesbury Avenue, she felt herself everywhere; not "here, here, here"; and she tapped the back of the seat; but everywhere. She waved her hand, going up Shaftesbury Avenue. She was all that. So that to know her, or any one, one must seek out the people who completed them; even the places. Odd affinities she had with

people she had never spoken to, some woman in the street, some man behind a counter—even trees, or barns. It ended in a transcendental theory which, with her horror of death, allowed her to believe, or say that she believed (for all her scepticism), that since our apparitions, the part of us which appears, are so momentary compared with the other, the unseen part of us, which spreads wide, the unseen might survive, be recovered somehow attached to this person or that, or even haunting certain places, after death. Perhaps—perhaps. [pp. 167–68]

Indirect as this statement is, qualified by Clarissa Dalloway's lack of any real theoretical power, reduced in Peter's mind to a theory she had "in those days," it does nevertheless suggest a view of life which is confirmed by the tale and the whole manner of telling it. This view implies that there is no clear boundary between the "inside" and the "outside," just as there is no clear boundary between Virginia Woolf's characters or between the author and her materials. The self, in this view, is not simply an ego bound by space and time, but the total context of the physical world that the self creates and/or embraces in its movement through life, a context that helps define the self and remains after the individual "appearance" has gone. Thus the former inhabitants of "A Haunted House" seem to live on; thus Mrs. Ramsay seems to return to the Isle of Skye ten years after her death.

Mrs. Dalloway, disturbed by her inability to really "know" people, troubled by the transitoriness of love, and haunted by a fear of death, feels somehow that there remains a vague transcendental unity. One consolation for her is that she feels she can live on through others, that life is a shared web of experience. Thus she "lives" in the memory of her friends and is in a real sense a part of their lives; she even "lives" through people she does not know but who have affinities with her personality: "somehow in the streets of London, on the ebb and flow of things, here, there, she survived, Peter survived, lived in each other, she being part, she was positive, of the trees at home . . . part of people she had never met . . . being laid out like a mist between the people she knew best." The "ebb and flow," the "mist" that connects people, what Mrs. Woolf would later call a "luminous halo," is not, however, a simple matter of associationist psychology. It implies a vision of an ultimate unity in life which can perhaps be expressed only through metaphors of water.[12] It represents, like the sense of unity expressed in *The Voyage Out,* a submission of the individual to an ultimate in Nature, and therefore offers a more profound and lasting answer to the anguish of death than the love of one's friends can provide. As we have seen, however, the submission or "embrace" which this view of life entails is often treated with ambivalence. Mrs. Woolf's novels are full of the desire to merge with the "hosts opposed to the ego." Many of her characters—Clarissa, Mrs. Ramsay, and Bernard are examples—feel they have to suppress the urge to die, even when there appears to be no clear reason for doing so.

Some sense of the elemental forces which lie beneath all life can be felt in a passage characteristic of Virginia Woolf, though not, perhaps, of *Mrs. Dalloway.* We are shown the skywriting airplane moving higher and higher, taking the wonder of the crowd with it, until it presents us with one of those landscapes which are at once panoramic and microscopic: "soaring over Greenwich and all the masts; over the little island of grey

12. Of course the "halo" around the self can also imply a valuable isolation. Clearly, Mrs. Woolf's characters—Clarissa Dalloway is an example—are jealous of their privacy; they sometimes wish to give up the struggle to live, but they also wish to survive, not as a "mist" but as their own unique and admirable selves. Thus Mrs. Woolf often tries—unsuccessfully, I think—to have her characters "die" and yet somehow remain alive. Clarissa "dies" through Septimus. Mrs. Ramsay "lives" through Lily. Neither instance represents a true solution to the problem that haunts the novels.

churches, St. Paul's and the rest till, on either side of London, fields spread out and dark brown woods where adventurous thrushes hopping boldly, glancing quickly, snatched the snail and tapped him on a stone, once, twice, thrice." All of Virginia Woolf's fiction attempts to indicate a universal, timeless sense of life which may be called truth or reality. Very often this truth is expressed through descriptions of nature—vast perspectives where we sense a beautiful but impersonal force that is destructive to individuals but seems to live in all things. In a more indirect sense, this vision of reality is expressed in the stylistic peculiarities of Mrs. Woolf's novels—in her fluid transitions, for example, or in her explorations of her characters' ostensibly trivial thoughts and memories, which link them in a community.

Mrs. Dalloway is no intense, talented, romantic young girl like Rachel Vinrace; but in her own way she is equally conscious of an elemental unity of feeling that is the basis for life. For Rachel, this unity is to be apprehended in music or sex; for Mrs. Dalloway, whose intense sexual feelings have been confined to her youthful love for Sally Seton, the sense of unity is reached by means of an elegant party: "What did it mean to her, this thing she called life? Oh, it was very queer. Here was So-and-so in South Kensington; someone up in Bayswater; and somebody else, say, in Mayfair. And she felt quite continuously a sense of their existence . . . and she felt if only they could be brought together; so she did it. And it was an offering; to combine, to create; but to whom?" Beneath the superficial characteristics of the socialite, Clarissa is as much an artist as Lily Briscoe. She creates, or at any rate discloses to herself if to no one else, a sense of unity out of apparent separateness or chaos. And no less than Rachel Vinrace, Clarissa wants to experience this sense of unity all the time; even, it sometimes seems, if such a unity can only be felt in the dissolution of personality or ultimately in death itself.

Furthermore, one cannot escape the conclusion that Virginia Woolf often had the same desire. Her style is in many ways a reflection of the will to achieve the unity in life that Mrs. Dalloway tenuously apprehends. And Septimus Smith is, of course, a concrete demonstration that Mrs. Dalloway is a part of "people she had never met." Smith, furthermore, has an added importance. I have already indicated in discussing *The Voyage Out* that the impulse behind a great deal of Mrs. Woolf's fiction is a kind of death-wish. One simply cannot experience the unity of life in any more than a tenuous and temporary way and still retain an individual identity. Therefore most of Virginia Woolf's characters are vouchsafed only moments of satisfaction: in the warm blur of a party or in the heat of artistic creation, in trances or reverie, in sexual passion or at the moment before sleep or death. Septimus Smith, however, has feelings of transcendent unity repeatedly and often; to the psychologists he lacks a sense of "proportion," and significantly he chooses to die rather than be healed in their way.

And his death has symbolic overtones. Later I will discuss the importance of rooms and windows in Mrs. Woolf's fiction and essays: here we have a character who forsakes his "room," his identity, by leaping out of the window to completely embrace the world beyond. (Virginia Woolf once attempted suicide by the same means. There are other parallels. Just as Septimus' doctor advises him to try "proportion," so in 1922 a doctor in Harley Street told Virginia Woolf, "Equanimity-equanimity-practice equanimity." [13]) Smith, however, like Rachel Vinrace and Mrs. Ramsay, has a partially redemptive death, in that he gives to Mrs. Dalloway, quite unawares, an acute sense of her unity with life. He is also in a way the "scapegoat" he considers himself, since Mrs. Dalloway experi-

13. Leonard Woolf, *Downhill All the Way: An Autobiography of the Years 1919–1939* (London: Hogarth Press, 1967), p. 51.

ences his death vicariously and gains a consolation from it. Virginia Woolf stressed the relation between these two characters in her notes on revisions for the novel: "Mrs. Dalloway seeing the truth. Septimus Smith seeing the insane truth." [14] In dying Septimus of course "lives on" through his alter-ego, Clarissa, who also feels that trees are like people, who also longs to communicate through a kind of universal love, and who also has a theory about death: "Death was an attempt to communicate; people feeling the impossibility of reaching the center, which, mystically, evaded them; closeness drew apart, rapture faded, one was alone. There was an embrace in death." Death, in this view, is transformed from the ultimate separation into the ultimate union, the most complete form of that embrace that Mrs. Woolf said she wanted her novels to show. Clarissa Dalloway is therefore able to experience Septimus' death as it really must have been, though she does not know the details of it. And, without forsaking the ultimate intactness of her self, she can climb the stair and look from her room into the one across the way, which had earlier seemed so separate, and feel a sense of unity with the woman there.

There are of course other parallels between Septimus and Clarissa, chiefly in terms of their struggle against Dr. Bradshaw and Miss Kilman. Both Bradshaw and Kilman are representatives of what Mrs. Woolf, in a long diatribe almost at the center of the novel, calls the "Goddess of Conversion." Mrs. Woolf makes a half-hearted attempt to disguise this lengthy passage as the thoughts of Rezia Smith, but the voice we hear speaking is clearly the author's: "Conversion," we are told, "feasts on the wills of the weakly, loving to impress, to impose, adoring her own features stamped on the face of the populace" (p. 111). Conversion, too, makes a unity of life, but it is anything but natural. It is the result of one ego trying to impose its will on

14. Woolf, quoted by Richter, *Inward Voyage,* p. 120.

another; it is, in other words, the exact opposite of the unity created by a sacrifice of the ego in characters like Rachel Vinrace and Clarissa Dalloway. Mrs. Woolf suggests that the spirit of conversion leads directly to British imperialism, to nationalism, and to oppressive institutions like Bradshaw's home for the mentally ill or Kilman's church. On a more personal level, conversion is the force behind the subjection of Mrs. Bradshaw to her husband, and behind Miss Kilman's attempt to take Elizabeth away from her mother.

In a way, Septimus Smith is justified in feeling that other people want him to die. Bradshaw wants to subdue other people's selves, to convert their identity to his own, and Septimus' last words, "I'll give it you" (added by Mrs. Woolf in the final page proofs of the book) are partly meant to acknowledge Bradshaw's design. In another sense, however, Septimus uses death to escape his doctors. His most serene moments come when he has a vision of himself as a "drowned sailor on a rock"; in this dreamy state, Septimus feels a certain "luxury": "even Holmes himself could not touch this last relic straying on the edge of the world, . . . who gazed back at the inhabited regions, who lay, like a drowned sailor, on the shore of the world" (p. 103). To escape having to submit his ego to the Goddess of Conversion, Septimus chooses to yield up his entire being; but there is perhaps also in his death something of what Mrs. Dalloway calls "an attempt to communicate." Just before he jumps from the window, Septimus notices an old man across the way staring at him—an image repeated in the scene where Clarissa Dalloway, contemplating Septimus' death, discovers that the old lady across the way is staring at her.

Doris Kilman, whose name has an almost painfully obvious significance, remains a somewhat less powerful oppressor than Bradshaw. Mrs. Woolf describes Bradshaw's victims as "Naked, defenseless," receiving the "impress of Sir William's will." Kilman would like to exert a similar strength, but she is less successful. Toward Mrs. Dalloway, she feels "an overmastering desire to overcome . . . If only she could make her weep; could ruin her; humiliate her; bring her to her knees crying. You are right!" (p. 138). And toward Elizabeth she has an agonized possessiveness: "If she could grasp her, if she could clasp her, if she could make her hers absolutely and forever and then die; that was all she wanted" (p. 145). But even though Miss Kilman hides away in an upper room, exhorting Elizabeth to prayer, even though she takes the girl on trips to the Army and Navy stores, she has far less power than Mrs. Dalloway fears. Elizabeth does not care much for clothes and parties, but that is not because of Kilman's influence. On the brief occasion when we share Elizabeth's thoughts, we discover that she was "delighted to be free" of Kilman: "The fresh air was so delicious. It had been so stuffy in the Army and Navy stores" (p. 149).

The novel therefore suggests a victory over more than one kind of death. On the one hand Clarissa Dalloway represents an alternative to Kilman's suffocating egoism: "Had she ever tried to convert anyone herself? Did she not wish everybody merely to be themselves?" And on the other hand, she vaguely apprehends an elemental unity in life which causes her to regard death as something other than oblivion. In both instances her love of parties is significant. The life of the socialite might appear simply another manifestation of egoism, but Mrs. Dalloway is quick to defend against this charge. She knows other people think "She enjoyed imposing herself"; actually, however, she regards her parties as an "offering" to "life." "After that," she thinks, "how unbelievable death was" (p. 135).

It should be noted, however, that the characters who are drawn to this sense of cosmic unity are cut off from ordinary personal relationships. We think of Clarissa Dalloway as the perfect socialite, but there is a good deal of the solitary, of Rachel Vinrace, in her as well. There is a certain asceticism and coldness about her retreats from people into her upper room, described almost as if it were a nunnery, where she sews, falls into dreams, and speculates on the unity of life. Significantly, she has to leave her party in order to experience unity with that woman across the way. Likewise, there is obviously a good deal of pain and pathos in the estrangement of Septimus from Rezia. The major characters have sacrificed one kind of closeness for another, which they feel is somehow more real.

In fact, however, were Mrs. Dalloway to experience such intense emotions for long she would have to die just as Septimus does, or at least sacrifice her social identity. Instead she seems to absorb Septimus' experience, and as a result she comes to terms with death. The novel, like so much of Virginia Woolf's fiction, is elegiac. Mrs. Dalloway, aging and in poor health, no longer fears death but embraces it. Indeed nearly all of Virginia Woolf's characters seem to be drawn toward a kind of death. Peter Walsh, for example, is capable of a comfortable solitude and a loss of personal identity that is deeply satisfying to him, though he also feels a need for ordinary relationships in the world of "fact":

> For this is the truth about our soul, he thought, our self, who fish-like inhabits deep seas and plies among obscurities threading her way between the boles of giant weeds, over sunflickered spaces and on and on into gloom, cold, deep, inscrutable; suddenly she shoots to the surface and sports on the wind-wrinkled waves; that is, has a positive need to brush, scrape, kindle herself, gossiping. What did the Government mean—Richard Dalloway would know—to do about India? [p. 177]

There is a need, Peter feels, to make direct contact with the surface appearances of life, to assert the ego. For him, Clarissa's party is a means for such contact, though for the hostess it has a different value. In either case, the natural abode for the soul seems to be somewhere down under the lovely water. And direct contact with others, after one has been submerged so long, is a harsh and abrasive experience. Such a process no doubt accounts for one of the effects we encounter fairly often in Mrs. Woolf's fiction: a smooth, liquid stream of sensibility abruptly interrupted by the violent contact of life outside in the form of a sound like a backfire or a doorbell. In a larger sense, this watery world, where identity is muted and the self seems to blend with the outside, where in solitude the individual feels at peace and harmony with an elemental form of life—this world *is* Virginia Woolf's style.

6

To the Lighthouse

I have said that *Mrs. Dalloway* is an elegiac novel and implied as much about *The Voyage Out*; the same term can be
applied with even more obvious justification to *To the Lighthouse*, which was not only conceived as an elegy[1] but is one
of the best in modern literature. This is not to deny that there
are other ways of looking at the story of the Ramsays; it has, for
example, affinities with the novel of manners, as Ralph Freedman has observed.[2] The portrait of an age past, of the summer
guests at the Isle of Skye, is one of the most affecting parts
of the book, and proof, if one needed it, that Mrs. Woolf could
create memorable characters. In the most comprehensive sense,
however, *To the Lighthouse* is about death—the death of loved
ones, the death of a beloved place and time. Like *Mrs. Dalloway*, it offers some consolation for death, and this consolation
is intimately related to Virginia Woolf's effort to depict what
she regarded as "life itself."

The method here is essentially the same as that used in *Mrs.*

1. Woolf, *A Writer's Diary*, p. 83.
2. Ralph Freedman, *The Lyrical Novel* (Princeton: Princeton University
Press, 1963), p. 227.

Dalloway, but it has become more complex and subtle. The text is divided into parts and sections, so that action seems not so much all of a piece. Still, the sense of temporal and qualitative unity, of a single voice that orders the whole, is if anything greater than in the previous book. Everything seems to be refracted through the medium of a prose which tends to blur distinctions. There is an increased tendency to suppress or muffle exterior actions or events; dialogue is usually reported indirectly or filtered through the sensibilities of the characters; even the details of setting have been reduced to a minimum. Time is also handled somewhat differently here than in *Mrs. Dalloway.* We still have an extensive study of a single day (the afternoon and evening of one day and the morning and noon of another ten years later) as well as the occasional flashbacks; we still feel, as Erich Auerbach puts it, as if events "cut loose from the present of the exterior circumstances and range freely through the depths of time." [3] But in this novel such an effect is not always tied to the activities of any individual memory, and the author sometimes confuses the order of events in a most ingenious manner.

The first section of "The Window" illustrates all these characteristics. Consider, for example, Mrs. Woolf's handling of the time sequence. Just after Charles Tansley stops outside the drawing room window where Mrs. Ramsay and James sit and parrots Mr. Ramsay's cold observation about the weather, Mrs. Ramsay begins to think about him: "She wished they would both leave her and James alone and go on talking. She looked at him. He was such a miserable specimen, the children said . . . She could not help laughing herself sometimes." She notes the way he turns everything around and makes it "somehow reflect himself and disparage them." This thought about the children leads, or seems to lead, to a reflection on the way the eight sons

3. Auerbach, *Mimesis,* p. 540.

and daughters run to their rooms after dinner to debate things
(p. 18). The paragraph describing the Ramsay children in their
rooms appears at first to be a part of Mrs. Ramsay's monologue.
It is a relatively elegant and coherent description, but it follows
quite naturally upon Mrs. Ramsay's thoughts about the children's criticisms of Tansley. We seem to pick up Mrs. Ramsay's
thought more directly again at the opening of the next paragraph: "Strife, divisions, differences of opinion . . . oh, that
they should begin so early, Mrs. Ramsay deplored."

Up to this point there has been no clear indication that the
time has changed, that we are no longer observing the thoughts
of Mrs. Ramsay as she sits by the window with James—though
a very scrupulous reader might be alerted by the reference to
dinner in the previous paragraph, since we have been told that
Mr. Ramsay and Tansley are out for an evening walk. But in
fact the time *has* changed, as we discover from these subsequent
lines, where I have underlined Mrs. Woolf's clues: "They were
so critical, her children. They talked such nonsense. *She went
from the dining room, holding James by the hand, since he
would not go with the others.*" The "others" are the other children, who, as we have been told, run up to their rooms after
dinner. A few lines on we read, "The real differences, she
thought, *standing by the drawing room window,* are enough,
quite enough." And the next paragraph begins, "Insoluble problems, they were, it seemed to her, *standing there, holding
James by the hand. He had followed her into the drawing
room, that young man they laughed at; he was standing by the
table, fidgeting.*" The young man is of course Tansley. What
is so odd about all this is that if we disregard these authorial
signposts, which supply only very indirect evidence that the
time has changed, and only after the fact, we might still be
reading Mrs. Ramsay's thoughts as they occurred in the early
evening. "That young man they laughed at" could be taken as
a reference to her thoughts as she sat by the window and felt

anger at Tansley. We are, however, reading about something that happened much earlier in the day, when Tansley followed Mrs. Ramsay from the dining room after dinner, and she invited him to come on an errand to the village. Is she remembering all this as she sits by the window? Apparently not, since there follows a treatment of the expedition to town, during which the pathetic Tansley falls under Mrs. Ramsay's spell and we see into his thoughts: "For the first time in his life," we are told as the first section draws to a close, "Charles Tansley felt an extraordinary pride . . . for he was walking with a beautiful woman. He had hold of her bag."

One would have to be a very careful reader not to be confused about the time sequence in these fourteen pages. The second section, however, clarifies things by bringing us back to where we were at the beginning:

> "No going to the Lighthouse, James," he said, as he stood by the window . . . Odious little man, thought Mrs. Ramsay, why go on saying that?

The "he" refers of course to Tansley, whose act, in light of Mrs. Ramsay's kindness to him earlier in the day, is shown to be not only insensitive but ungrateful.

As I have indicated, the episode of the visit to town is not presented from Mrs. Ramsay's viewpoint, so it cannot be her memory of the event. Obviously, it is the author who describes the excursion, altering the time sequence to write about something that occurred *before* the opening scene of the novel. But it is singularly difficult to determine just when Mrs. Ramsay's thought stream is abandoned; in fact, the transition takes place with the paragraph beginning, "Disappearing as stealthily as stags . . . the eight sons and daughters of Mr. and Mrs. Ramsay sought their bedrooms" (p. 18). But there is no real indication that this paragraph marks a shift to an earlier time; indeed, because we so quickly pick up Mrs. Ramsay's meditations on the critical temperaments of her children, the whole passage seems related to her observations just above about their criticisms of Tansley. Her thoughts in the evening and her thoughts earlier in the day are causally unified, and seem to follow immediately upon one another.

Instead of the sometimes overly-contrived transitions from present to past or character to character found in *Mrs. Dalloway* (and occasionally in *To the Lighthouse*) what we have here and in some other passages is an apparent absence of transition, as if everything belonged to the same place and time. If in the earlier novel it was hard to determine where the thoughts of a character stopped and the words of the author began, here there is an added confusion about what is past and what is present, what is part of a character's memory and what is being supplied by the author. Consider the thoughts (or statements?) of William Bankes, enclosed in a long parenthesis (pp. 50–51). What is described took place sometime in the past, but that is by no means immediately clear as we read the passage in its context. The "Time Passes" section of the novel is also rife with ambiguities. The effect of time passing is conveyed, but only indirectly; we watch the slow decay and then refurbishment of the Ramsay's summer house, we observe the cycle of the seasons and sense the timelessness of nature; but now and then we are notified of some event in the human world to which nature itself seems impervious. Ten years pass, but these years are encompassed in the framework of a single night: the section begins with the characters coming in from outside and preparing for bed, and ends with everyone reluctantly waking up to a new day. In between we encounter passages like this one:

> Should any sleeper fancying that he might find on the beach an answer to his doubts, a sharer of his solitude, throw off his bedclothes and go down by himself to walk on the sand,

no image with semblance of serving and divine promptitude comes readily to hand bringing the night to order and making the world reflect the compass of the soul. [p. 199]

This alliterative and slightly grandiose description seems to fit Mr. Ramsay. Such dramatic gestures are suited to his temperament, and the prose style suggests his erudition—Latinisms such as "promptitude" are uncommon in Mrs. Woolf's writing. But Ramsay is not named, and there is no indication that anyone performed the action described at any particular time. As a result, the walk on the beach can seem to belong to the night described in the first part of the novel, or to almost any summer night. In fact, we discover parenthetically a few lines later that time has passed and that Mrs. Ramsay is dead. Therefore the loneliness of the "sleeper" seems vaguely related to Mr. Ramsay's loss, but it remains an event that we cannot fix precisely in time.

To borrow another remark from Auerbach, Virginia Woolf's novels sometimes appear to be narrated by "those 'certain airs, detached from the body of the wind,' which in a later passage . . . move about the house." [4] It is impossible to illustrate the peculiarities of such a technique without quoting a fairly long passage. Here are Mrs. Ramsay and Charles Tansley as they walk to town in the first section of the novel:

It flattered him; snubbed as he had been, it soothed him that Mrs. Ramsay should tell him this. Charles Tansley revived. Insinuating, too, as she did the greatness of man's intellect, even in its decay, the subjection of all wives—not that she blamed the girl, and the marriage had been happy enough, she believed—to their husband's labours, she made him feel better pleased with himself than he had done yet, and he would have liked, had they taken a cab, for example,

4. Ibid., p. 532.

to have paid the fare. As for her little bag, might he not carry
that? No, no, she said, she always carried *that* herself. She
did, too. Yes, he felt that in her. He felt many things, something in particular that excited him and disturbed him for
reasons which he could not give. He would like her to see
him, gowned and hooded, walking in a procession. A fellowship, a professorship,—he felt capable of anything and saw
himself—but what was she looking at? At a man posting a
bill. The vast flapping sheet flattened itself out, and each
shove of the brush revealed fresh legs, hoops, horses, glisten-
ing reds and blues, beautifully smooth, until half the wall was
covered with the advertisement of a circus; a hundred horse-
men, twenty performing seals, lions, tigers . . . Craning for-
wards, for she was short-sighted, she read out how it . . .
"will visit this town." It was terribly dangerous work for a
one-armed man, she exclaimed, to stand on top of a ladder like
that—his left arm had been cut off in a reaping machine two
years ago.

"Let us all go!" she cried, moving on, as if all those riders
and horses had filled her with childlike exultation and made
her forget her pity.

"Let's go," he said, repeating her words, clicking them
out, however, with a self-consciousness that made her wince.
"Let us go to the circus." No. He could not say it right. He
could not feel it right. But why not, she wondered. What was
wrong with him then? She liked him warmly, at the moment. Had they not been taken, she asked, to circuses when
they were children? Never, he answered, as if she asked the
very thing he wanted to reply to; had been longing all these
days to say, how they did not go to circuses. [pp. 22–24]

In a minor way, this passage serves to illustrate something
that almost defines VirginiaWoolf's novels during this period.
She had an extraordinary understanding of how people's emo-

tions are always fluctuating, recognizing that in any brief space of time a number of small events, some of them random, some of them determined long before, continually modify the quality of our feelings and influence our slightest actions. Her novels depict not only the small motives which generate actions but also the formation of these motives. At the same time, however, she devotes comparatively little attention to the details of her characters' surroundings and even avoids the direct rendition of action. The result is the sketchlike quality that I have noted before. The physical details in the passage at hand are remarkably sparse—we are not told, here or anywhere, just what Mrs. Ramsay and Charles and the streets look like. We have only snippets of conversation and the colors in a circus poster. By contrast, however, she records every variation in the characters' emotions. A bit of flattery restores Tansley, inspires him to offer to carry Mrs. Ramsay's bag, then sends him off into a daydream. This mood in turn is interrupted by a random event—a circus poster which attracts Mrs. Ramsay. She, ever-sympathetic, feels pity for the one-armed paperhanger, but in the next instant the bright poster has made her almost girlish. Tansley tries to echo her enthusiasm for the circus but ends up feeling awkward and deflated. Mrs. Ramsay notices this and for a second she experiences sympathy for him. She asks him about his childhood, and once again the restoration process is under way.

Both characters have gone through a series of emotional fluctuations, and the reader becomes strongly aware of what Mrs. Woolf called the "tremor of susceptibility" in the self. I do not know of any other novelist who places such emphasis on all the fluctuations of feeling within a single scene—there are passages in *A Portrait of the Artist* that come close, but they have to do with a hypersensitive young boy under extreme emotional pressure, whereas Virginia Woolf is portraying relatively stable adults. This ability to isolate and dramatize all the little influ-

ences on feeling is the basis for William Empson's observation
that Mrs. Woolf shows the whole character behind every action.[5] Clearly, too, this style represents a variety of stream-of-
consciousness fiction. We have a fine sense of the texture of emotional life, of constant variations in mood, of the way thoughts
and actions are influenced by random sensations. But notice how
little of the passage actually refers to the texture of *consciousness*. Indeed, when one tries to define the author's relationship
to her characters in such a scene, one is in difficulty.

Some of the passage consists of the author's comment. The
first few sentences, for example, seem in part an objective statement about Tansley: "It flattered him, snubbed as he had been,
it soothed him that Mrs. Ramsay should tell him this." At
the same time, however, the narrator seems to imitate the
rhythm of Tansley's emotions; the repetition in "It flattered
him . . . it soothed him," sounds almost like a healing pulse.
There is just enough of Tansley himself in the sentence to make
it possible that he is thinking the words, or something like them.
It seems unlikely that he would be capable of such self-detach-
ment, but one cannot be completely sure (Mrs. Woolf's method,
whether she wills it or not, makes nearly all her characters seem
intensely self-conscious). At other times the passage is still more
ambiguous: "Yes, he felt that in her. He felt many things,
something in particular that excited him and disturbed him for
reasons which he could not give." The first sentence is probably Tansley, but what about the second? Is it the author commenting or the author simply reporting somewhat indirectly
what Tansley is saying to himself?

The passage goes on: "He would like her to see him, gowned
and hooded, walking in procession. A fellowship, a professorship, he felt capable of anything and saw himself—but what
was she looking at? At a man posting a bill." Here the author

5. William Empson, "Virginia Woolf," in *Scrutinies II*, ed. E. Richword
(London: Wishart and Company, 1931), p. 213.

is clearly reporting Tansley's thoughts, rendering them very indirectly but in a style that imitates their actual rhythm and shows how they are determined by trivial events like a man hanging a poster. In the same way, the passage renders nearly all of the conversation between the two characters indirectly: "Insinuating, too, as she did the greatness of man's intellect, even in its decay, the subjection of all wives—not that she blamed the girl, and the marriage had been happy enough, she believed—to their husband's labours, she made him feel better pleased with himself . . . and he would have liked, had they taken a cab, for example, to have paid the fare. As for her little bag, might he not carry that? No, no, she said, she always carried *that* herself." We hear both of the characters speaking in these lines, especially Mrs. Ramsay's chatter, but their conversation has been generalized and subordinated to the thoughts and feelings it stimulates in Tansley. It is characteristic of Mrs. Woolf that her characters often seem absorbed in thought or daydream, only half-conscious of the buzz of talk, the sights and sounds of the outside world. As a result of all this indirection and introspection, it is not always clear in scenes like this one how much is only thought and how much actually spoken—as with Tansley's thought about the cab, for example.

A similar ambiguity pervades the end of the passage, where we shift almost imperceptibly to Mrs. Ramsay's view: "He could not say it right. He could not feel it right. But why not she wondered. What was so wrong with him then?" We do not even recognize that we are reading Mrs. Ramsay's thoughts until we come to "she wondered." And who thinks "He could not say it right," Charles or Mrs. Ramsay or both of them together? The effect of such a transition is that Tansley's thoughts seem almost to flow into Mrs. Ramsay's mind, without any noticeable change in the point of view.

It is not uncommon for Virginia Woolf, as opposed to James, Conrad, Joyce, or Faulkner, to rely on this kind of multipersonal subjectivity. And in this particular novel the difference is especially apparent: even when characters are separated by great spaces, as when Lily is on shore while Ramsay and the children make for the lighthouse, we view the event from several different perspectives. In *Mrs. Dalloway* and *To the Lighthouse,* unlike most of *Ulysses,* the viewpoint is always shifting, while a qualitative unity is maintained through Mrs. Woolf's elegant prose. And this qualitative unity is a distinguishing characteristic. Even a passage like the one we have been considering, which combines authorial comment with the thought and speech of two different characters, reads like a single flow of words. Much of this effect derives from the indirection of the method and the author's careful blending of conventional rhetorical devices. Part of it, too, owes to the device of repetition, which serves not only to intensify the language and to beat out a rhythm but also to move the reader from one thing to another without any feeling of an intervening space. Repetition is, in fact, often essential to Mrs. Woolf's idiosyncratic transitions. Notice the litany, "Let us all go," "Let's go," "Let us all go to the circus," in the passage quoted earlier; it sounds a dissonant note, perhaps because it is almost the only quoted dialogue, and helps effect the transition from Charles' view to Mrs. Ramsay's.

I want to comment at some length on the implications such a style has for the meaning of the novel as a whole and for Virginia Woolf's view of life, but first we should consider in more detail how her style works to render individual consciousnesses. I have said that Virginia Woolf nearly always creates a sense of multipersonal subjectivity, emphasizing a total emotional life composed of the feelings of different characters; that is not to imply, however, that the reader is exposed only briefly to each individual mind. Indeed, Virginia Woolf has placed the characters of this novel in a situation where she can take full advantage of moods of reverie and meditation. We come upon Mrs. Ramsay idly measuring a stocking, Mr. Ramsay walking in the garden, Lily Briscoe musing over her painting. As David Daiches has pointed out, the holiday setting of the novel seems especially suited to an effort to develop, compare, and contrast the inner lives of the figures in moods of comparative isolation.[6] The result is a striking counterpoint between the major characters, and a carefully modulated stylistic unity.

Because of these frequent meditations, *To the Lighthouse* has been described as if it were a straightforward stream-of-consciousness novel; but again, one must qualify the use of the term. As in *Mrs. Dalloway,* there are passages which fit Humphrey's definition of indirect interior monologue, though the method used most often resembles his "omniscient narration." Erich Auerbach has, of course, exhaustively demonstrated the random play of Mrs. Ramsay's mind as she measures a stocking on her son James, and he has indicated how the passage is related to stream-of-consciousness literature; at the same time, he notes that what seems to be the voice of the author in a paragraph just following Mrs. Ramsay's thoughts is inseparable from the tone and style of the interior monologue:[7]

> Never did anybody look so sad. Bitter and black, half-way down, in the darkness, in the shaft which ran from the sunlight to the depths, perhaps a tear formed; a tear fell; the waters swayed this way and that, received it, and were at rest. Never did anybody look so sad. [p. 49]

Here, as elsewhere, the thoughts of the characters mingle with the thoughts of a barely defined narrator; and the passage makes us aware that the whole book is the product of one voice which at times assumes the role of a given character and approximates his patterns of thought.

6. David Daiches, *Virginia Woolf* (Norfolk, Conn.: New Directions, 1942), pp. 82–83.

7. Auerbach, *Mimesis,* pp. 530–32.

A more typical device in *To the Lighthouse* falls somewhere between a stylized report of consciousness and an authorial comment, as in the scene where Lily Briscoe, thinking about her canvas, is approached by William Bankes:

> Even while she looked at the mass, at the line, at the colour, at Mrs. Ramsay sitting in the window with James, she kept a feeler on her surroundings lest someone should creep up, and suddenly she should find her picture looked at. But now, with all her senses quickened as they were, looking, straining, till the colour of the wall and the jacmanna beyond burnt into her eyes, she was aware of some one coming out of the house, coming towards her; but somehow divined, from the footfall, William Bankes, so that though her brush quivered, she did not, as she would have done had it been Mr. Tansley, Paul Rayley, Minta Doyle, or practically anybody else, turn her canvas upon the grass, but let it stand. [p. 32]

The passage is devoted to the thoughts of a character, but the narrator takes a stance somewhere outside the mind, a stance that implies that the author (her language notwithstanding) is not attempting to dramatize the literal content of a consciousness. Notice the sentence, "Even while she looked at the mass, at the line, at the colour, at Mrs. Ramsay . . . she kept a feeler on her surroundings lest someone should creep up, and suddenly she should find her picture looked at." No attempt is made to verbalize Lily's thought; instead, the author merely characterizes her attitude. The same distance is suggested by the next sentence. Is Lily supposed to have thought this, or anything like it? She is aware of Bankes' approach, and perhaps she makes a conscious distinction between him and the others, but the rest of the information here seems provided by the author as a means of characterization. The technique, at least in terms of the depth and dramatic intensity of the psychological view, brings to mind the nineteenth-century novel.

The next paragraph continues in the same expository fashion: "They had rooms in the village, and so, walking in, walking out, parting late on door-mats, had said little things about the soup, about the children . . . so that when he stood beside her now in his judicial way (he was old enough to be her father, too, a botanist, a widower, smelling of soap, very scrupulous and clean) she just stood there" (p. 33). But the long sentence is broken by a parenthetical comment which seems to belong to Lily and to dramatize her instantaneous collection of impressions. Mrs. Woolf is fond of the parenthesis, but she does not, as Daiches implies, use it for only one purpose.[8] Sometimes it represents a shift in a character's thought, and sometimes it is used for remarks by the author. In this case the parenthesis seems to imitate Lily's thought; indeed, the whole sentence could be taken as an imitation of consciousness, a string of remembered details in apposition, broken by a parenthetical summation of Bankes' appearance. But the sentence only appears to be casual, and the concluding "she just stood there" makes for a consciously artful effect. Is Lily thinking all this, or is the author characterizing Lily by echoing her already-formed opinion of Bankes, thoughts she has had at some time, perhaps at several times, in the past? And even if we take the parenthesis as a report of Lily's consciousness at the moment when the scene is taking place, this one sentence hardly amounts to an interior monologue. Besides, midway through the paragraph, the author makes one of her subtle transitions and slips quite easily into William Bankes' view of the scene. Here again the functional device is repetition: "she just stood there. He just stood there. Her shoes were excellent, he observed . . .

8. Note also Daiches' interesting comment on Mrs. Woolf's use of the impersonal pronoun: "It indicates a certain agreement on the part of the author with the character's thoughts" (*Virginia Woolf*, p. 73). This is true to an extent, perhaps, but in the largest sense the repeated use of "one" gives her narration its highly ambiguous quality, so that the author seems to have merged with the characters.

Lodging at the same house with her, he had noticed, too, how orderly she was, up before breakfast and off to paint, he believed, alone: poor, presumably, and without the complexion or the allurement of Miss Doyle" (p. 31). We see Lily through Bankes' eyes, but it is not at all certain that the passage constitutes a dramatization of consciousness.

And passages like this one are not the exception but the rule in the novel. Virginia Woolf's technique is typically an artful mixture of exposition, rhetorical helps, approximations of actual thought, and omniscient commentary. She clearly has much in common with other stream-of-consciousness writers, but she depends heavily on the traditional descriptive language and the generalized overview of the nineteenth-century novel. Notice, however, that when she does discuss her characters from the vantage point of traditional omniscience, her voice lacks that tone of certainty that one finds, for example, in George Eliot. Much earlier, analyzing that long descriptive passage from *The Voyage Out,* I noted that the authorial personality seemed to give itself up to its subject as if captured by the hypnotic beauty of the landscape. This sympathetic yielding to the rhythm of her character's emotions is one of the chief determinants of Mrs. Woolf's style in *To the Lighthouse,* and one of the reasons it is so difficult to say when we are being told about her characters' minds and when we are being shown them.

Often, indeed, the style of *To the Lighthouse* can vividly suggest what a character feels even though the author is clearly not trying to report consciousness. For example, when Lily and William Bankes go walking just after the scene described above, Lily is preoccupied with a comparison of Bankes and Mr. Ramsay. A number of impressions of the two men crowd into her mind at once, and the author remarks, "to follow her thought was like following a voice which speaks too quickly to be taken down by one's pencil" (p. 43). We are supposed to

imagine a veritable jungle of impressions, and Virginia Woolf
assists us by enumerating some of Lily's thoughts, and adding:

> All of this danced up and down, like a company of gnats,
> each separate, but all marvellously controlled by an invisible
> elastic net—danced up and down in Lily's mind, in and about
> the branches of the pear tree, where still hung in effigy the
> scrubbed kitchen table, symbol of her profound respect for
> Mr. Ramsay's mind, until her thought which had spun
> quicker and quicker exploded of its own intensity; she felt
> released; a shot went off close at hand, and there came, flying
> from its fragments . . . . a flock of starlings. [pp. 43–44]

The emphasis on rhythm in this passage ("danced up and
down," "in and out the branches," "spun quicker and quicker,"
"exploded"), gives us a sense of what Lily feels: a powerfully
sexual emotion, unmistakeable as such even though—as usual
in Mrs. Woolf's novels—it is expressed only through the rhythm
and through some of the images. The metaphoric language
used here is really an elaboration of a technique first developed
in *The Voyage Out:* the author provides a poetic description of
a state of mind in order to express feelings which are essentially
nonverbal (or in this case perhaps too explicitly sexual). This
technique, used extensively in *Mrs. Dalloway* (as in the description of Lady Burton's mind as a spider's web), enables the
author to maintain her objective pose, making generalized,
sometimes even analytical statements about the character's attitude, while the reader is led to participate imaginatively in the
character's experience. In other words, Virginia Woolf gains
some of the advantages of a dramatic form without using the
more dramatic varieties of the stream of consciousness. Metaphor in the passage I have quoted is generally applied from
without, by the author; the only "private" metaphor, the only
image that comes directly from Lily's experience, is the picture

of the kitchen table hanging from the pear tree, which has a number of personal connotations for Lily, symbolizing, among other things, "her profound respect for Mr. Ramsay's mind." Except for the table and the pear tree, the imagery keeps us outside the literal stream of consciousness, and serves only to characterize Lily.

One advantage of this method is that it allows Virginia Woolf to portray intangibles that cannot be directly presented. But sometimes the descriptions of mental life become highly generalized, and metaphor serves not so much to take us beyond the verbal level as to keep us at a distance from the consciousness. Notice, for example, the treatment of Mr. Ramsay, who, near the end of the first section, wanders alone and observes his wife and child:

> He was safe, he was restored to his privacy. He stopped to light his pipe, looked once at his wife and his son in the window, and as one raises one's eyes from a page in an express train and sees a farm . . . a confirmation of something on the printed page to which one returns, fortified, and satisfied, so without his distinguishing either his son or his wife, the sight of them fortified him and satisfied him . . .
>
> It was a splendid mind. For if thought is like the keyboard of a piano, divided into so many notes, or like the alphabet is ranged in twenty-six letters all in order, then his splendid mind had no sort of difficulty in running over those letters one by one, firmly and accurately, until it had reached, say, the letter Q. [p. 56]

The first paragraph here is a comment on Ramsay's state of mind; it does not follow any train of thought and is handled in a conventional way. The author tells us that Mr. Ramsay raised his eyes "as one raises one's eyes from a page in an express train," and the image indicates that the view is from outside the character. The second paragraph elaborates the

theme of Mr. Ramsay's "splendid mind" from an omniscient
stance and develops a playful, ironic analogy. For the first
couple of sentences the passage suggests nothing more than a
slightly arch characterization of Mr. Ramsay's intellect, but the
viewpoint is less sharply-defined by the time we are midway
into the second paragraph: "he saw, but now far, far away,
like children picking up shells, divinely innocent and occupied
with little trifles at their feet . . . defenceless against a doom
which he perceived, his wife and son, together, in the window.
They needed his protection; he gave it them. But after Q?
What comes next?" (p. 57). This could be taken as an indirect
report of Ramsay's thought—the image of children fascinated
with trifles captures perfectly the patronizing attitude Ramsay
sometimes feels toward his family, and Mrs. Woolf is satisfied
to let the image make the point. But how is it that Ramsay has
been able to pick up the alphabet metaphor that the author has
seemingly developed independently? It seems likely that the
paragraph is meant to convey not snatches of indirect interior
monologue, but rather the author's comment on Ramsay's
thought. He has, we are told, an extremely well-ordered mind,
and he is in a highly meditative mood; Virginia Woolf could
have given him the kind of monologue she gives Mrs. Ramsay
in the fifth part, but instead she develops a series of elaborate
metaphors and similes, slightly ironic ones at that, which allow
her to maintain a certain distance from the character's consciousness while at the same time presenting him in a relatively
dramatic fashion. The objectivity of her approach is evident as
Ramsay goes on in a desperate attempt to arrive at a momentous
conclusion:

> If Q then is Q—R—Here he knocked his pipe out, with two
> or three resonant taps on the handle of the urn, and pro-
> ceeded. "Then R . . ." he braced himself. He clenched him-
> self.

Qualities that would have saved a ship's company exposed
on a broiling sea with six biscuits and a flash of water—
endurance and justice, foresight, devotion, skill, came to his
help. R is then—what is R? [p. 57]

The style here suggests Ramsay's mental strainings, but it is
clearly not a variety of internal monologue. Ramsay is not
thinking "If Q then is Q—R," nor is he self-consciously visu-
alizing himself as a sea captain—although he probably does,
somewhere in the back of his mind, feel proud of what he
regards as his manly heroism. The point is that the author is
the one who has developed the metaphor of the alphabet and
the analogy with the savior of a ship's company—a metaphor
and analogy which hold the reader outside Ramsay's highly
verbal patterns of thought. In Lily Briscoe's case, the metaphor
is applied from without in an attempt to get at qualities of
mind which are below the level of conscious verbalization.
Ramsay, who is at this moment wrestling with his intellect, is
thinking systematically, verbally. Metaphor is not used simply
to suggest that Ramsay's complex speculations defy description,
but rather because the author wants to comment on his thought:
she assumes the role of the tolerant, slightly condescending
outsider who, while aware that Ramsay's thinking is in one
sense "splendid," finds it somewhat childish and amusing as
well. Significantly, the "letter" he is straining to understand is
the initial letter of his own name.

The metaphorical approach to Ramsay's cogitations keeps the
author at a distance, and implies a blend of irony and affection.
Notice, for example, how the alphabet metaphor is replaced
by another elaborate comparison as Ramsay begins to feel
sorry for himself: "Feelings that would not have disgraced a
leader who, now that the snow has begun to fall and the moun-
tain top is covered with mist, knows that he must lay himself
down and die before morning comes, stole upon him, . . . He

would never reach R" (pp. 58–59). Again the reader is outside Ramsay's mind, and the passage is true to Ramsay's emotions (the image of the mountain-climber is right out of Leslie
Stephen's experience); but the language used to evoke Ramsay's
mood is so melodramatic that it seems to parody the kind of
heroism Ramsay thinks he exemplifies. Indeed, the section on
Ramsay ends with what can only be taken as a direct commentary by the author: "Who shall blame him, if, standing for
a moment, he dwells upon fame, upon search parties, upon
cairns raised by grateful followers over his bones? Finally, who
shall blame the leader of the doomed expedition . . ." (p. 60).
There are none of the customary authorial signposts in this
lengthy paragraph, nothing to suggest that Ramsay thinks any
of it; it is instead the author's mildly ironic summary, suggesting at once the remarkable depth of Ramsay's intelligence
and his human capacity for vanity and self-pity. The extrava-
gant rhetoric of "Who shall blame him?" works on two levels,
to reveal the pompous egotism behind Ramsay's self-image and
to warn the reader not to judge him too harshly.

The use of metaphor in *To the Lighthouse* is almost worth
a chapter to itself. Witness the scene between the Ramsays and
their son James, where the psychological interests are Ramsay's
compulsive need for sympathy, Mrs. Ramsay's attempts to provide it, and son James' violent anger with his father:

> Charles Tansley thought him the greatest metaphysician
> of the time, she said. But he must have more than that. He
> must have sympathy. He must be assured that he too lived
> in the heart of life; was needed; not here only, but all over
> the world. Flashing her needles, confident, upright, she
> created drawing-room and kitchen, set them all aglow; bade
> him take his ease there, go in and out, enjoy himself. She
> laughed, she knitted. Standing between her knees, very stiff,
> James felt all her strength flaring up to be drunk and

quenched by the beak of brass, the arid scimitar of the male, which smote mercilessly, again and again, demanding sympathy. [pp. 62–63]

The factual details, the exterior setting, the dialogue of the scene have been almost entirely suppressed. Our view of the scene seems to be a product of an unconventional technique, but not because we view experience by means of an internal monologue. The paragraph makes only a few brief notations about the mental attitudes of the characters, and the only time we actually see into a mind is in the last sentence, which comments upon James' feelings by developing a metaphor for them. The medium through which we view the scene is the ghostly authorial personality, who reports only bits of the action: "Charles Tansley thought him the greatest metaphysician of the time, she said"; "She laughed, she knitted." The narrator is interested not in a report of the scene's action, but in its rhythm, in the light, healing pulse of Mrs. Ramsay's sympathy contrasted to Mr. Ramsay's harsh, repeated demands for more. Virginia Woolf wants to convey the essence of the scene; thus she works toward a distillation of the event, sketching the scene in a few relevant details and using a rhythmic, metaphoric language, so that it partakes at once of the particular and the general. Virginia Woolf's impetus at these moments is less toward the dramatic than toward the emblematic; she tries to create a symbolic moment that transcends the event: "Flashing her needles, confident, upright, she created drawing room and kitchen, set them aglow; bade him take his ease there, go in and out, enjoy himself." The language here implies an omniscient author, who, with a few economical strokes, gives us the scene in one crucial image. Though James' attitude colors the entire paragraph, no attempt is made to reproduce his sensibility; one has only the sexual metaphor of the last sentence, which leaves a strong impression of the son's passionate antagonism toward his father. Virginia Woolf's poetic view of experience gives her writing much of this unique effect; one can apply terms like stream of consciousness and interior monologue to her later work, but only if the concepts are highly qualified.

In comparison with *Mrs. Dalloway, To the Lighthouse* displays a heightened degree of emphasis on what might be called the characteristics peculiar to Virginia Woolf. The technique depends upon a twofold abstraction; the thought processes of the characters are framed more and more by Virginia Woolf's summaries and metaphors, so that the reader perceives only the distillation of thought, the essence of character. Always, too, there is a clear feeling that the language of the novel has been formed by an omnipresent narrative voice which can take the raw materials of thought and develop from them the poetic motifs which serve to comment on the whole design. At the same time that this abstraction, this symbolization of the mental life is taking place, the physical context of the novel is becoming more and more tentative. From the time of *The Voyage Out* until the end of her career Mrs. Woolf made a habit of evoking symbolic settings, but in a work like *To the Lighthouse* those settings are realized primarily through the sensibilities of the characters. As a result, not only the thoughts, but also the immediate experience which gives rise to them, seem almost ethereal: as though the author wants to emphasize that every thought and every aspect of the physical setting has been carefully selected and endowed with a mysterious significance. This explains, no doubt, why *To the Lighthouse* has been subject to allegorical interpretations; the book is not an allegory, any more than *The Voyage Out* is, but in both works the incidents seem somehow emblematic. Detail has been used not as Arnold Bennett, or even Joyce, would use it; instead Virginia Woolf isolates only a few objects, like the brown stocking or the lighthouse, which become obsessive and symbolic. She is rela-

tively unspecific, and the overall effect is one of an intensely
unified experience shared by all of the characters and the author as well.

Virginia Woolf sees experience, then, as a constant rhythmic
flow, influenced by an undercurrent of emotion which tends to
unify things. Her style is meant to reflect a vision of life that
Mrs. Ramsay at one point remarks upon: "that community of
feeling with other people which emotion gives as if the walls
of partition had become so thin that practically . . . it was
all one stream, and chairs, tables, maps, were hers, were theirs,
it did not matter whose." But the other major quality of the
style, that emblematic beauty of which I have been speaking, is
no doubt determined as much by Virginia Woolf's memory of
her mother and father, who are transformed into "the symbols
of marriage, husband and wife." As Lily Briscoe observes, they
have become part of "that unreal but penetrating and exciting
universe which is the world seen through the eyes of love" (p.
76).

To the Lighthouse, more than any of the classic novels of its
historical period, is suffused with the feeling of an authentic
love. And love (though one might say this of nearly any strong
emotion in Virginia Woolf's novels) has a shaping, unifying
power; it works to subdue what Lily calls "the reign of chaos":

> Love had a thousand shapes. There might be lovers whose
> gift it was to choose out the elements of things and place
> them together and so, giving them a wholeness not theirs in
> life, make of some scene, or meeting of people (all now gone
> and separate), one of those globed compacted things over
> which thought lingers, and love plays. [pp. 295–96]

In this view, Lily Briscoe and Virginia Woolf are less important
as artists than as lovers—and the power of their love is exerted
to redeem things from loss and separateness, to "choose" things
and "place them together" by a kind of secondary imagination.

To stress the power of love alone is not, however, fully to express the quality of the novel, which is equally suffused with a weariness and a cosmic sadness. Virginia Woolf's major theme here, to slightly vary a formulation by David Daiches, is the effect of time and death on the human personality. And here, no less than in her other fiction, there is an implied contrast between two varieties of experience: on the one hand is an active life which is egocentric and time-bound, usually associated in this novel with the land and described by Virginia Woolf as a world of "facts," "surfaces," and "the masculine intelligence," a world of separateness, struggle, and death; and on the other hand is an immersed, passive life without any sense of personality or time, a watery world of emotion and feminine sensibility which makes of all experience a great unity and which, it is suggested, partakes of eternity. Of these two visions of life, Virginia Woolf makes the second predominate, perhaps because she regards it as ultimately more true, perhaps because it provides a way to overcome the fear of death. It is not valued exclusively, any more than Mrs. Ramsay, who embodies such a vision of experience, is valued exclusively over Mr. Ramsay, who is the great example of the active, masculine intelligence; but it is clearly the world with which Virginia Woolf feels an instinctive rapport.

There are many places in the novel where we sense the contrast between these two views of life, which at times seem to represent the male and female principles. They are, for example, clearly set off against one another toward the end of the first part of the book, when Mr. and Mrs. Ramsay sit reading in their room. She chooses a volume of poetry:

Slowly those words they had said at dinner, "the China rose is all abloom and buzzing with the honey bee," began washing from side to side of her mind rhythmically, and as they washed, words, like little shaded lights, one red, one blue, one yellow, lit up in the dark of her mind, and seemed leaving their perches up there to fly across and across, or to cry out and be echoed; so she turned and felt on the table beside her for a book.

> And all the lives we ever lived
> And all the lives to be,
> Are full of trees and changing leaves,

she murmured . . . she opened the book and began reading here and there at random, and as she did so she felt that she was climbing backwards, upwards, shoving her way up under petals that curved over her, so that she only knew this is white, or this is red. She did not know at first what the words meant at all.

> Steer, hither steer your winged pines, all beaten Mariners

she read and turned the page, swinging herself, zigzagging this way and that, from one branch to another, from one red and white flower to another, until a little sound roused her —her husband slapping his thighs. [pp. 183–84]

The state of mind described here is, of course, like that of Rachel listening to the lines from Milton in *The Voyage Out.* It is also reminiscent of the scene where Mrs. Dalloway falls asleep over her sewing; and there are many other examples. Mrs. Woolf is depicting a passive yielding of the self to a hypnotic rhythm, a yielding so total that Mrs. Ramsay ceases to understand the words she reads. The snatches of poetry, however, are significant. The poetry that runs through Mrs. Ramsay's mind is about the elemental constancy of life, part of a vision of nature that enfolds all human existence in a unity containing "All the lives we ever lived. And all the lives to be," a sense of eternity which provides a haven for "beaten Mariners." Just before this passage, Mrs. Ramsay is shown thinking vaguely, "There is something I want." What she

seems to want most of all, like Clarissa Dalloway and Rachel
Vinrace, is a kind of peace and rapture that is associated with
a unity so complete it entails the yielding up of life. Here, as
in several places in the novel, she seems on the verge of passing
out of life altogether. She is brought back—and it is a fine
touch—by the sound of Mr. Ramsay slapping his thighs.

We move from Mrs. Ramsay's mind to her husband's without
at first being aware we have done so, in another of those unobtrusive transitions characteristic of Mrs. Woolf. He is reading
a novel:

> His lips twitched. It filled him. It fortified him. He clean
> forgot all the little rubs and digs of the evening, and how
> it bored him unutterably to sit still while people ate and
> drank interminably . . . This man's strength and sanity,
> his feeling for straightforward simple things, these fisher-
> men, the poor old crazed creature in Mucklebackit's cottage
> made him feel so vigorous, so relieved of something that he
> felt roused and triumphant and could not choke back his
> tears.
>
> Well, let them improve on that, he thought as he finished
> the chapter. He felt that he had been arguing with some-
> body, and had got the better of him. They could not improve
> on that, whatever they might say; and his own position be-
> came more secure. [p. 185]

Ramsay's reaction to Walter Scott is in direct contrast to his
wife's reaction to poetry; it clearly stems from his active view
of life, his vitality, his (temporary) confidence in his own
vigorous masculine intelligence and its brisk, direct contact with
the world.

But neither view of experience is without defects. Mr. Ramsay's love of the active life, of the world of fact and masculine
intelligence, makes him self-pitying and obsessively fearful of
passing time and death. He is not usually as confident as we

find him here. Even Shakespeare, he notes, will one day be
lost utterly—how much sooner his own work? Mrs. Ramsay, on
the other hand, has no such obsessive fear, and her comparative
selflessness, her capability for sympathy and inner peace, is a
great source of consolation for her husband. (Like Charles
Tansley, he needs to be "fortified" by her.) There is something
possessive and prideful about her compulsive matchmaking and
love of good works, but these faults do not essentially alter the
impression we have of a generous and even creative person. At
the same time, however, she often has to will herself into life;
like so many of Mrs. Woolf's characters, she is prone to daydreams in which she feels herself merging with nature, and
only reluctantly does she return to the active world and her
family:

> To be silent; to be alone. All the being and the doing, ex-
> pansive, glittering, vocal, evaporated; and one shrunk, with
> a sense of solemnity, to being oneself, a wedge-shaped core
> of darkness, something invisible to others. Although she
> continued to knit, and sat upright, it was thus that she
> felt herself; and this self having shed its attachments was
> free for the strangest adventures. When life sank down for
> a moment, the range of experience seemed limitless. And to
> everybody there was always this sense of unlimited resources,
> she supposed; one after another, she, Lily, Augustus Car-
> michael, must feel, our apparitions, the things you know us
> by, are simply childish. Beneath it is all dark, it is all spread-
> ing, it is unfathomably deep; but now and again we rise to
> the surface and that is what you see us by. Her horizon
> seemed to her limitless. There were all the places she had not
> seen; the Indian plains; she felt herself pushing aside the
> thick leather curtain of a church in Rome. This core of dark-
> ness could go anywhere, for no one saw it. They could not
> stop it, she thought, exulting. There was freedom, there was
> peace, there was, most welcome of all, a summoning to-

gether, a resting on a platform of stability. Not as oneself
did one find rest ever, in her experience . . . but as a wedge
of darkness. Losing personality, one lost the fret, the hurry,
the stir; and there rose to her lips always some exclamation
of triumph over life when things came together in this peace,
this rest, this eternity; and pausing there she looked out to
meet the stroke of the Lighthouse, the long steady stroke,
the last of the three, which was her stroke, for watching them
in this mood always at this hour one could not help attaching
oneself to one thing . . . the long steady stroke, was her
stroke. Often she found herself sitting and looking, sitting and
looking, with her work in her hands until she became the thing
she looked at—that light, for example. And it would lift up
on it some little phrase or other which had been lying in
her mind like that—"Children don't forget, children don't
forget"—which she would repeat and begin adding to it.
It will end, it will end, she said. It will come, it will come,
when suddenly she added, We are in the hands of the Lord.
[pp. 99–101]

I have quoted this famous passage at length because it is a
locus classicus for a kind of experience which had an extraordinarily powerful hold on Virginia Woolf's imagination. It is,
as I have indicated before, an extension of the introspective,
trancelike states first explored in *The Voyage Out*. It involves
a loss of personality and an intimation of death and eternity,
and it also seems to represent one of the "shapes" of love. Mrs.
Ramsay feels she has drawn closer to an essential self which
can only be defined negatively, as a vast dark realm which
everyone has in common, apart from the external personality,
"what you see us by." Note that while the mood is subjective,
it is clearly not solipsistic—Mrs. Ramsay feels that "everybody"
has moments like this one. Again, as in similar passages, the
character feels herself merge with something outside, in this
case the beam from the lighthouse, which not only hypnotizes

her but actually seems to become the pulse of her life and the
stimulus to her thoughts. In this condition the fancy is liberated, much as it is when Rachel or Mrs. Ramsay read poetry;
thoughts seem to bubble up out of the unconsciousness—or
perhaps that vaguely defined region known as the sensibility.
But experience here, as William Troy has rightly observed, is
only *implicit* experience; active contact with the world has
been abandoned in favor of fanciful daydreams, which hardly
constitute "thinking," as Mrs. Ramsay herself is aware. Her
mind lies open, given over to the lighthouse itself, so much
so that "We are in the hands of the Lord" seems to her to
have come from someone else. She pulls halfway out of her
trance and muses on what has happened, while all the time a
steady rhythm, emphasized in Mrs. Woolf's prose, draws her
back toward a total yielding:

> It was odd, she thought, how if one was alone, one leant
> to inanimate things; trees, streams, flowers; felt they ex-
> pressed one; felt they became one; felt they knew one, in
> a sense were one; felt an irrational tenderness thus (she
> looked at that long steady light) as for oneself. There rose,
> and she looked and looked with her needles suspended, there
> curled up off the floor of the mind, rose from the lake of
> one's being, a mist, a bride to meet her lover. [pp. 101–02]

One sees in a passage like this Virginia Woolf's affinity with
Wordsworth, and indeed with the whole romantic movement.
The "mist" described here is not unlike Wordsworth's "cor-
respondent breeze" (though it is perhaps a more passive agent),
and it becomes a metaphor for a kind of imaginative power
which breaks down subject-object distinctions, enabling the
beholder to "see into the life of things." The experience, however, is much more explicitly erotic than anything one finds
in Wordsworth (in this sense it is more like the experiences of
mystics), and in some ways it presents a much greater threat to

the integrity of the personality than Wordsworth's divine moments. The image of the bride going forth to meet her lover recalls the lengthy passage I quoted from *The Voyage Out*, and again one cannot be sure if the image is something in Mrs. Ramsay's mind or if it is evoked by the author as a means of describing Mrs. Ramsay's feelings. Such an ambiguity seems, however, to be a part of the total effect, an implied desire for a perfect spiritual unity. The erotic aspect of this desire is further enhanced by the window-lighthouse symbolism that Mrs. Woolf's critics have often commented on; the portrayal of the window and the lighthouse as female and male objects effectively suggests Mrs. Ramsay's ecstatic embrace of the world outside the self as she sits by the window and gives herself over to the beam of the lighthouse.

Mrs. Ramsay knows, "with her mind"—that is with the conscious and active part of her being—that there is not a Lord. "There was no treachery too base for the world to commit; she knew that. No happiness lasted; she knew that." But in such moments of hypnotic yielding she has an intimation of eternity and a feeling of erotic ecstasy. Yet the vast world outside, which becomes her lover, is also a force of death.

> She looked at the steady light, the pitiless, the remorseless, which was so much her, yet so little her, which had her at its beck and call (she woke in the night and saw it bent across their bed, stroking the floor), but for all that she thought, watching it with fascination, hypnotized, as if it were stroking with its silver fingers some sealed vessel in her brain whose bursting would flood her with delight, she had known happiness, exquisite happiness, intense happiness, and it silvered the rough waves a little more brightly, as daylight faded, and the blue went out of the sea and it rolled in waves of pure lemon which curved and swelled and broke upon the beach and the ecstasy burst in her eyes and waves

of pure delight raced over the floor of her mind and she
felt, It is enough! It is enough! [pp. 103–04]

It is no wonder Mrs. Ramsay feels that "Always . . . one
helped oneself out of solitude reluctantly." In one sense these
moments do not represent total solitude at all. Mrs. Ramsay
is solitary, but she does not feel lonely; on the contrary, she
seems to have a heightened sense of her relation to the vast
world of nature, represented here by the sea. It is Mr. Ramsay,
an especially energetic and egocentric person who loves intellectual and physical action and requires real as opposed to
implicit experience, who suffers anguish from solitude, because
he is intensely aware of the ultimate isolation and separateness
of the personality. Mrs. Ramsay, however, is content and even
eager to relinquish personality and become simply a dark
shadow. In this more or less passive, withdrawn state, she
vibrates from a feeling of union with the world, and even death
itself becomes for her a source of delight.

Death, as Mrs. Dalloway observed, can be a kind of embrace.
And the embrace of the self with the world outside and beyond, which Virginia Woolf was so anxious for modern fiction
to show, is inevitably associated in her work with the feeling
of death or with the loss of any active life as an individual.
Obviously, an intense desire for unity, the desire to know even
one other person completely (as, for example, Lily Briscoe
wants to know Mrs. Ramsay), or, in a more cosmic sense, the
compulsive need to relate one's life spiritually to the vast power
of nature—all these things can result in the destruction of
individuality. Virginia Woolf herself was no doubt aware of
such implications in her work; she is not the first author to
make art out of a death wish.

Quite obviously, Mrs. Ramsay is ready to welcome death.
Even at her dinner party, the effort of playing hostess is at first
almost too much for her:

In pity for him, life being now strong enough to bear her
on again, she began all this business, as a sailor not without
weariness sees the wind fill his sail and yet hardly wants to
be off again and thinks how, had the ship sunk, he would
have whirled round and round and felt rest on the floor of
the sea. [p. 131]

Yet this same death wish is based on a view of experience
which can offer consolation for the brevity of life. This is not
to say that Mrs. Ramsay is unable to feel, as her husband always does, the fragility of the human condition:

> The monotonous fall of the waves on the beach, which for
> the most part beat a measured and soothing tattoo to her
> thoughts and seemed consolingly to repeat over and over
> again as she sat with the children the words of some old
> cradle song, murmured by nature, "I am guarding you—I
> am your support," but at other times suddenly and unex-
> pectedly, *especially when her mind raised itself from the
> task actually in hand,* had no such kindly meaning . . .
> made one think of the destruction of the island and its
> engulfment in the sea . . . made her look up with an im-
> pulse of terror. [p. 30; italics mine.]

When Mrs. Ramsay is absorbed in her task, half-hypnotized
by the rhythm of her knitting and the sound of the waves, she
feels consoled; but when she becomes actively conscious of
herself, the sea in turn appears remorseless and destructive.
Nature is in fact cruel and destructive to individuals, to people who live active lives in the world. But Mrs. Ramsay, like
so many of Virginia Woolf's characters, is able to see nature
from a different perspective, to understand that with all its
diversity and change it remains an order, a constant, impersonal life of which everyone is a part. In this view nature
subsumes individual lives but in some sense also carries them

on. It exists in a kind of fourth dimension where it is always raining and always fine.

Virginia Woolf's characters become aware of this duality in nature when they sink down into a "wedge-shaped core of darkness," losing all active experience and nearly all their sense of personality, drifting along on a stream of impressions. And Mrs. Ramsay, perhaps more than anyone else in Virginia Woolf's fiction, is identified with this relinquishing of self. She is always described as wearing gray or black; she has no first name; her past is obscure; and Lily Briscoe associates her with a darkness, a shadow which completes the light surfaces in her painting, a "triangular purple shape." It is true that she has an active life and a personality: she is a matchmaker and a practical nurse, an exceedingly beautiful but nearsighted woman who has seven children and who is worried about the poor, about her husband and children, about "her old antagonist, life." But the image of Mrs. Ramsay that Virginia Woolf most powerfully evokes is no different from the image in Lily Briscoe's imagination: a shadowy mother-with-child, seated in a window, knitting.

"So much depends," Lily thinks as she watches Mr. Ramsay sail to the lighthouse, "upon distance: whether people are near us or far from us." Toward the end of the book this idea appears several times, and it is clearly important to the understanding of Virginia Woolf's particular vision. But that vision is not to be explained simply in terms of actual distances in space; "near" and "far" simply express what in other contexts is suggested by surfaces and depths, the notion of two perspectives on human life. From one, life is understood in terms of particular times and places, and from the other, in terms of vast space and cosmic time. In the larger perspective, the terrible beauty of individual lives becomes merely "what you see us by"; everything is part of a great elemental process which is both beautiful and terrible, destructive of individual lives but

always living. I say "always" because there are few if any
passages in Virginia Woolf which even suggest that the process might ultimately have a stop. Her subject is always the
relationship of individuals to the great impersonal forces of
this process, to what is called in *The Waves* the "abysses of
time," or to the huge sexual trees and the rushing waters of
the jungle in *The Voyage Out*. Thus while Lily Briscoe is
standing on shore with tears of grief running down her face,
calling out for Mrs. Ramsay to return, for life to become something other than "startling, unexpected, unknown," the scene
shifts abruptly:

> [Macalister's boy took one of the fish and cut a square
> out of its side to bait his hook with. The mutilated body
> (it was still alive) was thrown back into the sea]. [pp. 277–
> 78]

This episode, I take it, is meant (in part) to be a parable for
the impersonal violence of nature, to indicate how very little
individuals matter in relation to the great sea. The same im-
personality is clearly expressed in the first part of the book,
when young Nancy Ramsay goes off alone to play by the water.
I have had occasion to mention this passage earlier, since it
has relevance with regard not only to the characters in *To the
Lighthouse,* but also to Virginia Woolf's role as the novelist:

> Nancy waded out to her own rocks and searched her own
> pools and let the couple look after themselves. She crouched
> down and touched the smooth rubber-like sea anemones
> . . . Brooding, she changed the pool into the sea, and made
> the minnows into sharks and whales, and cast vast clouds
> over this tiny world by holding her hand against the sun,
> and so brought darkness and desolation, like God himself
> . . . And then, letting her eyes slide imperceptibly above
> the pool and rest on that wavering line of sea and sky, on

the tree trunks which the smoke of steamers made waver
upon the horizon, she became with all that power sweeping
savagely in and inevitably withdrawing, hypnotized, and
the two senses of that vastness and this tininess . . . flowering within it made her feel that she was bound hand and
foot and unable to move by the intensity of feelings which
reduced her own body, her own life, and the lives of all the
people in the world, for ever, to nothingness. So listening to
the waves, crouching over the pool, she brooded. [pp. 118–
19]

Virginia Woolf, like Nancy, is always aware of what Norman
Friedman calls "double vision"—"that vastness and this tininess." [9] But the vastness hypnotizes her until she seems, again
like Nancy, to brood over her creations, "listening to the
waves." The same thing can, of course, be said of many of
her other characters, especially Mrs. Ramsay and Lily, who
seem barely able to rescue themselves from nothingness. They
are granted certain moments of apprehension, times when they
surrender their egos; they are blissfully transfixed, brooding or
hypnotized or half-asleep, and in such moods they seem to
become a part of the vastness and untouched by time and
fear.

Mrs. Ramsay experiences such a moment as she watches the
lighthouse, and also at her dinner party, under the spell of
candlelight, good food, and the warm, dimly-apprehended conversation of her guests: "There is a coherence in things, a
stability; something, she meant, is immune from change . . .
so that again tonight she had the feeling she had had once
today, already, of peace, of rest. Of such moments, she thought,
the thing is made that remains for ever after" (p. 163). This
suggests that there is a priori an eternity, and that such mo-

9. Norman Friedman, "Double Vision in *To the Lighthouse*," in *To the
Lighthouse: A Casebook*, ed. Morris Beja (London: Macmillan and Company, 1970), pp. 149–67.

ments of inner peace are a part of that eternity, or at least
demonstrate the individual's awareness of his relation to it.
Mrs. Ramsay feels that she is at the "still space that lies about
the heart of things, where one could move or rest." She has
an intimation of something very like Eliot's "still point of
the turning world." Her husband, at the other end of the table,
remains in the world of fact, saying something, we are not
told what, about "the square root of one thousand two hundred and fifty-three." Mrs. Ramsay, barely aware of the conversation, admires the "admirable fabric of the masculine intelligence." She luxuriates for a while, and then, we are told,
"she woke up" (p. 164).

Lily Briscoe has an analogous experience in the last part of
the novel, except that it is brought on not by the lighthouse or
a party, but by her painting, her attempt to capture her vision
of Mrs. Ramsay and the landscape. Her first work on the canvas is produced by a "dancing rhythmical movement, as if the
pauses were one part of the rhythm and the strokes another"
(p. 244). We are told that she has "exchanged the fluidity of
life for the concentration of painting." But what Lily actually
does in the act of painting is to exchange one kind of fluidity
for another. She finds herself at first "caught up in one of those
habitual currents which after a certain time experience forms
in the mind, so that one repeats words without being aware any
longer who originally spoke them" (p. 246). Like Mrs. Ramsay
before her, she falls into a kind of trance, and words and impressions rise up involuntarily in her mind. Her hand moves
"as if it had fallen in with some rhythm which was dictated
to her . . . by what she saw, so that while her hand quivered
with life, this rhythm was strong enough to carry her along
with it on its current." The painting and the meditation it
inspires is interrupted from time to time by the sight of old
Mr. Carmichael or Ramsay's boat, and Lily finds that "against
her will she had come to the surface" (p. 274).

Let me emphasize again that to describe such a technique one must adopt an extremely liberal definition of stream of consciousness. Indeed the whole point is that Lily no longer has a consciousness; the intense, dreamy emotion she feels is rendered through the voice of Virginia Woolf, who, by means of a series of intricate metaphors, tries to communicate not what Lily thought but what her experience felt like. Thus the passage is not a product of any concern with depth psychology or the psychopathology of everyday life; instead the author consciously avoids outlining the specific content of Lily's mind: "her mind kept throwing up from its depths, scenes, and names, and sayings, and memories and ideas, like a fountain spurting over that glaring, hideously difficult white space." The author—like Lily—is more impressed by the fountain, the hideous white space, and the rhythm of the series of thoughts than the actual content of the mind.

"For how could one express in words these emotions of the body," Lily thinks a bit later. "It was one's body feeling, not one's mind" (pp. 274–75). And that is no doubt one of Virginia Woolf's strongest rationales for limiting her use of the internal monologue. In addition, she wanted to describe the consciousness without ever entering into it; to do so would be to emphasize the separateness of things, the prison of the ego instead of the stream of life which blurs distinctions. The peculiar state of mind that she dwells on so lovingly in her novels is purely emotional; it has nothing to do with thinking in the accepted sense of the term, and it is valued precisely because it seems to dissolve the personality and vibrate according to an absolute rhythm.

With regard to Lily Briscoe, this rhythm is felt as the culmination of two powerful impulses: her deep-rooted desire to find and express a kind of unity and self-sufficiency in experience, together with her desire for an impossibly complete union with Mrs. Ramsay ("What art was there, known to love or cunning," she wonders, "by which one pressed into those secret chambers? What device for becoming, like waters poured into one jar, inextricably the same, one with the object one adored?" [p. 82]). I do not, however, want to attempt any reasoned explanation of Mrs. Ramsay's sudden appearance, sitting in the window before Lily; the effect, it seems to me, is extraordinarily mysterious and moving, especially in the way Lily wanders off over the lawn, abstractedly, wanting to tell Mr. Ramsay. Whatever psychological explanation one could offer for this momentary recapture of the past would be ir- relevant. The important thing is that Lily has her "vision"; about her painting "one might say, even of this scrawl, not of that actual picture, perhaps, but of what it attempted, that it 'remained forever.' " (The same words are used to describe Mrs. Ramsay's vision in the dinner party scene.) Lily has for a time almost *become* Mrs. Ramsay, or at least she has become a creator like Virginia Woolf, projecting herself imaginatively into her memory of another woman, so that through her love Mrs. Ramsay seems to live on.

Mrs. Ramsay "lives," then, because Mr. Ramsay and Lily have been able for a moment to recapture the past. It seems that not ten years but only a day has passed since the first section of the novel. Lily completes her painting; Mrs. Ramsay is in the window; Mr. Ramsay goes to the lighthouse; James feels a moment of joy and reconciliation with his father; the weather is fine after all. It is the past perhaps not so much re- captured as remade. There is, however, a suggestion of some- thing that goes beyond such temporary victories over death. Lily knows that she will die; surely Mr. Ramsay and the chil- dren know they will perish. Lily also realizes that her picture will moulder away in an attic. But the painting (more, in my view, than Mr. Ramsay's trip to the lighthouse), has been an "attempt at something," and that something is what survives. The painting has been an effort to recapture and know Mrs.

Ramsay in the most complete sense. "One wanted fifty pairs of eyes to see with," Lily thinks. "One wanted most some secret sense, fine as air, with which to steal through keyholes and surround her where she sat knitting, talking, sitting silent in the window alone" (p. 303). This is, of course, one way of describing just what Virginia Woolf's method has been; and though Mrs. Ramsay remains an enigma to Lily and to Virginia Woolf as well (consider all those passages where the author hovers around Mrs. Ramsay but seems unable to reveal her entirely), the effort itself is testimony to belief in something that is serene and permanent, a center from which the thoughts and emotions of our lives radiate. Lily's painting is, therefore, another example of the intense desire to lose the self through love or union that serves Mrs. Woolf as a primary theme in so much of her fiction.

But beneath this temporary joy and consolation a sadness runs. We hear throughout the final part of the book Lily's cry for Mrs. Ramsay and Mr. Ramsay's solemn chant, "we perished, each alone." At the end Lily testifies that she has *had* her vision, and she puts down her brush "in extreme fatigue." *To the Lighthouse,* more than any of Virginia Woolf's works, gives us a sense of the extraordinary effort demanded of individuals who want some permanence and who win a temporary but heroic victory through love. After losing herself momentarily, Lily Briscoe returns to life with the feeling that it has at least some continuity. Even Mr. Ramsay seems able to forsake his ego for a time. "The depths of the sea," he thinks, "are only water after all."

7

The Waves

Tout ce que le coeur désire peut toujours se réduire à la figure de l'eau.

Paul Claudel, *Positions et Propositions*

The subject of *The Waves,* as Bernard puts it in his summation, is nothing less than the "meaning" of life. The book implies, among other things, a theory of personality, a metaphysic, and another response to the agonizing fact of death—developed here by means of artfully composed soliloquies which rise out of six lives at various points, with a series of land and seascapes interposed. The nature descriptions, and to a large extent the soliloquies themselves, are a manifestation of that timeless unity Mrs. Woolf continually strives to render.

As is generally agreed, *The Waves* is Virginia Woolf's ultimate attempt to transform the customary world of the novel. Her "caricatures," as she called them, are not depicted through direct conversation or action. There is a certain superficial diversity among their voices—three are male, three female; Jinny is an extrovert, Rhoda an introvert, etc.—but in spite of these improbably symmetrical contrasts among six friends, one is most of all struck by the *sameness* of things in the book, the unrelieved poetic intensity with which every experience is presented, and the static atmosphere that is created as one soliloquy follows another.

In some ways *The Waves* seems a radical departure from the techniques of the earlier subjective novels. If the quality of the previous fiction was primarily determined by Virginia Woolf's ever-present voice, here there seems to be an attempt to limit that voice's function by building the novel around a series of direct quotations. The method has been defined as sustained interior monologue,[1] "a presentation of the purest psychological analysis in literature," [2] and an experiment which is the "most poetic" and "most firmly rooted in stream of consciousness" of all Mrs. Woolf's novels.[3] Whatever it is, the technique presents special problems for a writer who was never given to using dramatic methods. She felt keenly, as we have seen, that direct quotation from the mind would confine her novels too much within individual egos. Thus, amid her early notions about experimenting with the novel, she asked in her *Diary*, "Is one pliant and rich enough to provide a wall for the book from oneself without its becoming, as in Joyce and Richardson, narrow and restricting?" [4] In this instance, her solution to the problem is a highly stylized set of speeches, perhaps unlike anything else in fiction. The speeches often seem like one pervasive voice with six personalities; and, as one of Virginia Woolf's best critics, Jean Guiguet, has remarked, "to define that voice is to solve the whole problem of *The Waves*." [5]

It is easier to say what the convention is not than to say

1. Bowling, "What is the Stream of Consciousness Technique?," p. 339.
2. Humphrey, *Stream of Consciousness in the Modern Novel*, p. 14.
3. Melvin Friedman, *Stream of Consciousness: A Study in Literary Method*, p. 22.
4. Woolf, *A Writer's Diary*, p. 32.
5. Jean Guiget, *Virginia Woolf and her Works* (London: Hogarth Press, 1965), p. 284.

what it is. Quite clearly, the characters cannot be said to speak their lines in any literal sense, in spite of the quotation marks and the repeated use of the word "said." The artificiality of the technique is evident from the opening pages, where the language is highly stylized and the characters speak as with one voice:

> "I see a ring," said Bernard, "hanging above me. It quivers and hangs in a loop of light."
>
> "I see a slab of pale yellow," said Susan, "spreading away until it meets a purple stripe."
>
> "I hear a sound," said Rhoda, "cheep, chirp; cheep chirp; going up and down." [6]

Mrs. Woolf has the child Bernard suggest her theme in the very first line, in language that is strikingly reminiscent of the opening of Henry Vaughan's poem, "The World":

> I saw eternity the other night
> Like a great ring of pure and endless light.

The beginning of *The Waves* also resembles Virginia Woolf's approach to the beginning of the "Time Passes" section of *To the Lighthouse*:

> "Well, we must wait for the future to show," said Mr. Bankes, coming in from the terrace.
>
> "It's almost too dark to see," said Andrew, coming up from the beach.
>
> "One can hardly tell which is the sea and which is the land," said Prue. [p. 195]

James Hafley suggests that the peculiar form of *The Waves* has its origin in this passage. We have seen, however, that such

---

6. Virginia Woolf, *The Waves* (London: Hogarth Press, 1963), p. 5. Unless otherwise noted, all references are to this edition.

mysterious speech, which hints vaguely at deeply important meanings, is present in Virginia Woolf's novels from the first. It is the language lovers use in *The Voyage Out,* the whispered " 'It's you' . . . 'Oh it's you' " of boys and girls; and it characterizes many other litanies, such as "Let us all go to the circus" from the conversation between Mrs. Ramsay and Charles Tansley in *To the Lighthouse.*

In the case of *The Voyage Out* and *To the Lighthouse,* however, it is clear that the characters are actually speaking to one another. In *The Waves* the children cannot be said to literally speak the lines; although the sentences are nothing more than simple and direct statements of sense impressions, the diction, the rhythm, and the feeling of litany indicate that this is not speech in the usual sense of the term. This is not to say, however, that we should dismiss the idea that the characters are speaking to each other, as many of Virginia Woolf's commentators seem to do; if the characters are not actually speaking, they are to some extent communicating. Such formal parallel responses suggest, at least in this opening context, a fundamental, communal response to experience; and the syntax implies not so much a series of private thoughts as a sequence of announcements. Bernard, perhaps characteristically, makes very clear that he is aware of the others by turning from the declarative to the imperative: " 'Look at the spider's web.' " It might be true that the convention serves as an abstract representation of thought; but in some places it is at least equally possible to read it as an abstract representation of speech. One might, of course, say that while we are given only thoughts in *The Waves,* some of these thoughts are about to be transformed into speech; yet when dealing with a technique as strange and consciously artificial as this one, the basis for making such distinctions is not clear. In any case, the language is too well-ordered to be considered the direct thought-stream of the characters, and it is too sophisticated to be their speech.

The peculiar effect of this technique can be seen more clearly in some of the longer speeches which occur just after the children have chanted their reactions to the world they have wakened into. The first relatively long speech is made by Louis, a habitual solitary, who, as we learn later, is painfully aware that he is different from the others:

"Now they have all gone," said Louis. "I am alone. They have gone into the house for breakfast, and I am left standing by the wall among the flowers. It is very early, before lessons. Flower after flower is specked on the depths of green. The petals are harlequins. Stalks rise from the black hollows beneath. The flowers swim like fish made of light upon the dark, green waters. I hold a stalk in my hand. I am the stalk. My roots go down to the depths of the world . . . I am all fibre. All tremors shake me, and the weight of the earth is pressed to my ribs. Up here my eyes are green leaves, unseeing. I am a boy in grey flannels with a belt fastened by a brass snake up here. Down there my eyes are the lidless eyes of a stone figure in a desert by the Nile. I see women passing with red pitchers to the river; I see camels swaying and men in turbans. I hear tramplings, tremblings, stirrings round me." [p. 8]

Most definitions of interior monologue allow for a certain amount of artificiality in the technique, but one would have to stretch them considerably to make this passage fit. There is no disorder in Louis' speech, no sense of the texture of consciousness, which is fundamentally disordered, inchoate. Furthermore, though speaking in solitude, Louis manages to give us all the signposts that in the earlier novels are provided by the voice of the author. He informs us about the setting, about his age, and about his personal appearance. "I am alone. They have all gone into the house for breakfast and I am standing by the

wall among the flowers," he tells us; and, "I am a boy in grey
flannels with a belt fastened by a brass snake."

As for the rest of the speech, the rhythmic, metaphorical assertions sound more like Virginia Woolf at her most literary than
like Louis. " 'Flower after flower is specked on the depths of
green' " is a self-consciously poetic line. And it, together with
the sentences that follow, resembles the descriptive writing in
"Kew Gardens" or the interchapters of *The Waves*. Many of
the images are characteristic of Virginia Woolf's especially
feminine world: " 'The petals are harlequins,' " " 'The flowers
swim like fish made of light upon the dark, green waters.' "
One finds the oblique suggestions of fear and sexuality ("Stalks
rise from the black hollows"), and the hypersensitivity typical of
nearly all her writing ("All tremors shake me, and the weight
of the earth is pressed to my ribs"). There is even special sensitivity to light and color: "fish made of light" swimming on
"dark green waters." The assertions introduce at least one important image (the picture of the women at the Nile, which will
recur); they emphasize Louis' characteristic desire not to be
seen as painfully individual or foreign; and they suggest (however faintly) the relationship of an individual to the "depths
of the world." They are confined mostly to sense impressions,
but they are certainly not meant to be taken as either the speech
or the thoughts of Louis, who is far from a *litterateur*.

Nearly all the speeches in this novel are based upon simple
present-tense declarative forms like those in the passages I have
quoted. The syntax elsewhere in the text has more variety and
sophistication, but what the characters say is usually nothing
more than a declaration about themselves. The result, as David
Daiches has observed, is that "each character formalizes his impressions and attitudes into what for Virginia Woolf is quite a
rigid piece of prose." [7] The only exception to this formality is

7. Daiches, *Virginia Woolf*, p. 107.

the long last chapter, Bernard's "summing up," which is largely
a review of his life told in a wry, discursive, cafe-table chat
with a stranger (who seems more like one of Bernard's fictions than an actual listener). On the whole, however, the
method cannot help but create a certain feeling of detached immobility, the uncharacteristic rigidity that Daiches observes—
Virginia Woolf's prose both before and after *The Waves* conveys a sense of lightness and unceasing movement, of an actual
immersion in passing sensations.

This is not to say that *The Waves* is unrelievedly immobile.
One has only to read Jinny's soliloquy at the ball in chapter 3 to
see how much speed and sensual undulation Mrs. Woolf is
capable of injecting into the prose. As always, she is especially
concerned to give a sense of the different rhythms that underlie
emotional life. Also in chapter 3 there is a long speech by Rhoda,
who is at the same party but whose emotions—unlike Jinny's
—are those of fear, tension, mortification. Nevertheless her
words transmit a sense of variety, in her sudden leap of terror
when a man comes into the room and the wistful, dreamy state
she likes to drift into when alone. My point, simply, is that
within a relatively rigid formal principle, which she never forsakes, Mrs. Woolf is able to evoke remarkable contrasts of
mood.

But for the most part, this formal principle does inhibit flexi-
bility in the prose. The speeches suggest a certain detachment
from the actual events that produce them, a kind of formally
expressed wonder at the mystery of personality. Then, too, the
characters are in some ways immune to time. There is little or
no attempt in *The Waves* to make the prose adapt itself to the
growth of the characters (as Joyce, for example, alters his prose
style in *A Portrait of the Artist* to reflect the growth of Stephen
Dedalus). Though the characters' reactions to life evince a
growing complexity, their language remains always formal and
sophisticated. Furthermore, while the six voices are differen-

tiated by temperament, the fundamental character of their language is always the same; thus there is a sense in which the form of the novel tends to deny or qualify the content. Bernard, for example, is supposed to be a phrase-maker, the sort of personality who is always putting words between himself and experience; but when Susan observes this trait in him during their childhood, she speaks in the same sort of language he uses: " 'I am tied down with single words; you slip away; you rise higher and higher with words in phrases.' " " 'Now you trail away . . . making phrases. Now you mount like an air-ball's string, higher and higher through the layers of the leaves, out of reach.' " The earth-mother Susan speaks like a phrase-maker herself, as do all the characters. All the language in the book has the same remarkable sensitivity to rhythm and metaphor, the same characteristics of repetition and alliteration, even sometimes the same use of rhyme, euphony, and assonance.

In fact the separate voices often draw on the same body of imagery. As several commentators have noted, the book is filled with recurrent images or leitmotiv (like the "chained beast" that can be heard in the waves), and the six speakers are often described by what Harvena Richter calls "symbolic images," words or phrases which share an important characteristic and which become attached to individual characters. Thus Susan is repeatedly associated with hard, knotted things[8] and Bernard with stringy things. For example, in the passage I have cited above, Susan describes Bernard as an "air-ball's string." When Neville thinks of Bernard during their childhood, it is as "a dangling wire, a broken bell-pull, always twangling." In both cases Bernard is made to seem like something loose and pliable; the difference is that for Susan he is as attractive and elusive as the string of a floating balloon, whereas for Neville he is sometimes an annoyance, always chattering

8. Richter, *Inward Voyage*, pp. 166–67.

like a broken bell-pull. Yet the loose, stringy quality is somehow a part of Bernard's personality. He himself is shown thinking about his beloved phrases and sentences as "a string of six little fish."

Out of such differences and correspondences between images, Virginia Woolf establishes a web of relationships among the characters. But at the same time all the voices seem to be a part of the same medium, expressing themselves through a single highly artful style. One might ignore such a point and grant the convention, as some people grant that Othello and Hotspur are not poets, except that Virginia Woolf fills the novel with criticisms of word-play. Bernard's summation, as we shall see, is an explicit critique of the phrase-making that we have been told is one of his special character traits. It seems odd, therefore, to find the practice enshrined in the very medium of the novel, and one cannot help but feel that if Bernard is guilty so are all the others.

There are times when Virginia Woolf seems untrue to her characters, making them all speak with a peculiarly feminine sadness and wonder, as when Bernard the child says " 'The air no longer rolls its long, unhappy, purple waves over us,' " or when he excitedly declares " 'Let us take possession of our secret territory, which is lit by pendant currants like a candelabra.' " In neither case does he sound much like a child, but more especially he does not sound like a boy. Within the limits of her chosen means, however, Virginia Woolf is generally a remarkably convincing interpreter of six different personalities. The deep subjective views she presents demand an unusually clear apprehension, an ability to live within her people; and though she is not always able to project herself convincingly into her men, she often succeeds admirably (consider, for example, the soliloquy by Louis on p. 69).

The soliloquies can be taken as an expression of consciousness, albeit a highly artificial one. But to me they seem much too artificial to fit the definition of direct internal monologue, or even the definition of "soliloquy" set down by Humphrey. Even if we take the highly poetic language as thought, we have to admit that—partly because of the rhetorical signposts—the thought seems to be viewed from the outside, as if it were being commented upon by vaguely aloof, poetic observers. We hear Virginia Woolf's voice throughout the book, and that is no doubt why some readers have emphasized that she is speaking, and not the characters. Hafley, for example, says that the point of view is omniscient; "one person is arranging and telling everything," he says, and the "one person" he takes to be the author. He defines the method as "transcriptions of the feelings, perceptions, and thoughts of six persons by a central intelligence —that of the author." [9] Granted that one person arranges and tells almost any novel, and that Virginia Woolf's literary style shapes the voices of all the characters, nevertheless the text of the novel *says* that we are reading direct quotations from Bernard, Susan, Jinny, Neville, et al.; here, as in none of the other novels, an attempt is made to keep the form completely dramatic, to provide "a wall for the book from oneself." We are supposed to accept the illusion that the characters are speaking for themselves. If the consistency of style and tone is meant to suggest anything, it is not, I think, the presence of an omniscient author, but the underlying equivalence of the various characters. At the ending they are merged into Bernard, who becomes their spokesman and who says " 'there is no division between me and them' " (p. 205): they have achieved that ultimate synthesis which, I have tried to argue, Virginia Woolf sought to depict in her fiction.

Nevertheless most of the speeches seem strangely detached from their context in the narrative. Quite naturally, the convention has been compared to the Elizabethan stage soliloquy.

9. Hafley, *Glass Roof*, p. 108.

But there is at least one important difference: in Elizabethan drama the character must in some way step aside from the action in order to reveal himself. The events that determine the soliloquy always happen *prior* to the speech itself, and subsequent events do not occur until after the speech is over and the character has stepped back into the action of the play. In *The Waves,* however (with some important exceptions which I want to discuss later), life is going on as we read the soliloquy; the events which influence the content of the speeches are often taking place as the character speaks. All events, whether past or present, are conveyed to us by means of the soliloquy; and while the outer world has completely lost the hegemony it has in the conventional novel, there nevertheless remains a sense of the *simultaneity* of the active, objective world and the passive, subjective one—an effect one cannot find in Shakespeare, but one often associated with the stream-of-consciousness novel.

If we take the speeches as stylized quotations from the minds of the characters themselves, musing on their condition at specific points in space and time, these figures emerge as extraordinarily self-conscious. " 'On the outskirts of every agony sits some observant fellow who points' " (p. 176), as Bernard puts it in describing his mental life; and this observant fellow abiding in all our minds sometimes does give us the feeling that we are watching ourselves perform. Such an approach would account for the overly-contrived quality of many of the speeches, like the soliloquy by Louis quoted above—he is, after all, a highly self-conscious little boy. Still, this explanation is somewhat too naturalistic. It assumes that the characters are *always* introspective, not allowing for the many occasions in the novel when they are living purely instinctive lives, occasions when a mood of detached introspection is not really credible. One might consider Bernard's electric experience in the bath at the end of the first chapter:

"Water pours down the runnel of my spine. Bright arrows
of sensation shoot out on either side. I am covered with warm
flesh. My dry crannies are wetted; my cold body is warmed;
it is sluiced and gleaming. Water descends and sheets me
like an eel. Now hot towels envelop me, and their roughness,
as I rub my back, makes my blood purr. Rich and heavy
sensations form on the roof of my mind; down showers the
day—the woods; and Elvedon; Susan and the pigeon."
[p. 19]

To call this a variety of interior monologue would be tanta-
mount to accepting the feeling of detachment as literally a
part of Bernard's consciousness. The boy is at this moment
being struck by " 'arrows of sensation.' " It seems improbable
that he could at the same time step outside himself and generalize about the quality of his experience: " 'Rich and heavy sensations form on the roof of my mind.' " This is exactly the sort
of statement we have associated with the authorial voice in the
earlier novels, where again and again one finds Mrs. Woolf
commenting on the quality of sensation on the "roof" or "floor"
of her characters' minds—but here the remark is supposed to
come from someone named Bernard.

A similar passage occurs toward the beginning of the chapter, just after Louis' long speech. Jinny discovers Louis in the
bushes, impulsively kisses him, and says: " 'I dashed in, seeing
you green as a bush, like a branch, very still, Louis, with your
eyes fixed. "Is he dead?" I thought, and kissed you, with my
heart jumping under my pink frock like the leaves . . . I
dance. I ripple. I am thrown over you like a net of light. I lie
quivering flung over you' " (p. 9). Even if we allow that an
interior monologue may be very orderly, even if we do not
insist on a diction and syntax appropriate to the character, we
still cannot easily apply the term to a passage like this one.
Jinny is simply too young, too unself-conscious, to sensual, too

immersed in the experience to stand back and see herself as in a picture; an interior monologue must always be taken as true to the spirit, if not the letter, of the personality. We cannot assume that the diction, the metaphor, the poetic rhythms, the self-conscious tone are meant to imply an indirect report of thought unless we are prepared to admit that the consciousness implied is remarkably sensitive and relatively sophisticated. If the repeated use of the personal pronoun, the tendency of the characters to see themselves in clearly defined postures (" 'I lie flung over you.' ") implies anything about consciousness, it is that the ego of the speaker is extremely well-developed. And yet to accept this passage as interior monologue would be to deny what the rest of the novel seems to be saying about the development of the personality.

The various speeches are usually related—as they should be—to the poetic prose of the nature descriptions which preface each section. If the landscape, gradually illuminated by the rising sun, is supposed to serve as an analogy for the lives of the six characters, then one would think that the individual egos would be most strongly emphasized in the fifth section, where the sun is at its zenith and gives to everything *"its exact measure of colour"* (p. 105). Indeed, in the fourth, fifth, and sixth sections the characters repeatedly tell us that they are asserting their individuality, that they feel themselves separated by their individual personalities, and ultimately left alone by the death of Percival. And Bernard, in his summation, remarks on the gradual but steady secretion of the protective "shell" inside which the individual asserts his ego. If the convention Virginia Woolf has adopted as a means of describing the lives of these six characters is supposed to represent consciousness, then shouldn't it reflect in some way the gradual assertion of the ego, the separation of the six characters, as the rest of the novel seems to do? In fact, the convention does just the opposite; if we take the first section as a series of direct expressions of consciousness, then we have to conclude that the characters from birth have a clearly defined vision of themselves as personalities distinct from others. Very little stylistic change takes place in the speeches as the sun rises and the characters grow older. The sentences grow more complex, the speeches somewhat longer; content changes; but the essential form of assertion, "I see," "I feel," remains the same.

Of course one way to explain this apparent conflict between theme and style is to say that the several voices we hear do not actually represent first-hand accounts of consciousness at all. When we read the soliloquies we often have the feeling that the voices are vaguely disembodied, as though they are six "Masks," to use David Daiches' term—six characters manqué, representing six attitudes toward experience, or six facets of personality, who can take the raw materials of consciousness as they are felt in a given context and reinterpret these materials in a series of choral statements. Thus the novel presents Bernard's, Jinny's, Louis', Rhoda's, Neville's, and Susan's conscious lives *as seen by* six ghostly representatives of their personalities. The constantly repeated "I," especially as it occurs in the first chapter, often seems less a reference to actual children rooted in space and time than an indication of transcendent spokesmen, as in this speech by Neville as a boy:

> "Since I am supposed . . . to be too delicate to go with them, since I get so easily tired and then am sick, I will use this hour of solitude, this reprieve from conversation, to coast round the purlieus of the house and recover, if I can, by standing on the same stair half-way up the landing, what I felt when I heard about the dead man through the swing-door last night when cook was shoving in and out the dampers. He was found with his throat cut. The apple trees became fixed in the sky; the moon glared; I was unable to lift my foot up the stair. He was found in the gutter. His blood

gurgled down the gutter. His jowl was white as a dead
codfish. I shall call this structure, this rigidity, 'death among
the apple trees' for ever. There were the floating, pale-gray
clouds; and the immitigable tree; the implacable tree with
its greaved silver bark. The ripple of my life was unavailing.
I was unable to pass by. There was an obstacle. 'I cannot sur-
mount this unintelligible obstacle,' I said, and the others
passed on. But we are doomed, all of us by the apple trees,
by the immitigable tree which we cannot pass." [pp. 17-18]

This reads as if it were spoken by some adult Neville who
stands above the boy and interprets his experience. The language clearly does not belong to the boy, but with its talk of
" 'this hour of solitude, this reprieve from conversation,' " of
the " 'purlieus' " of the house, it suggests a fastidious temperament which is undoubtedly a part of Neville's developing personality. There is, however, something humorless and a bit
pompous about all this formality—if, that is, one views it as
coming from the boy himself. We accept such a tone and even
welcome it when reading, say, the adult Wordsworth, a man
of philosophic bent who strongly emphasizes that he is no
longer what he was as a boy. But when the boy himself speaks
in this manner one cannot be sure that there is not some irony
intended. Granted the formality of the convention, most of the
passage might be taken as a true reflection of what the boy
Neville feels at this particular moment of his life. His words
do convey rather accurately the way certain sights and sounds
adhere to one's memory of an event: "what I felt when I heard
about the dead man through the swing door last night when the
cook was shoving in and out the dampers." To this extent even
the style of the passage sometimes seems to reflect the stream of
consciousness. What seems especially odd and improbable, however, is the way the boy Neville is able to generalize about his
experience with the philosopher's hindsight: " 'we are doomed,

all of us . . . by the immitigable tree which we cannot pass.' "
It is also unlikely that Neville would be detached enough from
his experience at this point in time to be able to say " 'I shall
call this structure, this rigidity, "death among the apple apple
trees" forever.' " It is of course possible for a young boy to be
intensely aware of himself, but it does not seem plausible that all
the characters would speak in these detached, sometimes almost prophetic terms. Louis, for example, can say " 'I, who
shall walk the earth these seventy years, am born entire' "
(p. 28). And when Rhoda is lying in her bed at the end of the
first section, her voice comments, " 'out of me now my mind can
pour' " (p. 19). Or consider again the voice of Louis in the
first section, describing the children at prayer: " 'we pray that
God may keep us safe while we sleep, calling ourselves little
children' " (p. 18).

" 'We shall not always give out a sound like a beaten gong
as one sensation strikes and then another' " (p. 28), the boy
Louis says of the group. But how can he, as a " 'beaten gong,' "
possibly know this? Quite obviously, both the form *and* the
content of the statement serve to deny that it is spoken by a
boy. In fact, the voices in the opening section do not sound
like beaten gongs at all, unless one considers only the very
formal litany of sensations on the opening page. More often
the voices suggest an intimation of immortality, an eternal presence caught for a moment in a temporal, transient world; they
have assumed the role Virginia Woolf herself took in the earlier
novels. In *To the Lighthouse* the omniscient author describes
Lily Briscoe's state of mind by means of a simile: "her mind
kept throwing up from its depths, scenes, and names, and sayings, and memories and ideas, like a fountain spurting." In
The Waves the speaker changes, but the same kind of metaphorical generalizations are made, from what sometimes seems
to be the same omniscient perspective. Thus Bernard's voice
can characterize his own consciousness: " 'I am at liberty now

to sink down, deep, into what passes, this omnipresent, general life . . . The surface of my mind slips along like a pale grey stream reflecting what passes' " (p. 81).

And if we are never quite sure from what perspective we view life in these speeches, there is also an uncertainty at times as to whether Virginia Woolf's term, "soliloquy," aptly represents them. I have already pointed out how the characters seem to be communicating in the opening lines; the feeling that the children are talking to one another is even stronger in other places. Jinny's speech, quoted above, is addressed to Louis, and a moment later, when Bernard notices the jealous Susan pass, he seems to speak to Neville: " 'I shall follow her, Neville. I shall go behind her, to be at hand, with my curiosity, when she bursts out in a rage and thinks, "I am alone" ' " (p. 10). Bernard's self-characterization, his allusion to his curiosity, implies that at least this part of the speech is not spoken aloud; at the same time, it is typical of the soliloquy.

Not only is the language artificial, but the characters often seem bent on describing themselves as they talk. The suggested dialogues are always intimately self-revelatory, and if the characters do communicate they seem to need only fragmentary phrases. A good example of this comes when Bernard follows Susan to comfort her. She says, " 'I saw her kiss him . . . She danced in flecked with diamonds light as dust. And I am squat, Bernard, I am short' " (p. 10). Bernard answers her indirectly: " 'I saw you go . . . I heard you cry "I am unhappy." . . . And my hair is untidy . . . So I am late always.' " And Susan says " 'I love . . . and I hate. I desire one thing only. My eyes are hard . . . Yours grow full and brim and never break' " (p. 11). This kind of dialogue is probably meant to indicate that the real communication is taking place beneath the surface of what is actually said. Intuitive communication is of course often a subject of Virginia Woolf's fiction—one thinks of Helen and Ridley Ambrose, Clarissa

and Septimus, Mr. and Mrs. Ramsay, Orlando and Marmaduke
—but here for the first time the idea is explored in a completely dramatic form. I say "explored" because there are several occasions when the characters do not communicate, even
though they address one another. When Bernard and Susan
are together in the first section, they sometimes think and feel
like one person. " 'When we sit together close,' " says Bernard,
" 'we melt into each other with phrases. We are edged with
mist. We make an unsubstantial territory' " (p. 11). But as
the characters grow older, this sort of communion becomes
more and more infrequent. In the third chapter, for example,
Neville and Bernard feel that they must put on a public self
to talk together. Bernard is struck with the double nature of
his personality: " 'Bernard in public, bubbles; in private is
secretive' " (p. 55). And when Neville sees Bernard approaching, he says, " 'how painful to be recalled, to be mitigated, to
have one's self adulterated, mixed up, become part of another' "
(p. 60). Bernard can sense Neville's "private sorrow," his dis-
approval, but the two do not share as do the children of the
first chapter; instead Bernard becomes his jovial public self,
talks of Percival, and boasts to himself when he is successful
at amusing Neville.

By contrast, in the scene between Bernard and Susan in the
first section a nearly total communion is implied. The two
go exploring at "Elvedon," are frightened and exhilarated by the
creations of their vivid imaginations, and run back toward
home. Through all this they seem almost to be talking to one
another; this is one of the few scenes in the book where the
reader feels that one character has heard everything the other
has said—the others being the dinner party for Percival and
the penultimate section, when the aging characters meet for
another dinner party at Hampton Court. The speeches in this
section sometimes resemble real conversation:

"In this silence," said Susan, "it seems as if no leaf would ever fall, or bird fly."

"As if the miracle had happened," said Jinny, "and life were stayed here and now."

"And," said Rhoda, "we had no more to live."

"But listen," said Louis, "to the world moving through abysses of infinite space." [pp. 159–60]

Actually, the effect goes beyond that of conversation; one character seems to be finishing another's sentence. The sense of total communication is of course intentional. The novel tries to show six characters who are intimately related in the community of their childhood. As the characters grow older their separateness is magnified, their egos are asserted, and they resist at times the feeling of being "edged together." Toward the end of their lives they once again come into harmony; distinctions between them are blurred, and, eventually, because of the web of their common experiences, Bernard tells us that they all seem to live as a part of his life. In the childhood scenes, the dinner party for Percival, and the Hampton Court episode this sense of union, division, and reunion is brought sharply into focus, and the speeches seem to represent a shared experience rather than a group of soliloquies.

To speak of the characters grown older is to remember that *The Waves,* in spite of its rather static method, is a narrative. But the narrative events are never seen from above or related by an impersonal narrator; instead they are alluded to in the speeches. Here, for example, is the account of Bernard and Susan's adventure at Elvedon:

"Put your foot on this brick. Look over the wall. That is Elvedon. The lady sits between the two long windows, writing. The gardeners sweep the lawn with giant brooms. We are the first to come here. We are the discoverers of an un-

known land. Do not stir; if the gardeners saw us they would
shoot us. We should be nailed like stoats to the stable door.
Look! Do not move. Grasp the ferns tight on the top of the
wall."

"I see the lady writing. I see the gardeners sweeping," said
Susan. "If we died here, nobody would bury us."

"Run!" said Bernard. "Run! The gardener with the black
beard has seen us! We shall be shot! We shall be shot like
jays and pinned to the wall! We are in a hostile country. We
must escape to the beech wood. We must hide under the
trees. I turned a twig as we came. There is a secret path.
Bend as low as you can. Follow without looking back. They
will think we are foxes. Run!"

"Now we are safe. Now we can stand upright again. Now
we can stretch our arms in this high canopy, in this vast
wood. I hear nothing." [p. 12]

Within a dozen or so more lines, the children are back at home,
and we pick up Rhoda's soliloquy. We are accustomed to the
strange expansion of time that comes from an interior view, but
here the effect seems just the opposite. Obviously the children's
journey to Elvedon, their peek over the wall, and their swift,
then ambling return takes more time than is spent in the telling
(the whole episode takes about two pages). The speeches seem
to follow one another in a temporal sequence, but the effect is
more like a compression of time, a rapid montage that dissolves
from one speaker to the other and captures the essence of the
event. The reason for this quality is that the soliloquies in *The
Waves* are not direct quotations from the mind, not so much
rooted in a circumstantial context as are the more typical
stream-of-consciousness techniques. Whereas in *Mrs. Dalloway*
and *To the Lighthouse* Virginia Woolf, as the omniscient author, was able to step outside the random flow of consciousness
and explain the essence of thought and event, here the same

information is obtained from the speeches of the characters. In other words, the soliloquy in this novel is artificial not only because it is well-ordered and uses complex metaphor, but also because it often implies a very high degree of selectivity. The characters of the children, the whole scene at Elvedon, are supplied in those "few bold strokes" that Virginia Woolf refers to in her *Diary.* The narrative incident is not a sharply particularized event, but more like what Guiguet calls an "epitome." Here, perhaps even more than in *To the Lighthouse,* both the thoughts and the circumstantial context from which the thoughts arise have been elaborately abstracted.

I have emphasized the first chapter because it is in the opening parts of the novel that the technique departs most clearly from what we associate with direct internal monologue. As the novel progresses and the characters grow older and more solitary, however, an occasional set of speeches appears to rise fairly directly out of the consciousness. Yet a close look at such speeches indicates that they are at the very least an artificial means of depicting the mind's conversation with itself. Toward the end of the second section, for example, Bernard muses as he travels on a train:

"My method, nevertheless, has certain advantages over [Louis' and Neville's]. Neville is repelled by the grossness of Trumble. Louis, glancing, tripping with the high step of a disdainful crane, picks up words as if in sugar-tongs. It is true that his eyes—wild, laughing, yet desperate—express something that we have not gauged. There is about both Neville and Louis a precision, an exactitude that I admire and shall never possess. Now I begin to be aware that action is demanded. We approach a junction; at a junction I have to change. I have to board a train for Edinburgh. I cannot precisely lay fingers on this fact—it lodges loosely among my thoughts like a button, like a small coin. Here is the jolly old boy who collects tickets. I had one—I had one certainly. But it does not matter." [p. 50]

The first part of the passage is characterized by an exceptionally high degree of order. Humphrey says that soliloquy as it appears in *As I Lay Dying* and *The Waves* is "an arrangement of thought units *as they would originate in a character's consciousness,* rather than as they would be deliberately expressed." [10] This might be true of Faulkner, but it is seldom true of Mrs. Woolf. Except toward the end of this passage, with the arrival of the ticket collector, there is no feeling that the words are popping into Bernard's head without regard for order. Still, Bernard is a writer, a phrase-maker, certainly a different kind of personality than Faulkner's southern rural types; it is perhaps natural that his thought should be more orderly, even formal in structure. Besides, Bernard is in a reflective, presumably undisturbed state at the beginning of the passage, so that he is able to compose his thoughts. As the train begins to near the junction, his sentences become shorter. Thus far the soliloquy might seem in accord with Humphrey's definition, except for one thought that does not fit:

"I have to board a train for Edinburgh. I cannot precisely lay my fingers on this fact—it lodges loosely among my thoughts like a button, like a small coin."

If Bernard cannot recognize clearly that he must board the train, how can he say, no matter how artificial we allow the technique to be, " 'I have to board the train.' "? Such a statement assumes a consciousness of consciousness, an omniscience, a voice that is aloof from the Bernard who must change trains but is only dimly aware of his mission. The soliloquy, Humphrey says, "represents the psychic content and processes of a character directly from character to reader without the presence

10. Humphrey, *Stream of Consciousness in the Modern Novel,* p. 54.

of an author." [11] But if no author is implied in Bernard's
soliloquy, there does seem to be some intermediary between the
actual Bernard, riding on the train, and the reader. Here, as in
many other places in the novel, there is a strong suggestion that
the voices we hear are detached from their actual counterparts
and do not represent consciousness except indirectly. It is as if
Virginia Woolf were asking the reader to suppose that the six
types she has arranged in the novel can at any given moment
be represented by six detached spokesmen who are continually
going through a process of self-revelation. These voices seem to
inhabit a kind of spirit realm from which, in a sad, rather
world-weary tone, they comment on their time-bound selves
below. Even while the voices assert their personalities, they
imply knowledge of a life without personality, an undifferentiated world like the one described by the interchapters.

From the start of her career, Mrs. Woolf sought to develop
ways of describing consciousness without directly entering an
individual mind. Here, the omniscient voice of *Mrs. Dalloway*
and *To the Lighthouse* has been replaced by six detached
spokesmen, who, like waves, are part of a single medium. As
in the other novels, the outer world is suppressed or refracted
through the musings of the speakers, and the metaphoric language suggests not only mental states that are non-verbal, but
also the presence of a symbolizing imagination which can
transform the surface of life into something quite poetic. Thus,
if in *To the Lighthouse* the omniscient narrator can liken Lily
Briscoe's mind to a fountain, in *The Waves* Bernard can look
down on his own consciousness and make the same kind of
metaphoric comment. Likewise, as the setting in *To the Lighthouse* is always described so that it becomes symbolic, so also
in *The Waves* the outer world is refined until it becomes
ethereal. Guiguet makes a very important point when he ob-

11. Ibid., p. 56.

serves that the circumstantial context of the speeches in *The Waves* is often subjected to a "process of abstraction and compression," so that the events of the novel seem to be "epitomes, recomposed by the novelist outside space and time." [12] But he is wrong, it seems to me, when he implies that the technique constitutes a departure from that employed in the two previous novels. To some extent in *Mrs. Dalloway,* and often *To the Lighthouse,* we can see the method taking shape.

In *To the Lighthouse* an even higher degree of unity and coherence is imposed on mental life than in *Mrs. Dalloway,* which is already quite different in texture from the works of Joyce or Richardson; there is an ever-increasing tendency to place characters in meditative moods, and the transitions from one character to another are effected more and more smoothly; in addition, there is an increased use of metaphoric descriptions of thought. Style and tone, almost invariable in *Mrs. Dalloway,* are perhaps even more uniform in *To the Lighthouse,* largely because the author's commentary becomes so completely submerged in her descriptions of mental life. The exterior is increasingly suppressed or abstracted—dialogue and event are rarely presented directly in *To the Lighthouse,* so that the dreamlike atmosphere that sometimes pervades *Mrs. Dalloway* is heightened. Sometimes the sameness of tone and style, together with rapid and smooth shifts of perspective, can create the effect of two distinct personalities immersed in the same medium; the narrator's reports of the attitudes of characters often function like a series of choral responses. All this prefigures *The Waves,* where the suggestion of an underlying unity in life, the use of metaphor, the suppression or abstraction of narrative and dialogue, the choral effect, are utilized to the fullest extent.

12. Guiguet, *Woolf and her Works,* p. 377.

Virginia Woolf conceived of *The Waves* as a completely dramatic work. When it was done, she called it a play-poem, and this is in one sense a very good name for it. While the authorial voice of the earlier novels has been effaced, the devices that make them poetic have been retained. A wall has been erected between the author and the work, but at the same time Mrs. Woolf has avoided what she saw as the restrictiveness of a method that relied entirely on depicting the egos of the characters. In place of an omniscient narrator who refines the raw materials of consciousness, six disembodied voices (in the final analysis, one observant spirit) provide their own omniscient analysis. Their presence in the novel means that we think of the characters in metaphysical rather than psychological terms. *The Waves* cannot be reduced to a series of stylized quotations from the consciousness of six characters, though many critics take this approach. What the novel portrays is not simply the consciousness of Bernard, Susan, Jinny, Neville, Rhoda, or Louis, but their being; not their existence but their essence. Thus, in almost every respect, *The Waves* represents the ultimate refinement of Virginia Woolf's so-called subjective novels.

But we need to speculate on how this peculiar form seems to grow out of a feeling about "life itself." For *The Waves*—however we judge its merits as a novel or poem or play—is the purest and most ambitious treatment of those themes which preoccupied Mrs. Woolf in all her earlier fiction. It is, in fact, one of those works which seem to run into a dead end, in the sense that they generate an aesthetic crisis and call into question their very being. I have said that *The Waves* manifests that intense desire of Mrs. Woolf to express the timeless unity of all things through a kind of self-destructive love. It is also true, however, that *The Waves* questions whether language can serve such an end, raises doubts about its sometimes beautiful but over-cultivated prose, and pictures the character Bernard—who in this sense is very like Virginia Woolf—as a man trying to stave off a death he partly longs for by making lovely rhythmical phrases.

The individual lives to which the soliloquies attest are set off against the impersonal forces of nature, described as " 'out there,' " beyond the self. Bernard sometimes calls these forces " 'the enemy,' " and he explains his life largely in terms of his attempts to make a secure and orderly place where the enemy cannot touch him. He describes how his ego separated itself from those of the other children: " 'I felt my indifference melt. Neville did not melt. "Therefore," I said, "I am myself, not Neville," a wonderful discovery' " (p. 170). His notion of a personal identity (which, significantly, he rarely is able to sense), leads him to assert his ego in the face of anything that would destroy it. " 'I then became aware of the presence of those enemies who change, but are always there; the forces we fight against. To let oneself be carried on passively is unthinkable. "That's your course, world," one says, "mine is this" ' " (p. 170). The sense of life and individuality which Virginia Woolf sometimes calls the ego or the self is born out of an act of assertion; and it is, in fact, unthinkable to be "carried on passively" if one wishes to retain that active contact with the everyday world of relationships that we normally call living. Nevertheless we have already seen how many of Mrs. Woolf's characters—Mrs. Ramsay, for example—not only allow themselves to be carried along passively at times, but are strongly tempted not to resist, to remain bereft of personality, deriving a kind of ecstasy from their sense of union with the world and of "infinite possibility" in their dreams. Bernard himself has several such moments. After his engagement, for example, wandering through London, he is able to grasp the " 'splendid unanimity' " in life:

"I am at liberty now to sink down, deep, into what passes, this omnipresent, general life . . . I will let myself be carried on by the general impulse. The surface of my mind slips along like a pale-grey stream reflecting what passes. I cannot remember my past, my nose, or the colour of my eyes, or what my general opinion of myself is. Only in moments of emergency, at a crossing, at a kerb, the wish to preserve my body springs out and seizes me and stops me, here, before this omnibus. We insist, it seems, on living. Then again, indifference descends. The roar of the traffic, the passage of undifferentiated faces, this way and that way, drugs me into dreams; rubs the features from faces. People might walk through me. And, what is this particular moment of time . . . The growl of traffic might be any uproar—forest trees or the roar of wild beasts. Time has whizzed back an inch or two on its reel; our short progress has been cancelled. I think also that our bodies are in truth naked. We are only lightly covered with buttoned cloth; and beneath these pavements are shells, bones and silence.

"It is, however, true that my dreaming, my tentative advance like one carried beneath the surface of a stream, is interrupted, torn, pricked and plucked at by sensations, spontaneous and irrelevant, or curiosity, greed, desire, irresponsible as in sleep. (I covet that bag—etc.) No, but I wish to go under; to visit the profound depths; once in a while exercise my prerogative not to act, but to explore; to hear vague, ancestral sounds of boughs creaking, of mammoths, to indulge impossible desires to embrace the whole world with the arms of understanding, impossible to those who act. Am I not, as I walk, trembling with strange oscillations and vibrations of sympathy, which, unmoored as I am from a private being, bid me embrace these engrossed flocks . . . ?"
[pp. 81–82]

This passive, dreamy mood, so common throughout Mrs. Woolf's fiction, is inimical to any kind of activity whatever. It is misleading for Bernard to say that the alternative to action is exploration, since exploration implies a kind of being and doing which such a mood does not permit. Bernard even seems to regard his instinctive reactions—the wish to preserve his life, his simple curiosity, his admiration for someone's bag—as mildly annoying and sometimes even abrasive conflicts with his wish to " 'go under' " to the " 'profound depths.' " He feels, as he says later, " 'unmoored from a private being,' " and the value of this condition is that he is able to sense a great, timeless unity in life, to " 'embrace the whole world with arms of understanding, impossible to those who act.' "

As I have already noted, when this overwhelming desire to embrace the world becomes compulsive in Mrs. Woolf's writings, it amounts to a desire for a kind of death. Indeed, its association with death is made explicit in Bernard's description of another, similar moment when he is grown old and feels the end of life is near. As usual, the mood is brought on by some hypnotic rhythm, this time the clipping of barber's shears:

> "The hairdresser began to move his scissors to and fro. I felt myself powerless to stop the oscillations of the cold steel. So we are cut and laid in swathes, I said; so we lie side by side on the damp meadows, withered branches and flowering. We have no more to expose ourselves on the bare hedges to the wind and the snow; no more to carry ourselves erect when the gale sweeps, to bear our burden upheld; or stay, unmurmuring, on those pallid noondays when the bird creeps close to the bough and the damp whitens the leaf. We are cut, we are fallen. We are become part of that unfeeling universe that sleeps when we are at our quickest and burns red when we lie asleep." [pp. 198–99]

It is hard not to be mesmerized by the rhythms and the familiar associations of the imagery in this passage. Under close examination, however, the details seem excessively literary: " 'We have no more to expose ourselves on the bare hedges to the wind and the snow; no more to carry ourselves erect when the gale sweeps, to bear our burden upheld.' " And one would not have expected a writer in the modernist period to create lines like " 'stay, unmurmuring, on those pallid noondays when the bird creeps close to the bough and the damp whitens the leaf.' " Such prose, in fact, indicates the gulf between Mrs. Woolf's sensibility and that of her contemporaries in the post-Imagist phase. Worldweariness appears everywhere in her writing, and with it expressions of gratitude for moments of peace and re-union with the " 'unfeeling universe.' "

Bernard quickly adds, however, that he is " 'no mystic' "; he, perhaps like Virginia Woolf, is always impelled—if only by simple curiosity—to emerge from these moods and assert his ego. He feels a compulsive need to fight back against " 'the enemy,' " to bang his spoon against the table, to " 'measure' " things. And for Bernard the chief instrument for measurement is language, which he uses to defend himself against the fear of chaos. He speaks of the need to " 'fight' " with words: " 'It is the effort and the struggle, it is the perpetual warfare, it is the shattering and piecing together—this is the daily battle . . . the absorbing pursuit. The trees, scattered, put on order . . . I netted them under with a sudden phrase. I retrieved them from formlessness with words' " (p. 191). Thus, he says, he feels joy when he has " 'dispatched the enemy for a moment.' "

At the same time, Bernard knows that there is a hollowness in such victories. " 'Life,' " he notes sadly in almost the same breath, " 'is not susceptible perhaps to the treatment we give it when we try to tell it' " (p. 189). Indeed, the book is saturated with passages revealing an ambivalence toward language which, I have tried to indicate, is implicit in nearly all of Mrs. Woolf's writings. The children in the opening chapter describe words as though they were beautiful trinkets. " 'Those are white words,' " Susan says, " 'like stone one picks up by the sea-shore.' " " 'Those are yellow words, those are fiery words,' "

Jinny says. " 'I should like a fiery dress' " (p. 188). But words, in this view, are not only aesthetic objects; they are the signs of personality. Thus the maternal Susan likes " 'white' " words, the sensual Jinny likes " 'fiery' " ones. Furthermore, words help to form the earliest experiences by which the children sense order and separateness in the world around them. " 'Each tense,' " says Neville, " 'means differently. There is an order in this world; there are distinctions, there are differences in this world, upon whose verge I step' " (p. 15). Virginia Woolf makes explicit here what she implies in other contexts. Words, for her, represent an assertion of the ego, a means by which an individual personality is able to make its "appearance" known. But as Mrs. Ramsay notes, the "appearance" is only "what you see us by"; the reality lies somewhere down in those vague depths where one is divested of personality and the sense of distinctions, and where language—if it is present at all—has nothing to do with an active response to the world.

The " 'order,' " the sense of " 'distinctions' " which words impart is therefore at bottom a false or tenuous order. That is why the same Neville, grown a bit older, believes that Percival " 'understands' " Catullus. " 'Not the words,' " he observes, " 'but what are words?' " And that is why later, at the dinner for Percival, he feels the same thing even more intensely: " 'Yet these roaring waters . . . upon which we built our crazy platforms are more stable than the wild, the weak and inconsequent cries that we utter when, trying to speak, we rise; when we reason and jerk out these false sayings, " 'I am this; I am that!" Speech is false' " (pp. 98–99).

It is natural that most of the attack on the falsity of words should come from Neville and Bernard, the two characters who have chosen literary vocations. Both are profoundly convinced that words make false distinctions, and both have moments when they sense that the " 'roaring waters,' " the vast impersonal life outside, has more stability than the individual ego.

" 'Outside the undifferentiated forces roar,' " Bernard says. " 'Inside we are very private, very explicit, have a sense, indeed,
that it is here, in this little room, that we make whatever day
of the week it may be. Friday or Saturday. A shell forms upon
the soft soul, nacreous, shiny, upon which sensations tap their
beaks in vain.' " But, he adds:

> "It is a mistake, this extreme precision, this orderly and
> military progress; a convenience, a lie. There is always deep
> below it . . . a rushing stream of broken dreams, nursery
> rhymes, street cries, half-finished sentences and sights—elm
> trees, willow trees, gardeners sweeping, women writing—
> that rise and sink even as we hand a lady down to dinner.
> . . . There is nothing one can fish up with a spoon; noth-
> ing one can call an event. Yet it is alive too and deep, this
> stream." [p. 181]

Many of Bernard's arguments against orderly " 'lies' " are
extensions of the same reasoning one finds in essays like "Modern Fiction" and "Mr. Bennett and Mrs. Brown." *The Waves,*
however, applies these arguments not just to fiction but to the
way we live our lives, questioning any phenomenon—even
language itself—that is based on the principle that there are
such things as discreet individuals or discreet events. Reality,
in this view, is to be felt in what Bernard describes as the
steady stream of impressions in the consciousness, which, if
we give ourselves over to it, will show us how all of life is
composed of an element that can be divided only arbitrarily.

> "The crystal, the globe of life as one calls it, far from being
> hard and cold to the touch, has walls of thinnest air. If I
> press them all will burst. Whatever sentence I extract whole
> and entire from this cauldron is only a string of six little
> fish that let themselves be caught while a million others leap
> and sizzle. . . . How impossible to order them rightly; to

detach one separately, or to give the effect of the whole—again like music." [p. 182]

Virginia Woolf's distrust of "fact" extends even to a distrust of language as cognition, since language is a product of the ego, since it makes " 'proportions' " of things and is always at least one step removed from reality. Notice, too, that Bernard, like Virginia Woolf, like Pater or Mallarmé, sometimes longs for a medium that approximates music, that does not tend to emphasize the distinctions between things.

This love of the musical has appeared before in Mrs. Woolf's writings: one thinks of Rachel Vinrace's reaction to Milton and of Mrs. Ramsay's dreamy response to the poetry she reads. Neither of these women has any direct grasp of the meaning of the words, but there is something in the rhythm that puts the active will to sleep and lets the hearer drift along on a wave of associations until she feels at peace with the world outside. Before one is tempted to denigrate Virginia Woolf as a mere aesthete, however, one should recognize that her attitude toward "significant form" is sometimes just as ambivalent as her attitude toward cognition. Consider this familiar passage, spoken by Rhoda as she listens to a musical concert just after the death of Percival:

" 'Like' and 'like' and 'like'—but what is the thing that lies beneath the semblance of the thing? Now that lightning has gashed the tree and the flowering branch has fallen and Percival, by his death, has made me this gift. Let me see the thing. There is a square; there is an oblong. They place it very accurately; they make a perfect dwelling-place. Very little is left outside. The structure is now visible; what is inchoate is here stated; we are not so various or so mean; we have made oblongs and stood them upon squares. This is our triumph; this is our consolation." [p. 116]

This statement has been taken as praise of the artist's ability
to make a triumphant "dwelling-place" by means of the formal
relationships in his work.[13] But surely that assumption misses
the whole point; there is an extremely bitter irony in Rhoda's
words, almost a sneer at the pettiness of " 'squares' " and " 'oblongs,' " forms which leave " 'very little outside,' " but which
do, after all, leave something out. The " 'triumph' " and " 'consolation' " are fragile and pathetic. The " 'semblance of the
thing' " is not the thing itself, any more than Lily Briscoe's
painting was her vision.

That is why Bernard feels he cannot make the story of his
life a " 'globe, full of figures,' " and why he feels that language
is inadequate for his purposes. " 'I begin to long for some little
language such as lovers use,' " he says, and later he despairs
of his attempts: " 'what is the use of painfully elaborating
these consecutive sentences when what one needs is nothing
consecutive but a bark, a groan?' " (p. 178). This attitude,
however, develops in Bernard rather late in life. As a young
man he is given to phrase-making and is bent on discovering
his true identity. Marriage and middle age help him toward a
definition: " 'Tuesday follows Monday; Wednesday, Tuesday.
Each spreads the same ripple of well-being, repeats the same
curve of rhythm . . . So the being grows rings; identity becomes robust. What was fiery and furtive . . . is now method-
ical and orderly and flung with a purpose—so it seems' " (p.
186). All the while, however, Bernard has the sense that the
order and distinctions he perceives are false: " 'when I meet an
unknown person, and try to break off, here at this table, what
I call "my life," it is not one life that I look back upon; I do
not altogether know who I am—Jinny, Susan, Neville, Rhoda,
or Louis: or how to distinguish my life from theirs' " (p. 196).

I have mentioned that at two places in the book—the dinner

13. See Johnstone, *The Bloomsbury Group,* p. 366.

party for Percival in the fifth chapter and the meeting at Hampton Court toward the end—the six characters come together and experience that remarkable community of being that Bernard talks about. These occasions represent two very different moods. In the first the characters claim to be young and eager and expectant, insistent on the distinctions between them; in the second they are old, a bit sad, and weary of individuality. At the dinner for Percival Neville offers an extraordinary description of how it feels to eat roast duck, drink cool white wine, and gradually " 'lose all knowledge of particulars.' " Rhoda and Louis, describing themselves as " 'conspirators, withdrawn together to lean over some cold urn,' " observe that everyone has become " 'nocturnal, rapt,' " and that the party gives a sense of " 'drumming,' " as of " 'naked men with assegais' " (the same image that appears in the landscape description at the beginning of the chapter, to describe the violence of waves at noon).

Later in the novel, at Hampton Court, the process repeats itself, with important qualitative differences. We are told that " 'The fish, the veal cutlets, the wine . . . blunted the sharp tooth of egotism.' " The characters are " 'ready to consider any suggestion that the world might offer impartially.' " Suddenly a silence falls, and all six feel that " 'Our separate drops are dissolved; we are extinct, lost in the abysses of time, in the darkness.' " Again Louis and Rhoda draw aside, again calling themselves conspirators, and this time they hover around a real urn to watch the others walk in the gardens. They remark on how short a time the silence has been allowed to last: " 'They are saying to themselves, it is time, I am still vigorous . . . My face shall be cut against the black of infinite space.' " But of course such egoism (of which Mr. Ramsay displays one variety) is futile, and for a brief moment all the characters seem to understand that identity itself is a kind of illusion.

Louis and Rhoda fear death at the earlier party, when youthful egoism is at its height and the characters seem generally oblivious to the insignificance of personal identity in comparison to the vastness of time and space. At Hampton Court, however, the two " 'conspirators' " say they " 'cannot hear death anywhere.' " All the characters have grown older and seem more ready to give themselves up to the void outside themselves; even though enough of their identity remains for them to resist extinction as individuals, their struggle is comparatively feeble. Louis and Rhoda actually lament the failure to achieve death, and they have a vision of how beautiful it all would be if they were merged together in the dark forever. Here is the way they describe the others returning from their walk in the garden:

> "But now look, as we stand here, a ripple breaks on the horizon. The net is raised higher and higher. It comes to the top of the water. The water is broken by silver, by quivering little fish. . . . There are figures coming towards us. Are they men or are they women? They still wear the ambiguous draperies of the flowing tide in which they have been immersed."
>
> "Now," said Rhoda, "as they pass that tree, they regain their natural size. They are only men, only women. . . . I feel myself grappled to one spot by these hooks they cast on us. . . ."
>
> "Something flickers and dances," said Louis. "Illusion returns as they approach down the avenue. Rippling and questioning begin. What do I think of you—what do you think of me? Who are you? Who am I? . . . all the insanity of personal existence without which life would fall flat and die, begins again." [pp. 164–65]

Here the " 'naked men with assegais' " have aged; they can be described as " 'the relics of any army . . . coming back every night with their wounds, their ravaged faces.' " The waves beat a weary rhythm, not a violent one, and personal existence becomes an " 'insanity.' " The characters now seem ready to welcome the darkness, the undifferentiated forces that dissolve the ego.

Bernard, in his summing up, reviews the evening at Hampton Court and describes his " 'pugnacity' " in dispatching the enemy. This time, however, the impulse to rejoin the conventional world is more difficult for him to sustain, and the vast universe seems less and less an enemy. He recalls the walk in the garden with a kind of wistfulness: " 'When we returned from that immersion—how sweet, how deep!—and came to the surface and saw the two conspirators standing there it was with some compunction.' " He wonders, " 'Was this then, this streaming away mixed with Susan, Jinny, Neville, Rhoda, Louis, a sort of death?' " (p. 198). Age has brought him, if not full cycle, then at least to a point where he again senses an intermingling, " 'edged with mist,' " that he felt as a very small child. " 'I have lost in the process of eating and drinking and rubbing my eyes along the surfaces that thin hard shell which cases the soul' " (pp. 204–05). At Hampton Court, Bernard had come to a moment in his life when the " 'self,' " the phrase-maker, " 'the man who collected himself in moments of emergency and banged his spoon on the table,' " no longer put up any resistance at all; did not answer, in fact. At first, Bernard says, he felt a total desolation; then he began to perceive the world again, but in a different way: " 'I saw but was not seen. I walked unshadowed . . . Then, as a ghost, leaving no trace where I trod, perceiving merely . . . unable to speak save in a child's words of one syllable' " (p. 203).

What Bernard sees he cannot describe. Like the mystic, he can only testify to his experience or try to approximate it. " 'How describe the world seen without a self?' " he asks. " 'There are no words. Blue, red—even they distract, even they hide with thickness instead of letting the light through' ":

"But for a moment I had sat on the turf somewhere high above the flow of the sea and the sounds of the woods, had seen the house, the garden, and the waves breaking. The old nurse who turns the pages of the picture-book had stopped and had said, 'Look. This is the truth.'" [p. 204]

What Bernard has "seen" is what Virginia Woolf's prose description of house and garden and sea tries to suggest in the interchapters. A couple of pages later, Bernard tells his auditor that he has reached a stage in life when these moments come to him more often:

"I could go like a spy without leaving this place . . . I can visit the remote verges of the desert lands where the savage sits by the campfire. Day rises; the girl lifts the watery fire-hearted jewels to her brow; the sun levels his beams straight at the sleeping house; the waves deepen their bars; they fling themselves on shore; back blows the spray; sweeping their waters they surround the boat and the sea-holly. The birds sing in chorus; deep tunnels run between the stalks of flowers; the house is whitened; the sleeper stretches." [p. 207]

This passage, reminiscent of Mrs. Ramsay's dreamy excursions, has all the imagery of house and garden and sea that we find in the interchapters. The girl who "'lifts the watery firehearted jewels to her brow'" should be compared with the girl Virginia Woolf describes in the third descriptive passage.

Bernard has become so accommodated to "that vastness" outside that sometimes his individual life hardly matters. He cannot sustain this feeling very long, however; something always brings him back to himself. From the sense that he is "'capable of being everywhere on the verge of things,'" he is always returned to being "'an elderly man, rather heavy, grey above the ears.'" In the last pages of the novel he oscillates between the sense of having a special identity and that other

feeling of infinite possibility, until at the end he is convinced
that these very oscillations are part of some " 'eternal renewal' "
and that his habitual struggle against the enemy is futile but
noble. Guiguet has pointed out that the final words of the
novel, *"The waves broke on the shore,"* are a problem: "Does
this mean nothingness sanctioning the victory of time and
space, our enemies and our defeat, or does it mean eternity
sanctioning our victory over their vain and illusory opposition?" [14] The only answer I can give is that it suggests both,
that here as elsewhere Virginia Woolf sees death as a kind of
victory and a kind of defeat—a loss of the self, but at the
same time an ecstatic embrace.

Bernard's soliloquies, as to some extent all of Mrs. Woolf's
novels, express an alternating pride and agony over the ego,
the "little room" imposed upon us by time and space. Her
characters value that room, but they are unusually prone to
an impulse to exchange it for what they consider a vast dome
or cathedral, where space seems infinite and time is reduced
to the rhythm of changes in a great natural cycle. In their
private rooms they perceive time and space as forces that can
separate and destroy; but in those hypnotic moments when they
seem to lose personality and come to the verge of death, they
are empowered to see " 'the world without a self,' " without
any division between "I" and "thou." The wonder of that sight
not only removes their fear of dying, but makes them hesitate
to reenter the world.

Much of what Virginia Woolf tries to communicate is, by
definition, incommunicable. I had occasion to remark as early
as the discussion of *The Voyage Out* that the verbal order of
experience did not inspire in her the holy wonder that Joyce
sometimes bestowed upon it. She is a great verbal craftswoman,

14. Guiguet, *Woolf and her Works,* p. 397. See also his fine paragraph
on the theme of "anguish" in Mrs. Woolf, where he indicates the differences between her works and those of Bergson and Proust (pp. 396–97).

to be sure, but there is a vagueness about much of her language, reflecting her basic misgivings about the ego and about the words which are its signs. That is why the stream of consciousness is only a starting place for her explorations. She begins with the private self in order to escape from it or at least deny its primacy. She believes in an ultimate order of experience, which can be achieved only through a momentary embrace or immersion in that dark, often frightening world outside the self. The nature descriptions introducing the chapters of *The Waves* are supposed to approximate that experience, as are the six voices which often seem to be only one voice, unmoored from an immediate circumstantial context. The great paradox about *The Waves,* however, is that while it tries to deny the primacy of the self, it remains one of the most personal and idiosyncratic books in English literature. It is also, to my mind, a failure—though a highly interesting one. Like *Finnegans Wake,* it attempts to sustain a powerful lyric intensity over a wide-ranging novelistic terrain, and to imply a world where things are always changing yet always the same. To mention *The Waves* in the same breath as *Finnegans Wake,* however, is to point up Mrs. Woolf's shortcomings. Certain passages in *The Waves* are extraordinarily beautiful; with the possible exception of the last chapter, however, the prose is rather stifling in effect—the reader almost drowns in the language.

8

Orlando and the "New Biography"

In the interval between the demanding tasks of *To the Lighthouse* and *The Waves,* Virginia Woolf was occupied with *Orlando,* a mock biography inspired partly by her romantic friendship with Vita Sackville-West. The emphasis on fantasy allowed free rein to her naturally ornate, erotic style, and provided good material for sketches of vast, generalized landscapes. Perhaps more important, in pretending to write a biography Mrs. Woolf gave her prose some breathing room above the subjective deeps. As usual, she describes her central character in the third person and from an omniscient perspective; but here she chooses to look down through the eyes of a voluble, often unreliable narrator, a "biographer" who indulges in digressions and flights of description like the famous accounts of the Great Frost or the damp cloud descending over Victorian England. The voice of this narrator is highly flexible, capable of adapting with ease to all the inner emotional rhythms of Orlando's life; at times, however, particularly in the first parts of the book, it stands at a marked distance, observing its subject's behavior with wonder, puzzlement, or even blatant incomprehension. Orlando's conversations with herself are reported, but usually as well-ordered, logical meditations (see pp. 159–61). In general, *Orlando* employs the techniques of conventional omniscient narration, and, on the surface at least, its existence might imply that Mrs. Woolf had temporarily lost interest in the flow of mental life. Even the plot, granting its outrageousness, is more conventionally "novelistic" than Mrs. Woolf's previous work—certainly no one could charge that nothing happens in this book.

Ultimately, however, *Orlando* is as much about the inner life as any of Virginia Woolf's other novels. The difference is that here she chose to represent a chiefly internal, implicit experience as if it were objective and explicit. Instead of dealing with an inner life which is at least generally bound by an ordinary circumstantial context, she chose to imagine the racial or family memory in a character much like Vita Sackville-West, and then depicted that memory as a sequence of actual events. As have seen, she was fascinated with the mind's ability to think back to times before it even existed, and travel to places it has never been. Thus when Mrs. Ramsay sinks into a "core of darkness," she feels that she can go anywhere: "Her horizon seemed to her limitless. There were all the places she had not seen; the Indian plains; she felt herself pushing aside the thick leather curtain of a church in Rome." Orlando's experience has precisely this sort of limitless possibility, but it is presented straightforwardly, in a book that purports to be a biography.

This fanciful device, like all of Mrs. Woolf's experiments, represented another attempt to overcome the problem of isolation; it allowed her to suggest that the envelope surrounding individual lives is in some sense permeable, permitting some contact with what lies "outside." Hence we encounter a recognizable stream of consciousness only in the later chapters of *Orlando,* and find there that Virginia Woolf is no longer satisfied with the ordinary flotsam of the internal monologue—she is approaching those deeper, more communal regions Joyce treats in some parts of *Ulysses* and in *Finnegans Wake:*

"Sheets for a double bed," Orlando repeated dreamily, for a double bed with a silver counterpane in a room fitted with taste which she now thought a little vulgar—all in silver; but she had furnished it when she had a passion for that metal. While the man went to get sheets for a double bed, she took out a little looking-glass and a powder puff. Women were not nearly as roundabout in their ways, she thought, powdering herself with the greatest unconcern, as they had been when she herself first turned woman on the deck of the *Enamoured Lady.* She gave her nose the right tint deliberately. She never touched her cheeks. Honestly, though she was now thirty-six, she scarcely looked a day older. She looked just as pouting, as sulky, as handsome, as rosy (like a million-candled Christmas tree, Sasha had said) as she had done that day on the ice, when the Thames was frozen and they had gone skating—

"The best Irish linen, Ma'am," said the shopman, spreading the sheets on the counter,—and they had met an old woman picking up sticks. Here, as she was fingering the linen abstractedly, one of the swinging doors between the departments opened and let through, perhaps from the fancy-good departments, a whiff of scent, waxen, tinted as if from pink candles, and the scent curved like a shell round a figure —was it a boy's or was it a girl's?—young, slender, seductive —a girl, by God! furred, pearled, in Russian trousers; but faithless, faithless! [pp. 271–72]

As the story of Orlando's "life" reaches its conclusion, every sensation evokes a web of associations. The effect is extraordinary: the fall of every "atom"—the shopkeeper's talk, the glimpse of a reflection in a hand mirror, the scent drifting in through an open door—activates a "tremour of susceptibility."

The previous events of the tale are gathered up in a single moment, and, like Bernard in *The Waves,* Orlando knows the feeling of time "whizzed back an inch or two on its reel"; also like Bernard, she participates in other selves, even other sexes. In one sense the moment is poignant, because Sasha and youth are gone—yet in another sense it is a joyful and triumphant experience, because all time, all distinctions, all finality seem to have been overcome.

Such passages reveal the basic similarity between *Orlando* and Mrs. Woolf's other work—again she presents a victory over time and death, again she insists on the unity of experience. In this case, however, she was directly concerned with *historical* consciousness, and with an attack on the deadening empiricism of most biographical literature. If she felt that the novels of Bennett and Galsworthy had been weighted down by a superficial realism, she found the typical biography, with its slavish attention to facts, even more burdensome. The biographer's work is grounded in a tight little realm of detail and distinction, much like the everyday reality that grows up around characters in *The Waves*; biography, as it is usually practiced, deals with our "shell," not our soul, with our temporal, not our eternal being. In one sense, then, the historian's facts threaten our survival, so that Mrs. Woolf's playful satire of historicism in *Orlando* represents a perfectly serious attempt to show us a world which cannot be explained by fact, a world in which the changes wrought by historical process become merely "what you see us by."

All this is not to say that Virginia Woolf was uninterested in conventional historical writings—on the contrary, like everyone else in Bloomsbury, she was fascinated by them. But in *Orlando,* as in most cases where she deals with historical subject matter, she tries to create an imaginative unity between past and present, and in so doing exposes the relative emptiness of empirical data. Humanity, she seems to say, has always shared a common life; only the external circumstances of time and place make us seem different. She had touched on this theme many times before, especially in her essays. In "The Pastons and Chaucer," for example, she refuses to take the impersonal, scholarly point of view of a writer who is forever removed from medieval England. Instead she shows us how John Paston felt as he sat alone reading:

> For sometimes, instead of riding off on his horse to inspect his crops or bargain with his tenants, Sir John would sit, in broad daylight, reading. There, on the hard chair in the comfortless room with the wind lifting the carpet and the smoke stinging his eyes, he would sit reading Chaucer, wasting his time, dreaming—or what strange intoxication was it he drew from books? Life was rough, cheerless, and disappointing. A whole year of days would pass fruitlessly in dreary business, like dashes of rain on the window-pane. There was no reason in it as there had been for his father; no imperative need to establish a family and acquire an important position for children who were not born . . . But Lydgate's poems or Chaucer's, like a mirror in which figures move brightly, silently, and compactly, showed him the very skies, fields, and people whom he knew, but rounded and complete. Instead of waiting listlessly for news from London or piecing out from his mother's gossip some country tragedy of love and jealousy, here, in a few pages, the whole story was laid before him.[1]

"The Pastons and Chaucer" is no excavation of dead relics from the past. It recreates Paston before our eyes, presenting him as a character like Rachel Vinrace or Mrs. Ramsay, a sensitive person who exchanges rough life for dreamy solitude. Paston is also like the characters in *Between the Acts* who are troubled

---

1. Woolf, *Collected Essays*, 3:7–8.

by the fragmentary quality of ordinary life; he feels dependent on the piecemeal facts of "news" or "gossip," which have to travel across time and space. But when he retreats from active life and gives himself over to imagination, he can understand "the whole story." Moreover, just as the imagination of Chaucer redeems Paston, so the imagination of Virginia Woolf, who has absorbed both Paston and Chaucer, helps to redeem us. As we sit reading Mrs. Woolf's essay, we half share in Paston's experience. Like him, we overcome boundaries and seem to understand a life "rounded and complete." Without leaving our chairs, we take imaginative possession of an event that occurred hundreds of years before our birth.

This kind of triumph over space and time can be found everywhere in Virginia Woolf's writing, but in essays like "The Pastons and Chaucer," in *Orlando,* and subsequently in *Between the Acts,* it becomes more specifically the triumph of imagination over the historical process. Thus the many evident similarities between *Orlando* and *Between the Acts:* both deal with the realm of action and affairs and treat that realm with a good deal of comic irony; both use a magnificent country estate as a focal point, and end with night scenes in which a man and a woman move toward each other across a timeless, otherworldly landscape. In both Mrs. Woolf employs bits of parody and doggerel language, and adapts her familiar style to new techniques, with less emphasis on the watery language and single ghostly voice of her previous novels. Finally, both books present history as a kind of pageant, where the costumes change but the actors remain essentially the same.

Between the Acts, however, is occasioned by the events leading up to World War II, so that its darker moments always contain the tension of an impending brute violence. *Orlando* is in every sense a happier book, chiefly because it was prompted by a love for Vita Sackville-West and by Mrs. Woolf's longstanding interest in biographical literature. Indeed, to appreciate

Orlando fully, to understand a few of the motives behind its
technical peculiarities, one needs to know something of its background. One should recognize, for example, that it refers back
to Leslie Stephen's *Dictionary of National Biography,* that it is
contemporary with Lytton Strachey's anti-Victorian life studies
and his quasi-fictional *Elizabeth and Essex,* and that it looks
forward to Virginia Woolf's own attempt at biography in
Roger Fry. In addition, there are two less widely-known
Bloomsbury biographies which have a more direct bearing on
what Mrs. Woolf called her "writer's holiday": Harold Nicholson's *Some People,* and his wife Vita Sackville-West's *Knole
and the Sackvilles.* To read these books, together with Mrs.
Woolf's writings on biography, is to see that *Orlando* is not just
"about" her friends; it is, in part, both a response to their work
and a commentary on the relationship between "fact" and
imagination.

The only critic who has written at length about the "biographical" subject of *Orlando* is Leon Edel. In his Alexander
Lectures, published as *Literary Biography,* Professor Edel offers a long digression on what he calls Virginia Woolf's "fable
for biographers":

> The idea for the work appears to have been given to Vir-
> ginia Woolf by Lytton Strachey. One day at lunch, he told
> her . . . "You should take something wilder and more fan-
> tastic, a framework that admits of anything, like *Tristram
> Shandy.*" This fictional biography thus stems from a pre-
> eminent figure in modern biography. The acknowledgement
> . . . carries not only Strachey's name, but also that of an-
> other biographer, Harold Nicholson . . . who was to write
> a little volume on biography published by Leonard and Vir-
> ginia Woolf at the Hogarth Press. The plot thickens consid-
> erably when we note that Sir Harold Nicholson's wife is
> none other than Vita Sackville-West. And if we remind our-

selves that Virginia Woolf's father, Sir Leslie Steven, was the editor of the *Dictionary of National Biography,* we have a vision of Orlando in the cradle, grandfathered and uncled by a group of biographers.[2]

Edel might have added that Orlando also has an "aunt," since Vita Sackville-West was herself a talented biographer, and since *Knole and the Sackvilles* is Virginia Woolf's primary source for historical detail. Moreover, while Lytton Strachey may have planted the seeds that matured into Mrs. Woolf's book, her immediate inspiration was apparently Harold Nicholson's series of character sketches, *Some People.* The Elizabethan adventures in *Orlando* and even the use of illustrations in the early Hogarth editions probably owe something to Strachey's *Elizabeth and Essex,* but it is difficult to say just how much; both books were published in 1928, though Strachey had begun work in 1925, two years before *Orlando* was conceived. It was in October, 1927, that the specific idea for *Orlando* came to Mrs. Woolf. On Wednesday, October 5, she wrote in her *Diary*: "having done my last article for the *Tribune* . . . instantly the usual exciting devices enter my mind: a biography beginning in the year 1500 and continuing to the present day, called *Orlando*: Vita, only with a change about from one sex to another." [3] The "last article" she mentions was an essay-review of *Some People,* which appeared in the *New York Herald Tribune* on October 30, under the title "The New Biography." Just as the feminist didactics of *Orlando* can be connected with *A Room of One's Own* (1928), so the comic, hyperbolic style and the biographical satire can be demonstrated to follow from what Virginia Woolf had just written about Nicholson. But while the relationship between *Orlando* and *A Room of One's Own*

2. Leon Edel, *Literary Biography* (London: Rupert Hart-Davis, 1957), pp. 93–94.
3. Woolf, *A Writer's Diary,* p. 116.

has often been noted,[4] the essay on Nicholson and the similar but later discussion of Strachey, entitled "The Art of Biography," need more emphasis.

Virginia Woolf's review of *Some People* opens with an analogy which would ultimately produce the title *Granite and Rainbow* for one of her collections of essays: "if we think of truth as something of granite-like solidity and of personality as something of rainbow-like intangibility and reflect that the aim of biography is to weld these two into one seamless whole, we shall admit that the problem is a stiff one and that we need not wonder if biographers have for the most part failed to solve it."[5] In this sentence, Mrs. Woolf outlines the thesis that would preoccupy her in *Orlando* and in her subsequent essay on Strachey. Indeed, the dichotomy she presents here between biographical truth and human personality, between granite and rainbow, is akin to other antithetical structures at the heart of her writings—surface and depths, masculine and feminine, day and night, fact and imagination—and it cannot be underemphasized. The first term of each pair of contrasts always refers to something solid, distinct, mundane, and perishable; the second points to something disembodied, misty, visionary, and nearly eternal. The one is represented by Mr. Bennett, the other by Mrs. Brown. This kind of opposition is touched upon when Rachel Vinrace contemplates the difference between her inner life and the everyday world where "things went round and round quite satisfactorily to other people," or when the speaker in "The Mark on the Wall" contrasts the sea-green depths of consciousness with the Table of Precedency, or even when Mrs.

4. On the relation between *Orlando* and *A Room of One's Own*, see Dorothy Brewster, *Virginia Woolf* (New York: New York University Press, 1962), pp. 19–20; Winifred Holtby, *Virginia Woolf* (London: Wishart and Company, 1932), pp. 161–85; Aileen Pippett, *The Moth and the Star: A Biography of Virginia Woolf* (Boston: Little, Brown, 1953), p. 273.

5. Woolf, "The New Biography," *Collected Essays*, 4:229.

Ramsay reads poetry while Mr. Ramsay enjoys Walter Scott. In the context of the essay on Harold Nicholson, the familiar antithesis is posed as a problem for biographers: the biographer serves the world of factual truth, but his aim, in the words of Sidney Lee, is the "'transmission of personality.'" [6] Is it ever possible, Mrs. Woolf asks, to bring these conflicting notions together?

Some of her most intimate friends were trying to solve the problem by combining the roles of biographer and creative artist; in her essays on biography she applauded their efforts, even though she obviously did not believe they had succeeded. At least, she wrote, they had improved on the Victorian authors of what she calls the "old" biography. Both her review of *Some People* and her essay on Lytton Strachey make essentially the same points about the Victorians: nineteenth-century biographers distorted the personalities of their subjects because they were ploddingly factual and "dominated by the idea of goodness." [7] J. A. Froude's biography of Carlyle had helped alter the current fashion for ignoring the subject's sex life and permitting him "only a smooth superficial likeness to the body in the coffin";[8] and Edmund Gosse had dared to show that even his father had imperfections. But in Mrs. Woolf's eyes the first true revolutionary was Strachey, who was basically irreverent and possessed of "gifts analogous to the poet's," even if he did not have the poet's "inventive power." [9] Nevertheless, Mrs. Woolf argues that Strachey was successful only in *Queen Victoria*. *Eminent Victorians* she calls a set of "caricatures," whereas *Elizabeth and Essex,* one of Strachey's most ambitious works, she thinks went too far in flouting the limitations of biography. Victoria's life had been scrupulously authenticated,

6. Ibid., p. 229.
7. Ibid., p. 231.
8. Woolf, "The Art of Biography," *Collected Essays,* 4:222.
9. Ibid., p. 223.

but Strachey indulged himself in fictions about Elizabeth, who inhabited a strange and relatively obscure age. Thus, Mrs. Woolf says, Strachey's Elizabeth "moves in an ambiguous world, between fact and fiction, neither embodied nor disembodied." [10] Strachey had not achieved a synthesis of rainbow and granite, had not managed the fruitful exchange between the two worlds that Mrs. Woolf works for everywhere in her writings. In fact, she says, a true dialectic between those worlds is probably impossible. If the biographer "invents facts as an artist invents them—facts that no one else can verify—and tries to combine them with facts of the other sort, they destroy each other." [11]

Harold Nicholson's work revealed the same problems as Strachey's, though in certain ways it evidently struck her as more experimental and intriguing. His *Some People* is an eccentric but charming hybrid of a book, redolent of a secure English gentility more remote today than the mountains of the moon. It contains a series of character sketches based on Nicholson's experiences in the diplomatic service, and the early editions are prefaced with this brief, Puckish note: "Many of the following sketches are purely imaginary. Such truths as they may contain are only half-truths." [12] Like *Orlando, Some People* is a playful book, though not outrageously so. If it lacks high seriousness, it does convey some of the pleasures of light, sophisticated literature. Thus we meet such characters as Jeanne de Hénant, who is seen quoting Verlaine through the languid plumes of her cigarette smoke; Jeanne's mother, listening to the Alexandrine her daughter has quoted and "scratching the top of her bald brown head with a table fork," mumbles "Tu as des ideés saugrenues" (p. 97). Years later, Nicholson was to explain that Jeanne and her mother are "an exact description of a

10. Ibid., p. 225.
11. Ibid.
12. Harold Nicholson, *Some People* (New York: Oxford University Press, 1934). Unless otherwise noted, all references are to this edition.

French family in which I lived while preparing my examination for the Diplomatic Service . . . nothing fictional has been
introduced." [13] But the character of Jeanne is really no less
vivid than the essentially fictional "Miss Plimsoll," a governess
whose nose was "sharp and pointed like that of Voltaire. . . .
When the thermometer fell below 60° it turned scarlet: below
50° it assumed a blue tinge with a little white morbid circle
at the end; and at 40° it became sniffly and bore a permanent
though precarious drop below its pointed tip" (p. 11).

Virginia Woolf admired Nicholson's book even though she
recognized its essential slightness and fragility. Nevertheless,
she was troubled by the presence of characters like Miss Plimsoll, whom she suspected were fictional: "Even here," she wrote,
"where the imagination is not deeply engaged, when we find
people we know to be real, like Lord Oxford or Lady Colefax,
mingling with Miss Plimsoll . . . , whose reality we doubt,
the one casts suspicion upon the other. Let it be fact, one feels,
or let it be fiction; the imagination will not serve under two
masters simultaneously." [14] Thus, although she regarded Nicholson as an important example of the biographer as artist, who
had indicated a "possible direction," there remained for Virginia Woolf no author "whose art is subtle and bold enough
to present that queer amalgamation of dream and reality, that
perpetual marriage of granite and rainbow" which is the essence of a truthful depiction of personality.[15]

As I have said, Mrs. Woolf began *Orlando* with these issues
very much in mind. In a letter to Vita Sackville-West concerning the new book, she remarked, "it sprung upon me how I

13. Nicholson, "Author's Note" to *Some People* (London: Folio Society,
1951).

14. Woolf, "The New Biography," p. 234.

15. Ibid., pp. 234–35. Though Mrs. Woolf recognized Boswell's genius,
she regarded it as genius of an inferior kind. In "The Art of Biography,"
she wrote: "Even Dr. Johnson as created by Boswell will not live as long
as Falstaff created by Shakespeare" (p. 227).

could revolutionize biography in a night." [16] Of course she did
not even write a biography, much less revolutionize the form,
and it is difficult to say just how seriously she went about this
task. But clearly the ideas she had outlined in her essay on
Nicholson are central to *Orlando*; indeed, even the granite-
rainbow metaphor appears in one of the narrator's more significant digressions. Speaking of the difficulty of transmitting
Orlando's personality, the biographer-persona comments:

> Nature, who has played so many queer tricks upon us, mak-
> ing us so unequally of clay and diamonds, of rainbow and
> granite, and stuffed them into a case, often of the most in-
> congruous, . . . nature, who has so much to answer for be-
> sides the perhaps unwieldy length of this sentence, has fur-
> ther complicated her task and added to our confusion by
> providing . . . a perfect rag-bag of odds and ends within
> us . . . [and] has contrived that the whole assortment shall
> be lightly stitched together by a single thread. [pp. 73–74]

The narrator of *Orlando,* while trying to do his (or her) duty
as a biographer, is much troubled by all the complexities in
human personality that we typically find in Mrs. Woolf's
novels. In fact, *Orlando* is largely devoted to conflicts between
the biographer and the artist—conflicts from which the artist
always emerges victorious.

Even so, the book does have a kind of basis in biographical
fact. To see how Mrs. Woolf has adapted her historical sources,
one need only read Frank Baldanza's brief but excellent account in "*Orlando* and the Sackvilles." [17] As Baldanza shows,
Virginia Woolf drew heavily on Vita Sackville-West's *Knole
and the Sackvilles* (1922), a biography of the grand country

16. Woolf, letter to Vita Sackville-West, quoted by Pippett, *The Moth
and the Star,* p. 254.

17. Frank Baldanza, "*Orlando* and the Sackvilles," *PMLA* 70 (March,
1955):274–79.

estate which had been in possession of the Sackville family since 1566. The details used to describe Orlando's home, even down to the imagery itself, are mostly taken from Miss Sackville-West's account of Knole, although they have been freely adapted to the services of fiction. The person of Orlando is a composite of the Sackville family, merged at last into the figure of Vita Sackville-West, who, in 1927, won the Hawthornden Prize for her poem "The Land," which is quoted in *Orlando* and retitled "The Oak Tree." The early Orlando bears a superficial resemblance to Thomas Sackville, poet and author of *Gorbuduc,* who was appointed treasurer to Elizabeth and presented with Knole because, as legend has it, the Queen "wished to have him nearer to her court and councils." [18] Like Charles Sackville, the second Duke of Dorset, Orlando briefly loves a mysterious Russian lady. The gypsy girl he later takes for a wife in Constantinople is based on a real Pepita, a Spanish dancer who was Vita Sackville-West's grandmother and, like Orlando after his sex change, the subject of extensive litigation to determine the true heir of Knole.[19] Even the household servants at Orlando's estate—Mrs. Grimsditch, Mr. Dupper, Mrs. Stewkly, Nurse Carpenter, and Grace Robinson the blackamoor—can be found in *Knole and the Sackvilles*: they are listed in a catalog of the household at Knole under Richard Sackville, the seventeenth-century earl of Dorset.

But *Knole and the Sackvilles* was more than a sourcebook, and it seems to me that Baldanza's careful research does not indicate its full significance. Vita Sackville-West herself was too modest about the possible influence of her book. In 1955, she wrote that *Orlando* was inspired by Virginia Woolf's "own

18. Vita Sackville-West, *Knole and the Sackvilles* (London: Ernest Benn Limited, 1958), p. 50. Subsequent references to this edition will be cited in parentheses in the text.

19. The history of Pepita is not found in *Knole and the Sackvilles,* but in a later book by Vita Sackville-West, *Pepita* (Garden City, N.Y.: Doubleday, 1937).

strange conception of myself, my family, and Knole . . . They
satisfied her acute sense of the continuity of history." [20] The
"strange conception" was indeed Virginia Woolf's own, but it
was echoed and doubtless stimulated by what she had read in
Knole and the Sackvilles, like this passage about the garden at
the estate:

> . . . the garden, save for one small section where the paths
> curve in meaningless scollops among the rhododendrons, re-
> mains today very much as Anne Clifford knew it. . . . The
> white rose which was planted under James I's room has
> climbed until it now reaches beyond his windows on the first
> floor; the great lime has drooped its branches until they have
> layered themselves in the ground of their own accord and
> grown up again with fresh roots into three complete circles
> all sprung from the parent tree . . . the magnolia outside
> the Poet's Parlour has grown nearly to the roof, and bears its
> mass of flame-shaped blossoms like a giant candelabrum; the
> beech hedge is twenty feet high; four centuries have win-
> nowed the faultless turf. . . . The soil is rich and deep and
> old. The garden has been a garden for four hundred years.
> [p. 209]

Here was an ultracivilized representation of that nearly timeless
but often frightening natural unity Virginia Woolf tried to suggest in all her novels. In *Orlando* itself there is a whimsical reference to the oak tree which the hero has known since "Somewhere about the year 1588," and which is "still in the prime of
life" (p. 291).

Vita Sackville-West's comments on the significance of her
family history must also have struck a responsive chord in Mrs.
Woolf: "Such interest as the Sackvilles have," she wrote, "lies

20. Vita Sackville-West, "Virginia Woolf and *Orlando,*" *The Listener*
(Jan. 27, 1955), p. 157.

. . . in their being so representative. From generation to generation they might stand, fully equipped, as portraits from English history, . . . let them stand each as the prototype of his age, and at the same time as a link to carry on, not only the tradition but also the heredity of his race, and they immediately acquire a significance, a unity" (p. 41). Such a notion is a step—a large step perhaps, but only a step—from Virginia Woolf's fanciful conception of "portraits from English history" rendered through the life of a single person. Yet Miss Sackville-West continues in this vein, until a kind of sexual transformation seems implicit in what she says about her forebears. Not only were they a family of lovers and would-be poets, but the masculine side of the family had ceased to dominate by the eighteenth century. Looking at the portrait gallery in Knole, she writes:

> You have first the grave Elizabethan, with the long, rather melancholy face, emerging from the oval frame above the black clothes and the white wand of office . . . You come down to his grandson: he is the Cavalier by Vandyck . . . hand on hip, his flame-coloured doublet slashed across by the blue of the Garter . . . You have next the florid, magnificent Charles, the fruit of the Restoration, poet, and patron of poets, prodigal, jovial, and licentious . . . in his Garter robes and his enormous wig, his foot and fine calf well thrust forward . . . the crony of Rochester and Sedley, the patron and host of Pope and Dryden . . . you come down to the eighteenth century. You have on Gainsborough's canvas the beautiful, sensitive face of the gay and fickle duke . . . You have his son, too fair and pretty a boy, the friend of Byron, . . . the last direct male. [pp. 41–42]

I do not mean to suggest that the sexual theme of *Orlando* derives wholly or even chiefly from *Knole and the Sackvilles;* but a passage like this one must have provided food for Mrs. Woolf's imagination. There are no female portraits here, yet when one reads this description, it is as if a slow metamorphosis were overtaking a single representative of the Sackvilles, taking him through the ages and making him gradually more feminine in the progress.

If *Knole and the Sackvilles* supplied Virginia Woolf with historical detail and perhaps even suggested the themes and plot of *Orlando,* it also stood as another example of a biography to which she might respond. Like the "new" biography, *Knole and the Sackvilles* is a very personal book, characterized by what Mrs. Woolf called a "lack of pose, humbug, solemnity." [21] It is far from comic, but it talks fairly openly about the sex life of the Sackvilles, and focuses on domestic events rather than public careers. Miss Sackville-West is clearly more interested in her ancestors' poetry than in their politics, and hence her book is different from Victorian biography, where, as Virginia Woolf wrote, chapter headings such as "life at college, marriage, career" make "arbitrary and artificial distinctions." Like the new biography as Mrs. Woolf later described it, *Knole and the Sackvilles* is a small volume in which "the author's relation to his subject is different. He is no longer the serious and sympathetic companion, toiling . . . slavishly in the footsteps of his hero. Whether friend or enemy . . . he is an equal." [22]

But Vita Sackville-West's personal, sometimes even poetic little book about her family home is filled nearly to the brim with odd facts. One of the fascinations of *Knole and the Sackvilles* for anyone interested in English history is the large number of minor documents it quotes—letters; amateur poems; diaries; catalogs of members of the household; account-books

21. Woolf, "The New Biography," p. 232.
22. Ibid., p. 231.

with expenses dutifully entered in the margins; petitions; menus; inventories; official reports of parliament; receipts; even a sort of dictionary of thieves' slang, dated 1690, which was found scribbled on the back of an official paper. These quaint but often sober details are sometimes cited at great length, and even though Virginia Woolf had written that biographical "fact" gave "rest and refreshment" to the imaginative faculties, at least once in *Orlando* she clearly makes fun of Vita Sackville-West's charming pedantry. The source of her amusement is the fifth chapter of *Knole and the Sackvilles,* where, among sundry other documents, we find a list of "household stuff" dated July, 1624, and including "a pair of Spanish blankets, 5 curtains of crimson and white taffeta, the valance to it of white satin embroidered with crimson and white silk," "a yellow satin chair and 3 stools, suitable with their bukram covers," "a said bag, wherein are 9 cups of crimson damask laid with silver parchment lace," "2 brass branches for a dozen lights apiece," "6 pairs of mats to mat chambers with at 30 yards apiece," "2 walnut tree tables," and "a box containing 3 dozen of venice glasses." The list goes on for about two pages, after which Miss Sackville-West apologizes, "I fear lest the detailing of these old papers should grow wearisome" (pp. 100–02). In *Orlando* this passage is openly mocked; when the hero takes an interest in refurbishing his estate, Mrs. Woolf's biographer-persona attempts to verify the truth of his report by quoting a document:

He now set to work in earnest, as we can prove beyond a doubt if we look at his ledgers. Let us glance at an inventory of what he bought at this time, with the expenses totted up in the margin—but these we omit.

"To fifty pairs of Spanish blankets, ditto curtains of crimson and white taffeta; the valence to them of white satin embroidered with crimson and white silk. . . .

"To seventy yellow satin chairs and sixty stools suitable with
their buckram covers to them all. . . .

"To sixty seven walnut tree tables. . . .

"To seventeen dozen boxes containing each dozen five dozen
of Venice glasses. . . .

"To one hundred and two mats, each thirty yards long. . . .

"To ninety seven cushions of crimson damask laid with silver
parchment lace and footstools of cloth of tissue and chairs
suitable. . . .

"To fifty branches for a dozen lights apiece. . . ."

Already—it is an effect lists have upon us—we are beginning to yawn. [p. 101]

A passage like this one leads quite naturally to the issue of
parody in *Orlando*. Only with respect to this list can *Orlando*
be considered a parody of *Knole and the Sackvilles*. In fact it
is a parody at all only in a very limited sense.[23] The prose style
undergoes some changes, but the book has relatively little in
common with Joyce's "Oxen of the Sun." At most, one can
point to the mock preface and index, which mimic the form of
scholarly biography, and a few passages which allude to other
writings without really trying to imitate them. Here, for exam-

23. Harvena Richter, in *The Inward Voyage,* says that "Each chapter
of the novel contains parodies of literary genres or specific works belonging
to the period with which the chapter deals" (p. 155n). It is true that
Orlando contains scraps of poetry and references to drama and the novel—
the protagonist, after all, has been interested in literature for nearly four
hundred years. But I believe Harvena Richter uses the term "parody" too
loosely. She says that Marvell's "Upon Appleton House" forms the "parody-
pattern" for the opening chapters of *Orlando,* but I can see no evidence
for such a large claim. Likewise, she says Thomas Browne is being parodied
in chapter 2, but I can find only a few gently ironic references to Orlando's
love of melancholy and his reading of Browne (pp. 67–68). *Orlando* can
be read as a sort of history of English literature, but the prose style everywhere is recognizably Virginia Woolf's own.

ple, is a probable reference to *Lady Chatterley's Lover,* which was distributed privately in England in 1928:

> Surely, since she is a woman, and a beautiful woman, . . . she will soon give over this pretense of writing and thinking and begin at least to think of a gamekeeper . . . And then she will write him a little note . . . and make an assignation for Sunday dusk . . . all of which is, of course, the very stuff of life and the only possible subject for fiction. . . . love—as the male novelists define it—and who, after all, speak with greater authority?—has nothing whatever to do with kindness, fidelity, generosity, or poetry. Love is slipping off one's petticoat and—But we all know what love is. [p. 242]

And here Mrs. Woolf makes fun of her own writing in a reference to the novel she had just published:

> He saw the beech trees turn golden and the young ferns unfurl; he saw the moon sickle and then circular; he saw— but probably the reader can imagine the passage which should follow and how every tree and plant in the neighborhood is described first green, then golden; how moons rise and suns set; how night succeeds day and day night; how things remain much as they are for two or three hundred years or so, except for a little dust and a few cobwebs which one old woman can sweep up in half an hour; a conclusion which, one cannot help feeling, might have been reached more quickly by the simple statement that "Time passed" (here the exact amount could be indicated in brackets) and nothing whatever happened. [p. 91]

And yet, while mocking references do not make a parody, *Orlando* did serve to liberate Mrs. Woolf's prose; the author seems conscious throughout of the comic potential in her inherently ornate language. At one extreme, the style has a lively but slightly archaic quality, almost like an imitation of an eighteenth-century comic novel: "many a time did Orlando, pacing the little courtyard, hold his heart at the sound of some nag's steady footfall on the cobbles" (p. 55); "Seizing the pen with which his little boy was tickling the cat's ears, and dipping it into the egg-cup which served for inkpot, Greene dashed off a very spirited satire there and then" (p. 88). At the other extreme—what might be called the extreme of modernity—are two curious passages in the last chapter, where the narrator drifts into a sort of nonsense-language full of doggerel. It is as if the speaker were out on the edge of a mysterious terrain, talking aloud just to save the book from extinction. The first passage occurs when Orlando sits down to write and the biographer finds that there is nothing to say:

> Let us go, then, exploring, this summer morning, when all are adoring the plum blossom and the bee. And humming and hawing, let us ask the starling (who is a more sociable bird than the lark) what he may think on the brink of the dust-bin, whence he picks among the sticks combings of scullion's hair. What's life, we ask, leaning on the farmyard gate; Life, Life, Life! cries the bird, as if he had heard.
> [p. 243]

The second passage precedes the birth of Orlando's child. Here is a portion of it:

> Oh yes, it is Kew! Well, Kew will do. So here we are then at Kew, and I will show you to-day (the second of March) under the plum tree, a grape hyacinth, and a crocus, and a bud, too, on the almond tree; so that to walk there is to be thinking of bulbs, hairy and red, thrust into the earth in October, flowering now; and to be dreaming of more than can rightly be said, and to be taking from its case a cigarette or cigar even, and to be flinging a cloak under (as the rhyme

requires) an oak, and there to sit, waiting the kingfisher.
[p. 264]

Mrs. Woolf seemed fond of this new style. She wrote in her *Diary*, "I feel more and more sure that I will never write a novel again. Little bits of rhyme come in" (p. 122). And though of course she did continue to write novels, her interest in the strange new manner stayed with her; consider, for example, the oddly trivialized language she used later in *Between the Acts*. Significantly, the doggerel passages in *Orlando* occur when the biographer is faced with the problem of describing poetic and sexual creativity. In both cases he makes some attempt to represent mysterious powers which seem beyond his power or will to invoke directly; we have, for example, the bird's cry of "Life," and the highly sexual "bulbs, hairy and red, thrust into the earth." Perhaps in the largest sense, the narrator's babble signifies the inadequacy not only of biography, which cannot explore the most intimate and important parts of the subject's life, but also of language itself. There are suggestions of this idea elsewhere in Mrs. Woolf's fiction, particularly when her characters undergo a "dissolution." In *Orlando* there are similar moments, when the hero-heroine is described asleep, in a state of sexual rapture, or sunk in intense imaginative concentration. Toward the end of the book, these moments are described in a language that is almost as disembodied as Orlando herself, as if the biographer had come to the end of the tether. At one point Orlando seems to comment on the significance of the phenomenon: " 'And if I were dead,' " she exclaims upon rising from the poem she has been composing, " 'it would be just the same!' "

The typical writer of "old" biography, as described in Mrs. Woolf's essays, might echo Orlando's sentiments, though for different reasons: in his view, so long as the heroine is writing a poem instead of fighting a war or running for office, she might as well be a corpse. But the biographer of *Orlando* is not typical, though he sometimes claims to be. Even when he sounds most pompous or naive, one cannot be sure that he is unaware of his own ironies. At first he welcomes the opportunity to write about an aristocratic man of action: "Happy the mother who bears, happier still the biographer who records the life of such a one! Never need she vex herself, nor he invoke the help of novelist or poet. From deed to deed, from glory to glory, from office to office he must go, his scribe following after, till they reach whatever seat it may be that is the height of their desire" (pp. 16–17). In the next breath, however, the narrator confesses that Orlando is hardly the subject for a pedant's vicarious fantasies; Orlando wants to go to war, but he also has a poetic and feminine side: "Directly we glance at eyes and forehead, we have to admit a thousand disagreeables which it is the aim of every good biographer to ignore" (p. 17). The narrator of *Orlando* is certainly not a "good" biographer, and by the time we reach the end of the book, he has committed all sorts of heresies against scientific objectivity. Toward the end he remarks, "The true length of a person's life, whatever the *Dictionary of National Biography* may say, is always a matter of dispute. For it is a difficult business—this time-keeping; nothing more quickly disorders it than contact with any of the arts" (p. 275).

Orlando's biographer is probably best described as a mask, a pose which Mrs. Woolf can assume or drop at will. Thus chapter 2 opens with an ironic apology for the biographer's "difficulty": "Up to this point . . . documents, both private and historical, have made it possible to fulfill the first duty of a biographer, which is to plod, without looking to right or left, in the indelible footprints of truth . . . on and on methodically till we fall plump into the grave and write *finis* on the tombstone above our heads" (p. 62). But the previous chapter has not been concerned with "documents," and the biographer, there as elsewhere, seems more inclined to poetry than to history. For example, when Orlando drops off to sleep in the first chapter, overtaken by one of those hypnotic moods Mrs. Woolf depicts so often, we are told that "his limbs grew heavy on the ground; . . . by degrees the deer stepped nearer and the rooks wheeled round him and the swallows dipped and circled and the dragon flies shot past, as if all the fertility and amorous activity of a summer's evening were woven web-like about his body" (p. 21). Later in the chapter, the brilliantly hyperbolic description of the Great Frost is supposedly based on the evidence of "historians." But these historians are very different from ours; they tell us that "Birds froze in mid-air and fell like stones to the ground," and that in Norwitch, "a young country woman started to cross the road . . . and was seen by the onlookers to turn visibly to powder and be blown in a puff of dust over the roofs" (p. 33).

The official evidence of biographers, historians, and eye-witnesses is consistently mocked. In chapter 3, when Orlando is given a dukedom and the ambassadorship to Constantinople, where he "had a finger in some of the most delicate negotiations between King Charles and the Turks," we are, or should be, on the familiar public ground of the "old" biography. And yet, while the author previously related the details of Orlando's amours and the most intimate of his thoughts, at this stage in the hero's life "we have the least information to go upon." It seems that all the important documents relating to Orlando's career have been destroyed. "Often the paper was scorched a deep brown in the middle of the most important sentence." Obviously, the comparative dullness of public lives is being satirized here, but the author is perhaps making another point as well. In her essay on Strachey, Virginia Woolf had commented on the perishable quality of biography: "Micawber and Miss Bates" she wrote, "will survive Lockhart's Sir Walter Scott and Lytton Strachey's Queen Victoria. For they are made of more enduring matter. The artist's imagination at its most intense fires out what is perishable in fact; but the biographer must accept the perishable, build with it, imbed it in the very fabric of his work. Much will perish; little will live." [24] Hence rainbow turns out to be more durable than granite, just as, in a more famous antithesis, Mrs. Ramsay's spirit is more nearly eternal than Mr. Ramsay's reputation can ever be.

The biographer of *Orlando* occasionally tries to do justice to the facts, but maintains the pose only briefly. Likewise, he cannot be a servant of Victorian morality; Orlando's sex-change is reported in spite of the blandishments of Purity, Chastity, and Modesty. Even some of the more lively didactic passages are treated half-jokingly: "these moralities belong, and should be left to the historian, since they are as dull as ditch-water" (p. 137). Although there are occasions when Virginia Woolf's own literary mannerisms are made the butt of the narrator's jokes (pp. 64–65, for example), the interests of the would-be biographer are usually no different from Mrs. Woolf's typical concerns. For example, consider the book's fascination with the workings of consciousness. " 'What a phantasmagoria the mind is and meeting-place of dissemblables!' " Orlando declares to herself (pp. 160–61). The narrator has already confirmed this point by noting the "disorderly and circuitous way" the mind works and by describing in great detail the relations between sensations and ideas (pp. 93–94). When Orlando's attempts at composition are frustrated by images of his "lost Princess," we are given a long digression on the workings of memory (pp. 73–75). Later (pp. 90–92) there is an almost equally long discussion of the effects of duration, where we are told that "An hour, once it lodges in the queer element of the human spirit, may be stretched to fifty or a hundred times its clock length." But after noting that the disparity between clock

24. Woolf, "The Art of Biography," p. 227.

time and mental time "deserves further study," the narrator feels he must hurry on: "the biographer, whose interests are . . . highly restricted, must confine himself to one simple statement: when a man has reached the age of thirty, as Orlando now had, time when he is thinking becomes inordinately long" (pp. 91–92).

Toward the end of the book, in a passage where the biographer's mask is securely in place, the narrator speaks contemptuously of mere thought. But Virginia Woolf's irony could not be more transparent:

> Life, it has been agreed by everyone whose opinion is worth considering, is the only fit subject for novelist or biographer; life, the same authorities have decided, has nothing whatever to do with sitting still in a chair and thinking. Thought and life are as the poles asunder. . . . If only subjects, we might complain (for our patience is wearing thin), had more consideration for their biographers! What is more irritating than to see one's subject, on whom one has lavished so much time and trouble, slipping out of one's grasp altogether and indulging—witness her sighs and gasps, her flushing, her palings—what is more humiliating than to see all this dumb show of emotion and excitement gone through before our eyes when we know that what causes it—thought and imagination—are of no importance whatsoever. [pp. 240–41]

Virginia Woolf wrote *Orlando,* of course, partly to demonstrate the importance of thought and imagination. The biographer-persona, in spite of his disclaimers, does not ignore the imaginative or sexual life, nor even those oddly disembodied moments that are so much a part of Mrs. Woolf's novels; and for these reasons the book is neither a consistent parody of official Victorian biography nor a simple satire. The narrator may claim to have the instincts of a biographer, but he begins the book like a novel, in the midst of an action, and his attention is always focused on Orlando's private selves. Obviously, the book is meant to poke fun at the "old" biography in a good many ways. I have already mentioned the use of comic paraphernalia like the mock preface and index, the occasional pretended distrust of imagination, and the abortive attempts at pedantry; more important, instead of a chaste history of the public life of an English peer, the narrator unfolds the imaginative and sexual life of a sensitive youth who is miraculously transformed into a woman overnight. If, in spite of the narrator's fascination with personality, Orlando never seems as fully-developed as Miss Plimsoll or Queen Victoria, that is partly because Mrs. Woolf's characters always tend to merge with the narrator and become slightly disembodied, and partly because her book is a critique of all biography, both old and new. Perhaps at some point she really intended to make *Orlando* a model for the "new" biography. But from the start the book was controlled by a playful fantasy, and the result is reminiscent of any of Mrs. Woolf's novels: an exploration into a realm where it is hard to determine whether character or novelist is speaking, where radical distinctions and discontinuities (as between the eighteenth century and the nineteenth) are more apparent than real, where granite gives way almost entirely to rainbow.

Ultimately, Virginia Woolf does little to revolutionize biography and much to break new ground for writers of imaginative literature. In a far less comprehensive and ambitious sense, *Orlando* describes some of the same phenomena as *Finnegans Wake;* it accounts for vast periods of history through the experience of a single person who, we are told, has "a great variety of selves to call upon" (p. 278), and it openly declares that "the most successful practitioners of the art of life, often unknown people by the way, somehow contrive to synchronize the sixty or seventy different times which beat simultaneously in every normal human system" (p. 274).

In her essays, Virginia Woolf acknowledged the importance

of the biographer and showed her deep interest in his craft. But she placed him always after the artist, since in her mind "fact" was always inferior to imagination. To the question her contemporaries and friends were asking—whether biographical and imaginative truths could be combined, whether granite could be fused with rainbow—her answer was always a regretful negative. *Orlando* is another of these negative replies, since at every turn it is meant to show us the futility of biographical fact and the necessity for art in the depiction of personality.

A similar pattern lies, I think, behind the sexual theme of *Orlando,* about which I have said rather little because it has been treated so extensively elsewhere.[25] The book is often described as "androgynous," chiefly on the strength of Mrs. Woolf's plea for an "androgynous mind" in *A Room of One's Own.* Certainly Orlando is, from the moment we first see him, a sexually ambiguous figure; and certainly the author is concerned to show that the "masculine" and "feminine" temperaments are and should be mixed in every person. But could anyone argue that the mind that produced *Orlando* is truly androgynous, whatever its intentions? If Mrs. Woolf regarded Shakespeare as an androgynous mind and found "a little too much of a woman" in Proust,[26] what must we say of her work? *Orlando* pays tribute to the active, outgoing character, but ultimately it celebrates an introspective, poetic sensibility. Here, as in *A Room of One's Own,* Virginia Woolf's argument rests on the assumption that there are two inherently different worlds, masculine and feminine. She believed that these worlds ought to coexist; she fought discrimination against women, and she quite wisely observed that they would need money to write

25. The most detailed treatment is in Herbert Marder's *Feminism and Art* (Chicago: University of Chicago Press, 1968), pp. 110–16.

26. Virginia Woolf, *A Room of One's Own* (London: Hogarth Press, 1967), p. 156. Mrs. Woolf adds, "but that failing is too rare for one to complain of it."

books. But at the same time she was attracted to the passive, dreamy experiences which she repeatedly associated with femininity. Sometimes she was able to range back and forth between the two worlds of rainbow and granite (as in writing her biography of Roger Fry), but one of her major weaknesses is that she was never quite able to synthesize them. In the last analysis, she prefers one order of experience over the other.

9

The "Orts and Fragments" in *Between the Acts*

Between the Acts is, technically at least, an unfinished work, since Virginia Woolf never made whatever final revisions she might have considered necessary—the novel was published post-humously. Until recently it has received comparatively little attention, and it has never enjoyed the comfortable niche in undergraduate literature courses sometimes accorded *Mrs. Dalloway* and *To the Lighthouse*.[1] Probably Mrs. Woolf would be disappointed by its reputation. In November 23, 1940, the day she finished the manuscript, she wrote in her *Diary*, "I am

---

1. The book has had some distinguished advocates. Northrup Frye, for example, calls it Virginia Woolf's "most profound" work (*Anatomy of Criticism* [New York: Atheneum, 1967], p. 67). See also Warren Beck's "For Virginia Woolf," *Forms of Modern Fiction*, ed. William Van O'Connor (Minneapolis: University of Minnesota Press, 1948), pp. 243–53; and Allen, *The English Novel*, p. 338. Two recent discussions of the novel's themes are useful: Ann Yanko Wilkinson, "A Principle of Unity in *Between the Acts*," *Criticism* 8 (Winter 1966):53–63; and Renee Watkins, "Survival in Discontinuity—Virginia Woolf's *Between the Acts*," *Massachusetts Review* 10 (Spring 1969):356–76.

a little triumphant about the book. I think it's an interesting attempt at a new method." [2]

But the "new method," when it has been discussed at all, has usually been looked on with disfavor. Thus Dr. Leavis has written that Mrs. Woolf's "mannerisms" are characterized by an "extraordinary vacancy and pointlessness," and Melvin Friedman has described the book as a "stream of consciousness novel" that fails because it does not adopt "the system itself." [3] *Between the Acts,* however, is not an impressionistic hodge-podge, and it should not be attacked for failing to conform to a rather amorphous genre. It is, in fact, a successful experiment which contains some of Mrs. Woolf's best writing.

The criticisms that have been applied to *Between the Acts* may grow out of the book's somewhat disjointed quality, which is characteristic of modernist classics like *The Waste Land* and *Ulysses* but not of Mrs. Woolf's other novels. There are no chapters, but the text is divided into what might be called "scenes" of various lengths, separated from one another by blank spaces. Those idiosyncratic and artful transitions that one finds everywhere in *Mrs. Dalloway, To the Lighthouse,* and *The Waves* are conspicuously absent in this novel. *Mrs. Dalloway* also lacks chapters and has blank spaces to mark some transitions, but the spaces serve only to break up an otherwise unceasing flow of words; and an image or idea that precedes a space is nearly always repeated at the beginning of the next scene to maintain the rhythm and help us bridge the gap. In *Between the Acts* the rhythm is not continuous; we have only fragments of action and character, little vignettes strung together, calling to mind the "orts and fragments" of which (we are told) life seems to be composed. Though the order of

2. Woolf, *A Writer's Diary,* p. 331.

3. F. R. Leavis, "After *To the Lighthouse,*" *Scrutiny* 10 (January 1942):295–97; Friedman, *Stream of Consciousness: A Study in Literary Method,* p. 208.

these passages is probably not arbitrary, and though they are held together loosely by the time sequence, one could rearrange several of the scenes without any noticeable change in the effect.

Let us consider a relatively innocuous example of such a scene. It occurs early in the book, and begins with this paragraph:

> The nurses after breakfast were trundling the perambulator up and down the terrace; and as they trundled they were talking—not shaping pellets of information or handing ideas from one to another, but rolling words, like sweets on their tongues; which, as they thinned to transparency, gave off pink, green, and sweetness. This morning that sweetness was: "How cook had told 'im off about the asparagus; how when she rang I said: how it was a sweet costume with blouse to match"; and that was leading to something about a feller as they walked up and down the terrace rolling sweets, trundling the perambulator.[4]

The paragraph is in many ways typical of Mrs. Woolf. It illustrates her almost hypnotic rhythms, a certain air of grace and cultivation, and a distance from the nurses that is suited to an English lady of the upper middle class. It also reflects her love of fragile, pretty, feminine images: "They thinned to transparency, gave off pink, green, and sweetness." Furthermore, one is struck by the paragraph's artfully symmetrical structure. It is made up of two compound-complex sentences of almost exactly equal length, so that the first period divides the paragraph neatly in half. Two phrases from the first sentence, "trundling the perambulator" and "rolling words, like sweets on their tongues," are picked up and repeated in the last sentence, with only a slight variation, as if they were part of a

4. Virginia Woolf, *Between the Acts* (London: Hogarth Press, 1969), p. 15. Unless otherwise noted, all references are to this edition.

refrain which served to round off the picture neatly: "rolling sweets, trundling the perambulator." This affection for repeated phrases and symmetry has been, in previous novels, a pronounced characteristic of Mrs. Woolf's style.

What is interesting about the paragraph is not, however, its virtuosity or neatness, but rather that the effect of neatness has been accomplished in spite of a scene based largely on tenuous and fragmentary elements. The nurses have no particular destination in mind as they trundle, and we are allowed to hear only trivial snatches of their conversation; phrases, as usual in Mrs. Woolf's novels, have become detached from their immediate contexts, so that we catch only vague and poetic fragments; they are pieces, "sweets," which seem to be blown to us on the wind. What gives this scene its wholeness, what connects all the fragments, is the rhythm, which the artist (in a manner reminiscent of La Trobe and her gramophone) renders through a little prose-poem.

The paragraph stands at the opening of a scene about two pages long, a scene containing almost all of the mannerisms that are typical of Mrs. Woolf's style. In the paragraph which follows, for example, the narrator presents a descriptive commentary on the grounds around Pointz Hall. It is characterized by the peculiar voice that dominates texts as diverse as *The Voyage Out* and *To the Lighthouse,* where the author becomes at times a ghostly observer, speaking almost as if she were one of her characters: "It was a pity that the man who had built Pointz Hall had pitched the house in a hollow . . . The terrace was broad enough to take the entire shadow of one of the great trees laid flat. There you could walk up and down, under the shade of the trees." The reader is almost hypnotized by the view, until the narrator breaks the spell by turning again to the nurses, who are calling out to the child George. Suddenly, without any apparent transition, we assume George's sensibility as he grubs among the flower-beds. The hypersensitive imagery here is reminiscent of the opening of *The Waves*. Indeed a "monster" appears, in the form of old Oliver, coming out from behind a bush with a newspaper wrapped round his nose. Lyricism gives way to terror and then comedy as Mrs. Woolf shifts the reader's perspective. Faced with Oliver and his big Afghan, Sohrab, the child bursts into tears. Oliver, in some ways reminiscent of Mr. Ramsay, walks away muttering to himself, " 'A cry-baby—a cry-baby.' " As he tries to read his newspaper we see into his mind:

> He tried to find his line in the column, "A cry-baby—a cry-baby." But the breeze blew the great sheet out; and over the edge he surveyed the landscape—flowing fields, heath and woods. Framed, they became a picture. Had he been a painter, he would have fixed his easel here, where the country, barred by trees, looked like a picture. Then the breeze fell.
>
> "M. Daladier," he read, finding his place in the column, "has been successful in pegging down the franc . . ." [pp. 18–19]

At this ellipsis, the scene ends. There is, in fact, no other novel by Mrs. Woolf that uses the ellipsis so freely. In *Between the Acts* it appears everywhere, as if to emphasize the tenuous and fragmentary quality of life.

There is nothing exceptional about this episode; though it is a fine scene in itself, though it furthers the delineation of setting and character in minor ways, though it suggests (as do many other scenes) that war broods over the horizon, in retrospect it is not one of the most important moments in the novel. Furthermore it has no clear relationship with what follows—a blank space and a shift to Isa, who is in her room combing her hair and contemplating her face in the mirror. One aspect of the technique used here needs emphasis, however, because there are very few examples of it in Mrs. Woolf's earlier work. I am speaking of her frequent quotations. These bits of dialogue, nearly always partially freed from their context, point to the apparent aimlessness and the disconnected quality of life; at the same time, the normal banality of everyday language is replaced by that oddly disembodied, poetic effect I have mentioned already:

> " 'How cook had told 'im off about the asparagus; how when she rang I said: how it was a sweet costume with blouse to match.' "

> " 'Come along, George.' "

> " 'Good morning, sir,' a hollow voice boomed at him from a beak of paper."

> " 'Say good morning, George; say "Good morning, Grandpa." ' "

> " 'Heel! . . . heel, you brute! . . . Heel! . . . You wild beast . . . you bad beast.' "

> " 'A cry-baby—a cry-baby.' "

> " 'M. Daladier . . . has been successful in pegging down the franc . . .' " [pp. 15–19]

This peppering of fragmentary quotations throughout the scenes is perhaps the most distinctive attribute of the novel. Nearly every page is filled out with just such "orts and fragments"; the one I have quoted, in fact, is a relatively mild example of the sort of mixture found everywhere—lines of poetry, orders to the grocer, comments on the weather, quotes from newspapers, etc. The effect is distinctly analogous to that " 'stream of broken dreams, nursery rhymes, street cries, half-finished sentences and sights' " that Bernard describes in *The Waves*. Here, however, the stream is not simply talked about but rendered—it is plain that it exists neither in an individual consciousness nor in any objective situation: it is made of the whole context of a given scene, and developed into a kind of harmony by the author. Perhaps here, for the first time, Virginia Woolf was able to make her technique evoke the sense of unity that concerned her all along—without the correlated sense of retreat from being and doing, of immersion in water with only muffled sounds audible from above. *Between the Acts,* does not sacrifice the "outside" world, either to the narrative voice or to the sensibilities of the characters. Objective events are shown to have the same texture as internal monologues, so that everything, inside and out, in this person and that, combines to make what Mrs. Ramsay called a "single stream."

We might consider how this technique works at another place in the novel—the conversation between Isa, Mrs. Swithin, and Oliver, on pp. 22–40. Actually these pages contain two scenes, since the conversation in the library is briefly interrupted with a shift to the villagers working in the barn; for my purpose, however, I will treat only the scene in the library. It opens with Old Oliver alone, drowsing in an armchair, dreaming of youth and India:

> The dream hand clenched; the real hand lay on the chair arm, the veins swollen but only with a brownish fluid now.
> The door opened.
> "Am I," Isa apologized, "interrupting?" [p. 24]

This technique, this moment, is again characteristic of Virginia Woolf: the author steps back from the character whose dream she has described to view him from the outside, like a ghostly but unprivileged observer; then, as quietness descends, and just as the dreamer seems to be on the verge of extinction, there is a sudden intrusion. The scene goes on with Oliver contemplating his daughter-in-law.

> Many old men had only their India—old men in clubs, old men in rooms off Jermyn Street. She in her striped dress con-

tinued him, murmuring, in front of the book cases: "The moor is dark beneath the moon, rapid clouds have drunk the last pale beams of even. . . . I have ordered the fish," she said aloud, turning, "though whether it'll be fresh or not I can't promise. But veal is dear, and everybody in the house is sick of beef and mutton. . . . Sohrab," she said, coming to a standstill in front of them. "What's *he* been doing?" [pp. 24–25]

Oliver's meditation, as described in this passage, has an ordered quality, but Isa's remarks are as disordered and fragmentary as any internal monologue. Oliver observes that Isa's son is a crybaby. Isa only turns to the bookshelves and says, " 'The library's always the nicest room in the house.' " Now she picks up the *Times* and reads an item about the rape of a girl—the shock is compounded because the item intrudes on her meditations about *The Faerie Queene,* Keats, the *Kreutzer Sonata,* and the relics of English civilization that the library holds. Mrs. Swithin comes in with a hammer and nails, and more casual remarks on the weather follow, interwoven with Isa's thoughts and a paragraph by the narrator, who seems to look up at the sky with her characters: "There was a fecklessness, a lack of symmetry and order in the clouds, as they thinned and thickened. Was it their own law, or no law, they obeyed?"

The clouds, however, are no more "feckless" than the apparently random play of conversation in the library. " 'It'll rain, I'm afraid,' " Mrs. Swithin says. " 'We can only pray.' " Oliver sniffs, " 'And provide umbrellas.' " Seeing the nurses out the window, and wanting to avoid another quarrel over religion, Mrs. Swithin abruptly starts talking about Isa's children:

"Oh there they are—the darlings!"
The perambulator was passing across the lawn.
Isa looked too. What an angel she was—the old woman!
Thus to salute the children; to beat up against those immensi-

ties and the old man's irreverences her skinny hands, her laughing eyes! How courageous to defy Bart and the weather!

"He looks blooming," said Mrs. Swithin.

"It's astonishing how they pick up," said Isa.

"He ate his breakfast?" Mrs. Swithin asked.

"Every scrap," said Isa.

"And baby? No sign of measles?"

Isa shook her head. "Touch wood," she added, tapping the table. [pp. 31–32]

The expression "Touch wood" makes Mrs. Swithin curious: "What's the origin—the origin—of that?" " 'Superstition,' " says Oliver, still brooding over how Lucy Swithin's skull could hold a "prayable being." He looks under "Superstition" in the encyclopedia, while Lucy flushes and begins talking about the fish with Isa—would they be fresh? This topic leads to thoughts and observations about the sea:

"Once there was no sea," says Mrs. Swithin. "No sea at all between us and the continent. I was reading that in a book this morning. There were rhododendrons in the Strand; and mammoths in Piccadilly."

"When we were savages," said Isa.

Then she remembered; her dentist had told her that savages could perform very skillful operations on the brain. Savages had false teeth, he said. False teeth were invented, she thought he said, in the time of the Pharaohs.

"At least so my dentist told me," she concluded.

"Which man d'you go to now?" Mrs. Swithin asked her.

"The same old couple; Batty and Bates in Sloane Street."

"And Mr. Batty told you they had false teeth in the time of the Pharaohs?" Mrs. Swithin pondered.

"Batty? Oh not Batty. Bates," Isa corrected her.

Batty, she recalled, only talked about Royalty. Batty, she

told Mrs. Swithin, had a patient a Princess.

"So he kept me waiting well over an hour. And you know, when one's a child, how long that seems."

"Marriages with cousins," said Mrs. Swithin, "can't be good for the teeth." [pp. 38–39]

Mrs. Woolf has been accused of being humorless; certainly there are critics, Dr. Leavis among them, who are not amused by *Orlando*. A passage like this one, however, is full of such gentle and subtle comedy that it is hard to see how anyone could fail to enjoy it. Yet I suspect that passages like this encouraged Leavis to charge the book with "vacancy." The point to be emphasized is that the conversation in the library has become more than ever a stream directed by accident and association. Mrs. Swithin stops. " 'How did we begin this talk' she counted on her fingers. 'The Pharaohs. Dentists. Fish . . . Oh yes, you were saying, Isa, you'd ordered fish. And I said, "That's the problem . . ."' "

So the scene ends, trailing off into another ellipsis. The conversation has doubled back upon itself, as conversations have a way of doing, and is ready to start out again on another aimless course, determined by those "pellets of information" dropped casually by this person or that. Perhaps this effect is what Melvin Friedman refers to when he says that the "devices" of stream of consciousness have been applied from the "outside." [5] The form of the inner life, with all its random play of associations and images, is here shown to be the form of life itself, and the novel reveals that we inhabit neither private nor public worlds, but rather some hazy, shifting ground in between. Furthermore, beneath all the apparent triviality, important issues are being raised: Lucy Swithin's brave little defiance of the weather and her remarks on dinosaurs in Piccadilly have profound ramifications. One could list at length the tri-

5. Friedman, *Stream of Consciousness: A Study in Literary Method*, p. 208.

umphs of this scene—the fine, quiet comedy between Lucy and
Oliver; the daydreams, which seem to be spun out at a moment's notice and then abruptly shattered; the inane, easy
chatter of relatives in a library, chatter which keeps verging on
poetry. Virginia Woolf was not without her limitations as a
novelist, but in moments like this she truly was extending the
boundaries of Jane Austen's work. Few writers in English fiction can reveal so dramatically the quiet and sometimes terrible
power and beauty that lie beneath everyday domestic relationships.

Mrs. Woolf's artistry in such a scene has something in common with La Trobe's theatrical, that odd conglomeration of
doggerel, scraps of verse, and parodies of British drama. Built
upon "orts and fragments" itself, the pageant is not only an
interpretation of history but also a means by which harmony
is created. It merges people, brings the fragments together and
makes them "all one stream." That is why so many of the
descriptions of the audience are a synthesis of bits and pieces;
even when the play is over and the audience leaves there is a
sense of community:

> "And what about the Jews? The refugees . . . the Jews
> . . . People like ourselves, beginning life again . . . But
> it's always been the same. . . . My old mother, who's over
> eighty, can remember. . . ." [p. 145]

The method here is very different from that used to convey
the height of the audience's emotion, as they think about the
music in unison at the close of the play. But even here, where
the style is intended to give a sense of dispersion, the passage in-
timates a kind of harmony. Art, then, if we may take La Trobe
as a type of the artist, has an affirmative end; it bridges gaps,
holds things together, merges people, and its greatest enemy
is the awful space between acts.

Virginia Woolf's anxiety over discontinuity and fragmentation and her attempts to depict unity in the face of this anxiety are equally implicit in the title of her book. She had originally planned to call it *Pointz Hall* (to represent the continuity of history through an English country estate, as in *Orlando*), but the title she finally chose is more appropriate. From the first, Mrs. Woolf was in love with inaction, and throughout her novels she asserts the value of that "embrace" of the world which, as Bernard says, is " 'impossible to those who act.' " This novel purports to be about what happens—or exists— in the space between actions; but here there is not so much a weariness with life as an uneasy incipience, as if some great event were hovering, about to take place. Leonard Woolf describes a somewhat similar mood in his account of the months before World War II: "There was in those days an ominous and threatening unreality, a feeling that one was living in a bad dream and that one was on the point of waking up from this horrible unreality into a still more horrible reality . . . There was [an] incessant feeling of . . . impending disaster." [6] He pictures war itself as "a cosmic rail station waiting-room, with nothing to do but wait endlessly for the next catastrophe" (p. 10).

Most of the characters in the novel seem to be aware that some new act is about to begin, and that it threatens what had appeared to be the permanent round of their lives, just as a flight of military aircraft suddenly interrupts Reverend Streatfield's request for contributions to the local chapel. But this impending something—the war—is usually presented quite indirectly. Thus in the scene I have just described, Isa Oliver dreamily browses over the newspaper in the library (in the same disengaged way that Mrs. Ramsay reads poetry), and the words suddenly take on meaning; the vision of horror that leaps out of the paper is specifically military in character:

6. Leonard Woolf, *The Journey Not the Arrival Matters: An Autobiography of the Years 1939–1969* (London: Hogarth Press, 1969), p. 53.

as her father-in-law had dropped the *Times,* she took it and
read: "A horse with a green tail . . ." which was fantastic.
Next, "The guard at Whitehall . . ." which was romantic
and then, buildings word upon word, she read: "The troopers told her the horse had a green tail; but she found it was
just an ordinary horse. And they dragged her up to the barrack room where she was thrown upon a bed. Then one of
the troopers removed part of her clothing, and she screamed
and hit him about the face. . . ."

That was real; so real that on the mahogany door panels
she saw the Arch in Whitehall; through the Arch the barrack room; in the barrack room the bed, and on the bed the
girl was screaming and hitting him about the face, when the
door (for in fact it was a door) opened and in came Mrs.
Swithin carrying a hammer. [p. 27]

As Mrs. Swithin chatters about the summer pageant and the
weather, the hammer she holds becomes linked in Isa's mind
with an impending terror:

Every summer, for several summers now, Isa had heard
the same words; about the hammer and the nails; the pageant
and the weather. Every year they said, would it be wet or
fine; and every year it was—one or the other. The same
chime followed the same chime, only this year beneath the
chime she heard: "The girl screamed and hit him about the
face with a hammer." [p. 29]

Giles, Isa's stockbroker husband, is acutely aware of the war
in Europe, and he is furious at his immobility, at the absurdity
of going on as usual when some decisive act is called for: "Had
he not read in the morning paper, in the train, that sixteen men
had been shot, others prisoned, just over there, across the gulf,
in the flat land which divided them from the continent? Yet
he changed [for dinner]." When Mrs. Swithin sits on the lawn

and muses on the view ("'It'll be there . . . when we are not.'"), Giles squirms, raging mentally at "old fogies who sat and looked at views over coffee when the whole of Europe—over there—was bristling . . . At any moment guns would rake that land into furrows; planes splinter Bolney Minster into smithereens and blast the Folly. He, too, loved the view. And blamed Aunt Lucy, looking at views, instead of—doing what?" By the end of the novel Giles himself has done no more than crush a garden snake and initiate a meaningless affair with Mrs. Manresa, that earthy, even gaudy visitor who arrives unexpectedly at the pageant.

The novel places the reader in a kind of limbo between historical events, and between two sexual acts as well: in the interludes between the acts of the pageant, Isa daydreams about the gentleman farmer Haines, and while her husband is lured off by Mrs. Manresa she makes half-hearted overtures to the effete William Dodge. There is relatively little indication that the marriage between Giles and Isa will be significantly affected by these flirtations, but the last page of the novel leaves us in suspense. The coming act—it is not explicitly described as sexual —is to be in some way a *first* act, or at least a repetition of all acts between men and women. In this sense it will determine the continuity of life:

> The great hooded chairs had become enormous. And Giles too. And Isa too against the window. The window was all sky without colour. The house had lost its shelter. It was night before roads were made, or houses. It was the night that dwellers in caves had watched from some high place among the rocks.
>
> Then the curtain rose. They spoke.

The fall of night in Virginia Woolf's novels is often made to suggest the beginning of history, but then history is never presented in her work as anything but a kind of fashion: "What you see us by," as Mrs. Ramsay says; hence the possibility of containing all history in one sexual relationship.

Between the Acts is built on that attempt at a masculine-feminine dialectic which is so much a part of Mrs. Woolf's fiction; the important historical events, if La Trobe can be taken as an authority, are not wars but loves. Hence the three plays that make up the "acts" of the summer pageant (they can be read as parodies of Shakespeare, Congreve, and Gilbert and Sullivan) are all at bottom the same play about love between the sexes. To underscore the sense of historical continuity, three sets of male-female relationships are established within the story proper, each representing a different period of history but each fundamentally the same. The first is contained in the eighteenth-century portraits which hang facing one another in Pointz Hall. On the one hand is an ancestor who holds the reins of his horse and seems to chafe at having to pose. (" 'If you want my likeness, dang it sir, take it when the leaves are on the trees.' ") Opposite him is an anonymous lady who leans elegantly on a pillar and leads the viewer's eye "through glades of greenery and shades of silver, dun and rose into silence." The male-female roles are characterized here as in Mrs. Woolf's other novels; even small details like the fact that the male figure "has a name" and is a "talk producer" are typical and significant. Reinforcing this statement about the elemental distinctions between the male and female, we have a nineteenth-century couple, Mr. Bartholomew Oliver, late of the Indian Civil Service, and his sister, Lucy Swithin:

Old Bartholomew tapped his fingers on his knee in time to the tune. . . . He looked sardonically at Lucy, perched on her chair. How, he wondered, had she ever borne children? . . .

She was thinking, he supposed, God is peace. God is love. For she belonged to the unifiers; he to the separatists. [p. 140]

The third couple are, of course, the twentieth-century figures, Giles and Isa—she dreamy and always murmuring fragments of verse, he, like the other males, impatient to do something. The confrontation of these two at the end represents the major "act" of the novel, the next great historical event; but that act is only about to take place as the novel ends. Indeed, even their infidelity to one another is not yet an accomplished fact.

These, then, are two important implications of the title: we are between wars and between two decisive acts in the lives of an archetypal male and female; in both cases the security of Pointz Hall is threatened, and in both cases an important event seems imminent, so that Giles and Isa continually have the feeling that the future is "disturbing our present." But there is a third and perhaps transcendent implication that helps us understand more clearly the impulses behind Mrs. Woolf's experimentation with the form of the novel. The title suggests, as Geoffrey Hartman has noted, that the book is about unfilled spaces;[7] more specifically, it is about the anxiety that grows from an effort to discover a continuity and unity in life. The great problem that animates this novel, as indeed all Mrs. Woolf's novels, is whether to deny or accept the terrible sense of separation between things. What is threatened here is not only the continuity of English civilization and the continuity of the relationships at Pointz Hall, but the continuity of life itself. By positing a world and a family hovering between acts, Virginia Woolf creates an air of uncertainty—and not only about metaphysics, for the voice that speaks like a mechanical god from the bushes at the end of La Trobe's pageant is hardly convinced of the moral value of human beings.

Nevertheless doubts are always being dispelled by vaguely affirmative notes. That "megaphonic, anonymous" voice, speaking to the audience at first in clipped sentences and then in dog-

7. Geoffrey Hartman, "Virginia's Web," *Chicago Review* 14 (Spring 1961):28.

gerel, is pretty clearly the voice of Miss La Trobe, and it is not
difficult to hear Virginia Woolf speaking too: *"All you can see
of yourselves is scraps, orts and fragments? Well then listen to
the gramophone affirming . . ."* (p. 220). What the gramophone affirms is harmony and unity, and it does this largely
through the power of art, which unites the audience: "Com-
pelled from the ends of the horizon; recalled from the edge of
appalling crevasses; they crashed; solved; united. And some re-
laxed their fingers; and others uncrossed their legs." As the
audience leaves, the gramophone mutters *"Dispersed are we,"*
but it adds, *"let us retain whatever made that harmony."*

But something more than La Trobe's art or Lucy Swithin's
religion is needed to make a meaningful continuum out of our
lives. We are told that there is a unity, a continuity extending
from the dinosaurs to the Victorians to us. But there is an active element in history, and the absence of action, the paralysis
that Giles Oliver feels, is made to seem a genuine evil. Some
act is required, some means to crush the "monstrous inversion."
Whether the act will take place is another matter, but the pro-
jected "act" between Giles and Isa seems to represent a hope
for the continuity of humanity. Though Mrs. Woolf herself
has more in common with Lucy Swithin and Miss La Trobe,
with Isa the dreamy wife, it is clear that the harmony she
seeks is incomplete without Giles and old Oliver, that some
kind of androgynous synthesis is necessary.

Virginia Woolf's visions of unity and her peculiar sort of
"feminine" aestheticism offer at best a limited compensation for
the uncertainties of life. But *Between the Acts* recognizes the
limitations of her philosophy more clearly than any of her previous novels. In spite of its warm comedy, in spite of its optimis-
tic notes, it leaves us on the brink of an action; and the technique, even granting that the book is in some sense unfinished,
indicates a certain unwillingness to improve on life by shaping
its random flux into a neat pattern. I have said that the novel

appears random and disjointed in contrast to her other, rather
obviously symmetrical books. One thinks of the voyage out–
voyage in symbolism of her first novel; of the almost improbably ordered day in the life of Clarissa Dalloway, ending as
primly and neatly as a ballroom dance; of the single day described in *To the Lighthouse,* completed after the space of ten
years during which "time passes"; and of still another day,
marked by the rising and setting sun in the purple chapters of
The Waves. Between the Acts is also concerned with the
events of a single day—or at least it might easily have been.
The first, very short scene, a little over a page and a half, describes a conversation during "a summer's night." All the rest
of the narrative is devoted to the following day, as if the author
were deliberately avoiding an easy symmetry.

And this slightly disordered, asymmetrical quality is carried
over into the depiction of individual scenes, as I have noted
already. Even Miss La Trobe's play leaves us with the feeling
that the tidy structure had to collapse at the last minute. A
prologue and a parody of an Elizabethan comedy; a prologue
and a parody of a Restoration comedy; a prologue and a parody
of a Victorian comedy—and then suddenly we come to the
last act, which isn't there, and we have to make do with a mirror and a megaphone. It is as if the closer we get to "life itself," the life of the moment, the less consolation art has to offer.
In other words, what Leavis and Friedman have taken to be
the absence of structure is in fact a conscious faulting of structure, a questioning of the power of "significant form" that runs
far deeper than Lily Briscoe's feeling that her vision is past or
Bernard's criticism of words and compacted shapes—deeper
because the criticism is embodied in the very form of the work,
as in no other novel by Virginia Woolf.

Mrs. Woolf's whole art is aimed at creating or revealing a
world where there are no discrete events and in that sense no

"acts." To place the emphasis on acts is to become fragmented; therefore from the first her style was designed to affirm a continuity between things, to show that life cannot be arbitrarily divided, that we are not paralyzed, and that we only seem to be forever poised on the brink. In this novel, however, the plot, the style, and the structure reflect the tension of doubt. Imagine for a moment that time could become slow enough for us to sense a great gap between the ticks of the clock. In those spaces between ticks, between acts, as it were, it is quite possible and perhaps even inevitable to wonder, fearfully, whether or not the next tick will come—and if it comes, whether it will resemble the ones that preceded it, or herald a whole new order. In such a condition, all order, all meaning is in suspension, awaiting the next stroke, the next act. The problem is much the same if it is expressed in terms of space, for we do not know what is going on "over there," just as in the novel we do not know what is happening across the channel. There was a time, Mrs. Swithin keeps noting, when the channel was not there and England was joined to the continent. Not so now; all we get are items in the newspaper, country gossip, and an ominous swoop of military aircraft. Everybody is in some sense isolated, fragmentary, and words must not only be spoken, but also travel across space in order to be heard. The two characters who come nearest to representing Mrs. Woolf's own values are both "unifiers," but they are also slightly absurd figures, portrayed with an ironic objectivity. Thus Lucy Swithin, a whimsical, Victorian old lady, keeps fingering her crucifix; and Miss La Trobe sweats behind a tree, trying to bring her audience into a state of harmony, frustrated when the actor's words are blown away.

The novel does affirm the existence of meaning, continuity, unity, even if only in tenuous ways, as in the scene where Mrs. Swithin looks into a deep pool and broods on the nature of fish:

"Ourselves," she murmured. And retrieving some glint of faith from the grey waters, hopefully, without much help from reason, she followed the fish; the speckled, streaked and blotched; seeing in that vision beauty, power, and glory in ourselves.

Fish had faith, she reasoned. They trust us because we've never caught 'em. But her brother would reply: "That's greed." "Their beauty!" she protested. "Sex," he would say. "Who makes sex susceptible to beauty?" she would argue. He shrugged who? Why? Silenced, she returned to her private vision; of beauty which is goodness; the sea on which we float. Mostly impervious, but surely every boat sometimes leaks? [pp. 239–40]

The watery metaphor, that image of total unity so often employed by Mrs. Woolf, is not stressed in this novel; in fact in this passage she seems to regard it with somewhat wistful amusement. But a kind of stream is implied, nevertheless, in the orts and fragments that represent the substance of most of the individual scenes. It is Mrs. Swithin's view of history that the novel ultimately supports: history understood not as a cycle or even a significant progression, but as a framework for the constant play of what Isa describes as love, hate, and peace. Only the surfaces of our lives change; nature, as the villagers tell us, *"is always the same, summer, winter, and spring."* This view, of course, can be deduced from all of Mrs. Woolf's novels. In this last book, however, there is a happier sense of the importance of cultivation, the digging and delving that give the earth its serene, permanent aspect. This very recognition of the importance of action brings some fear and doubt with it. Mrs. Swithin's view is qualified by her amusing, genteel religiosity. Virginia Woolf herself made a habit of attacking the official Christianity of the Victorians, and Bartholomew Oliver is by no means an unsympathetic character when he snorts at Mrs.

Swithin's crucifix. Art itself is brought into question more deeply than in any of Mrs. Woolf's other novels—even the artist La Trobe questions her own sincerity, and, when the pageant is over, finds herself in need of a drink. There is just enough doubt, in fact, to lend an air of suspense as the curtain rises at the end.

10

Conclusion

Rooms and windows play a special role in Virginia Woolf's fiction, as most readers are aware. She emphasizes the need to find "a room of one's own," and her novels are full of scenes where the central character, usually after some active contact with the city streets or large groups of people, returns to his room—Rachel Vinrace's room on board ship, Jacob's room, Clarissa Dalloway's upstairs room—to take pleasure in the solitude. Usually the room has a window: thus Septimus Smith takes his life by jumping out of a window, Mrs. Dalloway looks out her window and wonders about the woman across the way, and of course Mrs. Ramsay is always associated with the window that provides a title for one of the major sections in *To the Lighthouse*. The simple action of a character rising from his chair to go to the window and contemplate what lies outside becomes a kind of allegory for some of Mrs. Woolf's major themes, functioning even in her essays, notably *A Room of One's Own*. Without denying the widely accepted fact that literary symbols are what they symbolize and therefore cannot be abstracted or fully explained, let me comment on the suggestiveness of this typical scene in terms of Mrs. Woolf's chief interests as a novelist. My text is one of her essays, where the scene is used as a metaphor for the artist's relationship to the world. She is addressing a young poet in the form of a letter, and she envisions herself standing in his room, gazing out the window as he agonizes over the composition of a poem. "While you write . . . I will withdraw a little and look out of the window. A woman passes, then a man; a car glides to a stop and then—but there is no need to say what I see out the window, nor indeed is there time, for I am suddenly recalled . . . by your cry of rage or despair." [1] Her advice to the poet is to get up and come to the window beside her:

> All you need now is to stand at the window and let your rhythmical sense open and shut, open and shut, boldly and freely, until one thing melts in another, until the taxis are dancing with the daffodils, until a whole has been made from all these separate fragments. . . . Then let your rhythmical sense wind itself in and out among the street—until it has strung them together in one harmonious whole. That perhaps is your task—to find the relation between things that seem incompatible yet have a mysterious affinity, to absorb every experience that comes your way . . . to re-think human life into poetry and so give us tragedy again and comedy by means of characters not spun out at length in the novelist's way, but condensed and synthesized in the poet's way. [p. 191]

This passage says a good deal about Mrs. Woolf's own aims as a novelist (particularly in *The Waves*), even though in the same essay she distinguishes herself from poets and claims ignorance of their craft. Notice that she does not say that comedy and tragedy ought to be abandoned, something that many readers of her more famous essay, "Modern Fiction," seem

1. Virginia Woolf, "Letter to a Young Poet," *Collected Essays,* 2:185.

to believe she advocates. Rather she says that the poet must "re-think human life into poetry." The notion of a single rhythm stringing together all the fragments on the street, making them "melt in another" and become a "harmonious whole" might be taken as an important guide to the motive behind her style.

Throughout Mrs. Woolf's work, the chief problem for her and for her characters is to overcome the space between things, to attain an absolute unity with the world, as if everything in the environment were turned into water. This desire for absolute union can be expressed in both physical and spiritual terms, and in Mrs. Woolf it nearly always has sexual connotations (cf. the first sentence of the passage I have quoted). The generally erotic nature of her art has never received proper emphasis from critics, though many have pointed to lighthouses, pocket-knives, bodies of water, and windows as evidence of sexual symbolism. She has been portrayed as a prudish lady, a "peeper," as Wyndham Lewis once called her. It is true that her novels are often reticent about sex (Lytton Strachey's chief criticism of *To the Lighthouse* was that it avoided reference to copulation—a remark that tells as much about Strachey as it does about Mrs. Woolf), and sometimes she is manifestly prudish, as in *The Voyage Out*. This does not mean, however, that her work is sexless. On the contrary, her prose is full of erotic impulses, and sexual themes are major elements in all her books. Again and again she either hints at or explicitly portrays homoeroticism: consider, for example, St. John Hurst, Clarissa Dalloway, Lily Briscoe, Neville, Orlando, and William Dodge. Mrs. Woolf's indirection in some of these cases may reflect her concern for decorum, or Bloomsbury's proclivity to a love that even in the twenties was careful to speak its name. On the other hand, when she does portray sexual emotions, she often injects an element of fear. Her nervous, barely concealed eroticism is,

I have tried to indicate, related to the wish to find some permanent, all-embracing union: in effect, to the death-wish.

The room-window symbols are important aspects of this desire. Throughout her fiction and essays, Virginia Woolf uses the room as an objectification of individual personality, to suggest the ultimate isolation of the individual ego, bound in by walls. She is aware that while privacy and solitude are important, they can lead to insensitivity, loneliness, and despair—hence the importance of the window in her writings. She is always fighting a battle with the ego, and for her the window suggests a means to reach the world outside; even, at times, a means to dissolve the sense of individuality and merge with the anonymous movements she can see on the street. But there is a tension in her work between, in her own terms, a "creation" of the world and an "embrace" of the world. In her "Letter to a Young Poet," Mrs. Woolf is saying that poetry should become a less subjective and purely personal expression, that it should express life outside the window as novels do, though in its own terms. In the passage quoted above, the artist who stands at the window and sees a unity in the movement of figures on the street is "creating" a world through the effort of imagination. We should remember, however, that Septimus Smith leaps through a window to die, and that Mrs. Ramsay also wants to die for a moment as she broods on the lighthouse outside her window: here the wish to forsake the ego is pictured as a suicidal "embrace" of the world, an embrace which is actually a retreat from active life. The desire to retain individuality in Mrs. Woolf's work is always qualified, and sometimes overcome, by the desire to attain the "mysterious affinity" with all things.

Whether we are inside looking out or outside looking in (like Lily Briscoe in *To the Lighthouse*), we do not perceive the mystery through the window without at least a partial loss of ourselves or the ones we love. But in Virginia Woolf's fiction this loss it compensated for by a momentary glimpse of some reality beyond ourselves, and a consolation for death:

> Bonamy crossed to the window. Pickford's van swung down the street. The omnibuses were locked together at Mudie's corner. Engines throbbed, and carters, jamming the brakes down, pulled their horses up. A harsh and unhappy voice cried something unintelligible. And then suddenly all the leaves seemed to raise themselves.
>
> "Jacob! Jacob!" cried Bonamy, standing by the window. The leaves sank down again.
>
> "Such confusion everywhere!" exclaimed Betty Flanders, bursting open the bedroom door.[2]

In this example, from the last page of *Jacob's Room,* the consolation is less powerful than the pain of loss and the failure to attain a perfect knowledge and unity with another person. But there is something in the rise of leaves outside the window, a momentary intimation of unity beneath all the confusion.

Virtually all the technical peculiarities I have treated in this study—including self-consciously lovely prose rhythms; an easy and almost superficially artful symmetry in everything from paragraphs to plots; a feeling for graceful sketches; imagery of water, air, and insect life; particularly unobtrusive transitions; an ambiguous relationship between the narrator and the characters—are meant to produce an effect of complete unity when applied to the essentially fragmentary and chaotic flotsam of everyday life. Indeed, something analogous to these blurred distinctions, these visions of unity and order, is directly experienced by the characters. Repeatedly they are shown thinking together in large anonymous groups, or brooding in

2. Virginia Woolf, *Jacob's Room* (London: Hogarth Press, 1965), p. 176.

solitude until they experience a "dissolution" of personality and a sense of union with the objects around them.

The recurrent room-window symbolism is simply another way for Mrs. Woolf to state the unresolved tension between two worlds of experience that is the source of her art. On the one hand is the world of the self, the time-bound, landlocked, everyday world of the masculine ego, of intellect and routine, where people live in fear of death, and where separations imposed by time and space result in agony. On the other hand is a world without a self—watery, emotional, erotic, generally associated with the feminine sensibility—where all of life seems blended together in a kind of "halo," where the individual personality is continually being dissolved by intimations of eternity, and where death reminds us of a sexual union.

Mrs. Woolf did not wish to dispense with either of these worlds, but it was the second that held her imagination and inspired her to evolve a highly personal technique. Her interests are metaphysical, her typical moods elegiac. Like the English romantics before her, she feels encompassed by a world of process and death, and her art is an attempt to reach, through the power of imagination, a totally impersonal world, a world out of time. The major figures in her novels are all "unifiers," wanting to "embrace the world with arms of understanding." But her problem is that such an "embrace," an intense desire for a kind of ultimate rhythm, for knowledge of and union with something outside the self, can be realized only in death or one of its surrogates, like hypnosis or sleep. That is why she often seems to be striving to work out some kind of compromise between a basic inclination to inhabit the world and a spontaneous impulse to depart from it. Another of her problems is expressed by Bernard in the epigraph I have chosen for this study: language, the index of an observing personality, can never describe a reality that subsumes the self. Much of

Mrs. Woolf's experimentation therefore grows out of an attempt to suggest a world she could never directly describe. She remains a highly original and gifted writer, trying to evoke the kind of experiences most novelists avoid entirely.

Perhaps she was aware that the heart of her fiction was silence. In the later half of her career she made tentative efforts to find a new kind of language, represented by the monotonous, declamatory monologues in *The Waves* and the doggerel passages in *Orlando* and *Between the Acts*. In this respect she has something in common with Joyce and Beckett, who for quite different reasons had their own conflicts with words. For Joyce, the solution lay in an avoidance of his own voice, an overmastery of English with mimicry and solecism. For Beckett, the answer was passive resistance and ultimately retreat into elemental French.[3] Virginia Woolf's struggle with language grew out of different sources, and, at least partly because of her innate good manners, it had far less radical results. Nevertheless, like some other modern authors, she seems to be contending against the very medium of her art.

Her contention with the novel has its roots in her psyche. If one reads Leonard Woolf's autobiography or the *Writer's Diary,* one suspects that her mind was always on the verge of mysticism or madness. Even her conversations, as her husband describes them, tended to break suddenly into lyrical descriptions that were somewhat alien to ordinary conversation.[4] I have already mentioned that in her diary she records having felt, during one of the "breakdowns" that affected her throughout life, a "loss of character and idiosyncrasy as Virginia Woolf" coupled with a sense that she was "more attuned to existence" (p. 97). A similar emotion is described elsewhere as

3. See Ihib Hassan, "Joyce-Beckett: A Scenario in Eight Scenes and a Voice," *Journal of Modern Literature* 1 (1970):7–18.

4. Leonard Woolf, *Beginning Again: An Autobiography of the Years 1911–1918* (London: Hogarth Press, 1964), pp. 30–31.

"a consciousness of what I call 'reality,' . . . something abstract; but residing in downs or sky . . . in which I shall rest and continue to exist." And, she adds, "I would like to express it, too" (p. 130).

Her attitudes toward "reality" are very like the ones described in R. D. Laing's little book on the phenomenology of schizophrenia, *The Divided Self*. Laing says that schizophrenics often feel they are merging with or being engulfed by the outside world. For example, he tells of one young man who, walking in a park among the lovers, "began to feel a tremendous oneness with the whole world." This oneness, however, resulted in a strange terror: "the loss of identity involved in this merging or fusion of his self . . . He knew of no half-way stage between radical isolation . . . or complete absorption into all there was. He was afraid of being absorbed into Nature, engulfed by her . . . yet what he most dreaded, that also he most longed for." [5] One might also compare the descriptive passages in Mrs. Woolf's novels, and the experiences of her characters, with another of Laing's patients, a girl who employed a "magical camouflage" to defend against anxiety: *"It struck me that if I stared long enough at the environment that I would blend with it and disappear"* (Laing's italics).[6] Still another patient explained that she "had to die to keep from dying."

I do not mean to become overly clinical in discussing Mrs. Woolf. After all, seer and madman are often united in one person, whose role changes according to the onlooker's point of view. Laing reminds us that "Ezekiel, in Jasper's opinion, was a schizophrenic." Mrs. Woolf's psychosis is by now an established biographical fact, but I am less concerned with the why of her behavior than with the how of her presence in the

5. R. D. Laing, *The Divided Self* (Baltimore: Penguin Books, 1970), p. 73.
6. Ibid., p. 110.

world. Furthermore, I do not want to leave the impression that she was literally mad or caught up in a mystic vision as she wrote. Even the near-frenzy which often accompanied her more creative moments was always replaced by an Apollonian mood when she went back to revise and reorder.

My point, simply, is that her special experiences had special consequences for her art. In nearly everything she wrote, we can sense a kind of "divided self," or perhaps it is better to call it a division between a feeling of selfhood and a feeling of selflessness. And though I have stressed the fact that her unusual novels represent to some degree a flirtation with death, I should note that they are also acts of courage and love. In all her work, she tried to affirm the unity of our lives and to break down what she called in her *Diary* the "screen-making" habit of the human personality. This habit, she acknowledges, "is so universal that probably it preserves our sanity. If we had not this device for shutting people off from our sympathies we might perhaps dissolve utterly; separateness would be impossible" (p. 99). Nevertheless, she adds, in a coda that might serve as an epigraph to all her writings, "the screens are in the excess, not the sympathy."

Bibliography

A *Bibliography of Virginia Woolf*, by B. J. Kirkpatrick (London: Rupert Hart-Davis, 1957) is the guide to primary sources. Good bibliographies of secondary material may be found in Hafley, Guiguet, Richter, and "Criticism of Virginia Woolf: A Selected Checklist with an Index to Studies of Separate Works," compiled by Maurice Beebe, *Modern Fiction Studies,* February, 1956, pp. 36–45. The Berg Collection of the New York Public Library has many of Virginia Woolf's manuscripts, in addition to her complete diaries.

Primary Sources

Between the Acts. London: Hogarth Press, 1969.
Collected Essays. 4 vols. London: Hogarth Press, 1966–67.
The Common Reader. New York: Harcourt, Brace, 1953.
Contemporary Writers. New York: Harcourt, Brace, 1966.
Flush: A Biography. London: Hogarth Press, 1968.
A Haunted House and Other Stories. London: Hogarth Press, 1967.
Jacob's Room. London: Hogarth Press, 1965.
Mrs. Dalloway. London: Hogarth Press, 1968.
Night and Day. London: Hogarth Press, 1966.
Orlando: A Biography. London: Hogarth Press, 1964.
A Room of One's Own. London: Hogarth Press, 1967.
The Second Common Reader. New York: Harcourt, Brace, 1960.
Three Guineas. London: Hogarth Press, 1952.

To the Lighthouse. London: Hogarth Press, 1967.
Virginia Woolf and Lytton Strachey: Letters. Edited by Leonard Woolf and James Strachey. New York: Harcourt, Brace, 1956.
The Voyage Out. London: Hogarth Press, 1965.
A Writer's Diary. Edited by Leonard Woolf. New York: New American Library, 1968.
The Years. London: Hogarth Press, 1965.
The Waves. London: Hogarth Press, 1963.

Secondary Sources

(This list is selective, and devoted mainly to items about Virginia Woolf or her circle.)

Annan, Noel Gilroy. *Leslie Stephen: His Thought and Character in Relation to His Time.* London: Macgibbon and Kee, 1951.
Auerbach, Erich. *Mimesis.* Translated by Willard Trask. Princeton: Princeton University Press, 1953.
Baldanza, Frank. *"Orlando* and the Sackvilles." *PMLA* 70 (1955): 274–79.
Beck, Warren. "For Virginia Woolf." In *Forms of Modern Fiction,* edited by William Van O'Connor. Minneapolis: University of Minnesota Press, 1948.
Benjamin, Anna S. "Towards an Understanding of the Meaning of Virginia Woolf's *Mrs. Dalloway." Wisconsin Studies in Contemporary Literature* 6 (1965):214–27.
Bennett, Joan. *Virginia Woolf: Her Art as a Novelist.* 2d ed., rev. Cambridge: Cambridge University Press, 1945.
Bradbrook, M. C. "Notes on the Style of Mrs. Woolf." *Scrutiny* 1 (1932):33–38.
Beja, Morris, ed. *Virginia Woolf, To the Lighthouse: A Casebook.* London: Macmillan, 1970.
———, ed. *Psychological Fiction.* Glenview, Illinois: Scott, Foresman, 1971.
Bevis, Dorothy. *"The Waves:* A Fusion of Symbol, Style and Thought in Virginia Woolf." *Twentieth-Century Literature* 2 (1956):5–20.
Blackstone, Bernard. *Virginia Woolf: A Commentary.* New York: Harcourt, Brace, 1949.

Bowling, Lawrence E. "What is the Stream of Consciousness Technique?" *PMLA* 65 (1950):333-45.

Brewster, Dorothy. *Virginia Woolf.* New York: New York University Press, 1962.

Chambers, R. L. *The Novels of Virginia Woolf.* Edinburgh: Oliver and Boyd, 1947.

Chastaing, Maxime. *La Philosophe de Virginia Woolf.* Paris: Presses Universitaires de France, 1951.

Daiches, David. *Virginia Woolf.* Norfolk, Connecticut: New Directions, 1942.

Edel, Leon. *Literary Biography.* London: Rupert Hart-Davis, 1957.

————. *The Modern Psychological Novel.* New York: Grosset and Dunlap, 1964.

Doner, Dean. "Virginia Woolf: The Service of Style." *Modern Fiction Studies* 2 (1956):1-12.

Empson, William. "Virginia Woolf." In *Scrutinies II,* ed. E. Rickword. London: Wishart and Company, 1931.

Forster, E. M. *Virginia Woolf.* New York: Harcourt, Brace, 1942.

Freedman, Ralph. *The Lyrical Novel.* Princeton: Princeton University Press, 1963.

Friedman, Melvin J. *Stream of Consciousness: A Study in Literary Method.* New Haven: Yale University Press, 1955.

Goldman, Mark. "Virginia Woolf and the Critic as Reader." *PMLA* 80 (1965):275-84.

Graham, John. "Time in the Novels of Virginia Woolf." *University of Toronto Quarterly* 17 (1949):pp. 186-201.

Guiguet, Jean. *Virginia Woolf and her Works.* London: Hogarth Press, 1966.

Hafley, James. *The Glass Roof: Virginia Woolf as Novelist.* Berkeley: University of California Press, 1954.

Hartman, Geoffrey H. "Virginia's Web." *Chicago Review* 13 (1961): 20-32.

Hildick, Wallace. "In That Solitary Room." *Kenyon Review* 27 (1965):302-17.

Holroyd, Michael. *Lytton Strachey.* 2 vols. London: Heinemann, 1967.

Holtby, Winifred. *Virginia Woolf.* London: Wishart and Company, 1932.

Humphrey, Robert. *Stream of Consciousness in the Modern Novel.* Berkeley: University of California Press, 1959.

Johnstone, J. K. *The Bloomsbury Group*. London: Secker and Warburg, 1954.

Leaska, Michell A. *Virginia Woolf's To the Lighthouse: A Study in Critical Method*. London: Hogarth Press, 1970.

Leavis, F. R. "After *To the Lighthouse*." *Scrutiny* 10 (1942):295–98.

Love, Jean O. *Worlds in Consciousness*. Berkeley: University of California Press, 1970.

Marder, Herbert. *Feminism and Art: A Study of Virginia Woolf*. Chicago: University of Chicago Press, 1968.

Mellers, W. H. "Mrs. Woolf and Life." *Scrutiny* 6 (1937):71–75.

Nathan, Monique. *Virginia Woolf*. Translated by Herma Briffault. New York: Grove Press, 1961.

Pippett, Aileen. *The Moth and the Star: A Biography of Virginia Woolf*. Boston: Little, Brown, 1953.

Rantavaara, Irma. *Virginia Woolf and Bloomsbury*. Helsinki: Annales Academiae Scientiarum Fennicae, 1953.

Rosenberg, Stuart. "The Match in the Crocus: Obtrusive Art in Virginia Woolf's *Mrs. Dalloway*." *Modern Fiction Studies* 13 (1967): 211–20.

Richter, Harvena. *The Inward Voyage*. Princeton: Princeton University Press, 1970.

Schaefer, Josephine O'Brien. *The Three-Fold Nature of Reality in the Novels of Virginia Woolf*. London: Mouton, 1965.

Sprague, Claire, ed. *Virginia Woolf: Twentieth Century Views*. Englewood Cliffs, New Jersey: Prentice-Hall, 1971.

Thakur, N. C. *The Symbolism of Virginia Woolf*. New York: Oxford University Press, 1965.

Troy, William. "Virginia Woolf: The Poetic Method." *Symposium* 3 (1932):53–63.

———. "Virginia Woolf: The Poetic Style." *Symposium* 3 (1932): 153–66.

Wilkinson, Ann Yanko. "A Principle of Unity in *Between the Acts*." *Criticism* 8 (1965):53–63.

Woodring, Carl. *Virginia Woolf*. New York: Columbia University Press, 1965.

Woolf, Leonard. *Sowing: An Autobiography of the Years 1880–1904*. London: Hogarth Press, 1960.

———. *Growing: An Autobiography of the Years 1904–1911*. London: Hogarth Press, 1961.

———. *Beginning Again: An Autobiography of the Years 1911–1918*. London: Hogarth Press, 1964.

————. *Downhill All the Way: An Autobiography of the Years 1919-1939.* London: Hogarth Press, 1967.
————. *The Journey Not the Arrival Matters: An Autobiography of the Years 1939-1969.* London: Hogarth Press, 1969.

Index

Virginia Woolf's works are indexed under their titles. Works by other authors are indexed under the authors' names.